HOW TO REBUILD THE BIG-BLOCK CHEVROLET

Tony E. Huntimer

CarTech®

CarTech®

CarTech®, Inc.
39966 Grand Avenue
North Branch, MN 55056
Phone: 651-277-1200 or 800-551-4754
Fax: 651-277-1203
www.cartechbooks.com

Edit by Paul Johnson
Layout by Monica Bahr

ISBN-13 978-1-932494-53-2
Item No. SA142

Library of Congress Cataloging-in-Publication Data

Huntimer, Tony E.
    How to rebuild the big-block Cheverolet / by Tony Huntimer.
       p. cm.
    ISBN 978-1-932494-53-2
    1. Chevrolet automobile—Motors—Maintenance and repair. I. Title.
    TL215.C5H86 2009
    629.25'040288—dc22
                                    2008038323

Printed in China
10 9 8 7 6 5 4 3 2 1

On the Title Page:

Engine dynamometers allow builders to verify the performance of a particular engine and its equipment setup. At Edlebrock, a big-block Chevy with the company's latest fuel-injection system is dyno tested.

On the Back Cover:

Upper Left: Big-block cylinder head offerings have changed dramatically in the last few years. Companies offer mild heads to full-on drag racing heads with CNC porting.

Upper Right: During the assembly process, the crankshaft is placed in the block. The crankshaft is a sensitive component and needs to be treated with care and never dropped.

Middle Left: Before the piston and rod assemblies can be installed in the block, the engine assembler must install the piston lock rings over the piston wrist pins.

Middle Right: The camshaft is carefully guided into the block, so the lobes don't make harsh contact with block.

Bottom Left: A special installation tool is used to install the harmonic balancer, and a torque wrench is used to tighten the retaining bolt to the proper torque specification.

Bottom Right: A base gasket is placed on the intake manifold, the carburetor is placed over the manifold studs, and then the retaining nuts are properly torqued.

OVERSEAS DISTRIBUTION BY:

Brooklands Books Ltd.
P.O. Box 146, Cobham, Surrey, KT11 1LG, England
Telephone 01932 865051 • Fax 01932 868803
www.brooklands-books.com

Brooklands Books Aus.
3/37-39 Green Street, Banksmeadow, NSW 2019, Australia
Telephone 2 9695 7055 • Fax 2 9695 7355

CONTENTS

*A*CKNOWLEDGMENTS

I enlisted invaluable help from family and friends to complete this book on building big-block Chevy engines. I'd like to thank all of the people who helped in one way or another or influenced my life in some manner to give me the ability to pass this information onto others. I hope I didn't leave anyone out and that I spelled every name correctly. To start, I'd especially like to thank my wife, Vikki Bristol-Huntimer, for giving me the support I needed to write this book. In no specific order, I'd also like to thank Robert and Maureen Cera, Slim, Yetta, Ken, Linda and the entire Huntimer Family, Steve and Martha Sanford, Cliff S. Witham, Jim Witham, Paul Caselas, Tracy Edmonds, Jeff Harwell, Chris Mead, Ed Matthews, Chris Fogarty, Doug Bracey, Vic DeLeon Sr. and Jr., Ben Lingard, Ben Chase and the rest of the crew at Goodies Speed Shop, Keith Spain, Paul Johnson, the late Steve Hendrickson, Travis Thompson, Jeff Smith, Douglass R. Glad, Steven Rupp, Nick Licata, Smitty Smith, Rick Roberts, Jan Dwyer, Jason Snyder, Ken Sink, Patrick Chaves, Chris Schueller, Keith Morita, Chris Raschke, Wade Caldwell, Trish Yunick-Brown, Kevin Bennett, Chris Endres, Todd Ryden, Robert Stewart, Michael Demurjian, Mark W. Campbell, Chase Knight, Victor Moore, Barry Grant, Mike Stasko, Chris Douglass, Brian Clarke, Chris Ouellette, Paul Hauglie, Mike Osterhaus, Lake C. Speed Jr., Jeff Theobald, Larry Atherton, David Rex, 84 Lumber and crew, Scott Sulprizio, Chrissy Witter, David Barker, Scott Walters, Remington Moore Sr. and Jr., Jay Rowlands, Bob Folwer, Cort Charles, Larry Callahan, Robert Loftis, Marilyn Patton, Mrs. Reid, Dave Monyhan, Randy Oldham, John Rankin, Don of DDM, Bret Bowers, Ray Wold, Kevin Stearns, Jon Mikelonis, Mike Zimmerman, Mike Bosley, Karl Chicca, Mark Deshetler, Mark Zanella, Cliff Burton, James Hetfield, Lars Ulrich, Kirk Hammett, Bill Koppinger, Kyle Tucker, Sue Elliot, Kyle Fickler, and Tom Dobruck.

This book could not have been written without the advice, guidance, invaluable time, and skilled hands—trained from years of racing and real world application—of Paul Caselas, Tracy Edmonds and crew at Goodies Speed Shop, Bob Gromm, Dave Wiley and crew at Gromm Racing Heads, Balancing & Engine Machine, Robert Cancilla at Robert Cancilla Machines, and Rick Santos and crew at S&S Automotive.

WHAT IS A *WORKBENCH* BOOK?

This Workbench Series book is the only book of its kind on the market. No other book offers the same combination of detailed hands-on information and revealing color photographs to illustrate engine rebuilding. Rest assured, you have purchased an indispensable companion that will expertly guide you, one step at a time, through each important stage of the rebuilding process. This book is packed with real world techniques and practical tips for expertly performing rebuild procedures, not vague instructions or unnecessary processes. At-home mechanics or enthusiast builders strive for professional results, and the instruction in our Workbench Series books help you realize pro-caliber results. Hundreds of photos guide you through the entire process from start to finish, with informative captions containing comprehensive instructions for every step of the process.

Appendixes located in the back of the book provide essential specification and rebuild information. These include diagrams and charts for cylinder firing order, torque sequences and specifications, piston ring gap alignment, and timing belt/chain alignment. In addition, general engine specifications, including compression ratio, bore and stroke, oil pressure, and many other specifications, are included.

The step-by-step photo procedures also contain many additional photos that show how to install high-performance components, modify stock components for special applications, or even call attention to assembly steps that are critical to proper operation or safety. These are labeled with unique icons. These symbols represent an idea, and photos marked with the icons contain important, specialized information.

Here are some of the icons found in Workbench books:

 Important!—Calls special attention to a step or procedure, so that the procedure is correctly performed. This prevents damage to a vehicle, system, or component.

 Warning—Indicates a step or set of directives that must be closely followed in order to prevent catastrophic damage and/or bodily harm to the rebuilder.

 Torque Fasteners—Illustrates a fastener that must be properly tightened with a torque wrench at this point in the rebuild. The torque specs are usually provided in the step.

 Use Special Tool—Illustrates the use of a special tool that may be required or can make the job easier (caption with photo explains further).

Performance Step—Indicates a procedure or modification that can improve performance. Step most often applies to high-performance or racing engines.

 Critical Inspection—Indicates that a component must be inspected to ensure proper operation of the engine.

 Precision Measurement—Illustrates a precision measurement or adjustment that is required at this point in the rebuild.

 Professional Mechanic Tip—Illustrates a step in the rebuild that non-professionals may not know. It may illustrate a shortcut, or a trick to improve reliability, prevent component damage, etc.

 Documentation Required—Illustrates a point in the rebuild where the reader should write down a particular measurement, size, part number, etc. for later reference or photograph a part, area or system of the vehicle for future reference.

 Tech Tip—Tech Tips provide brief coverage of important subject matter that doesn't naturally fall into the text or step-by-step procedures of a chapter. Tech Tips contain valuable hints, important info, or outstanding products that professionals have discovered after years of work. These will add to your understanding of the process, and help you get the most power, economy, and reliability from your engine.

HISTORICAL REVIEW OF THE BIG-BLOCK CHEVROLET

The 427-ci Mark II V-8 was a giant-killer that put Chevy back on top in NASCAR, albeit briefly. Tom McIntyre purchased the only complete 427-ci "Mystery V-8" engine (Mark II; produced in 1963) known to be in existence from a Smokey Yunick auction. Unfortunately, any history on this specific engine was lost when Smokey passed away on May 9, 2001. (Courtesy Jeff Smith and Source Interlink)

The greatest engines designed by automotive manufacturers since the 1950s were first introduced in the most brutal performance environment: motorsports. The big-block Chevy engine was no different.

Chevrolet previously offered the Mark I Big-Block engines, which were better known as the 348, 409, and 427 "W" engines. It's been written that these "W" engines were great performers but lacked power and longevity for stock car racing. Since Chevrolet was heavily involved in racing during the 1960s, it dedicated a team of engineers to develop a special new engine that would put the competition to shame. It wouldn't be the first or last time GM, Ford, or Chrysler built specific parts for racing and labeled them as a low-production powerplant, so they could upset the competition. The Chevy "Mystery Motor" debuted on February 22, 1963, for the Daytona 500. The factory called this engine the Mark II, and eventually it became the big-block Chevy engine we know. That day, all eyes at the track were on Junior Johnson's Chevrolet as he won the first qualifier. Johnny Rutherford knocked down qualifier number 2 with a big-block thundering between the front fenders of his Chevrolet as well. The big-block proved to be so much more powerful than the previous big-block (known

as the W-block 348-409) that the competition didn't know what hit them. In the May 1963 *Hot Rod* magazine's Ray Brock wrote, "[Chevrolet's 427 Mystery V-8] sure rocked the racing fraternity," and, "Junior Johnson shook up the observers behind the pit wall with a practice lap above 168 mph." Chevy's best lap in 1962 of 153 mph had been officially obliterated! Ford and Chrysler were up in arms.

In the mid 1960s, Chevy was backing out of racing and wasn't able to follow through with parts to support the big-block, so the big-blocks of that era were only a taste of what was to come. It wasn't until 1965 that the big-block returned to the scene as the Mark IV, which was essentially a refined Mark II. The engine was downsized to 396 cubic inches and was stuffed between the fenders of the lightweight 1965 Corvette as a factory-installed option. America's first sports car had finally been turned into a muscle machine. Since that time the big-block Chevy has been powering trucks with its high-torque output and powering some of the greatest muscle cars in history.

Racers on almost all motorsports fronts have found ways to unleash massive amounts of power from the big-block Chevy.

The canted-valve design carried over from the Mark II to the Mark IV big-block, which was referred to as the porcupine engine because the valves in previous engines were parallel to each other. The valves in the new big-block were canted away from each other so larger diameter valves could be utilized in the combustion chamber. This canted design allowed the larger valves to open toward each other, instead of two smaller valves that would open side by side toward the piston in the same space. This new design made a lot more air flow, which equated to a lot more power.

Rumor has it that, in order for Chevrolet to run the Mark II on the banks of Daytona that day in 1963, the engine had to be a production engine and it had to be available to the public. This in turn led to the sale of one or two Mark IIs to Ford, which could be how a few Ford engines were then soon developed with canted valves like the Mark II.

Parts Identification

The big-block Chevy has been offered in many sizes. The factory offerings of the Mark IV were 366-, 396-, 402-, 427-, and 454-ci displacements. Later on, GM introduced Gen V, VI, and VII in 496-, 502- and 572-ci sizes. There aren't any stop signs or speed limits in the Chevrolet Skunkworks division, so bigger big-blocks may be coming after this book is written.

What's a 402 and What's a 400 Big-Block?

The 396, 427, and 454 are some of the most popular and recognizable big-block powerplants ever built.

Since it was a truck engine, the 366 doesn't get much press, and it's uncommon to see them. The 402 is more common but only dyed-in-the-wool big-block aficionados know what they are. The 402 is a factory .030-inch overbored 396 that was offered as a big-block starting in 1970. The 396 gained consumer recognition and popularity in the 1960s. There are a couple of urban legends as to why Chevrolet increased the bore size from the 396 to 402, but no one knows the definitive answer. Starting in 1970, the 396-powered Camaros, Novas, and Chevelles were wearing 396 badges on the fenders but the actual displacement was 402 cubic inches. The emissions tag on the radiator shroud

The block casting numbers are located on the bell housing mounting flange behind the driver-side head. These numbers specify the year the engine was produced, two- or four-bolt main, and size. Unfortunately these numbers are not all as correct as you'd like them to be because Chevrolet didn't always change the markings when casting its big-blocks. Engines denoting "HI PERF" frequently have "PASS" (passenger car) attributes. For the most complete casting number database on the Internet, go to www.racehome.com/bbc.htm.

When the big-block first hit the scene in 1963, its head design was a departure from previous Chevy engines. The valves were canted to accommodate larger valves for better breathing and more power. The small-block head in the background has the typical parallel valve arrangement.

This is one mixed-up big-block. It's labeled as a "TRUCK" and "PASS" high-performance block. The casting number pad behind the driver's side had numbers stamped, not cast-in. The numbers didn't show up in any database. It's possible this is a "dealer replacement" block.

stated 402 cubic inch. Maybe the bean counters and marketing departments got together and decided not to mess with sales and let the public call the 402 a 396. The worst part about this debacle is that the full-size Chevrolets, such as the 1970 and 1971 Monte Carlos and Caprices were equipped with a 402 and were marketed as the "Turbo-Jet 400." To add insult to injury for getting parts to fix your "400," the same model year Chevrolet also offered the "Turbo-Fire 400" (an actual 400-ci small-block) in the same cars in which they offered the Turbo-Jet 400. The marketing department stopped this nonsense in 1972 when badges and marketing materials were switched to "402."

Blocks

There are many different big-blocks. Early on, there were two Mark IV Tall Deck (10.2-inch) big-blocks used in heavy-duty trucks, they were the 366-ci Tall Deck (3.935-inch bore x 3.76-inch stroke) and the 427 Tall Deck (4.251-inch bore x 3.76-inch stroke). The shorter, 9.8-inch deck height Mark IV big-blocks were more standard, with fac-

tory offerings as 396 (4.094-inch bore x 3.76-inch stroke), 402 (4.126-inch bore x 3.76-inch stroke), 427 (4.251-inch bore x 3.76-inch stroke) and 454 (4.251-inch bore x 4.00-inch stroke).

Tall Deck

The early tall deck (10.2-inch) Mark IV blocks are harder to find than standard 9.8-inch deck blocks. While these tall deck engines are usually torque monsters, they produce very little top-end power unless they are rebuilt with the right parts; high-flow heads, large valves, high duration cams, etc. Drag racers seek out these tall deck blocks because they want to punch out a huge bore and cram a big-armed stroker crank in the main caps. You need to check your block casting numbers to identify your block before starting your project. A tall deck engine may not be suitable for your application. Because the deck of the block is taller, the heads are farther apart, which requires a special wider intake manifold or adapter spacers to bolt a standard deck intake manifold. These engines are wider and taller, and you may run into problems fitting one in your engine compartment under the hood. For a typical street car, it takes more money to get respectable power output from a tall deck Mark IV block, rather than a standard deck block. If you have any concerns about using a tall deck for your application, check with your machine shop or speed shop for advice.

Standard Deck

Chevrolet literally made tons more standard 9.8-inch deck big-blocks than they did tall decks. The factory installed 9.8-inch deck

The back of this block is what you would typically see on all blocks. Almost all Mark IV blocks contained "HI PER PASS," but don't be fooled by these letters. If the block had "HI PERF" cast behind the timing cover, you might have a high-performance block. Castings were never 100-percent reliable.

height blocks in Corvettes, Camaros, Novas, Chevelles, El Caminos, Impalas, Monte Carlos, and full-size and standard-duty trucks. These are the most popular of the big-blocks. The Mark IV only changed slightly from 1965 to 1991, when the Gen V replaced it. Other obvious differences are the all aluminum ZL-1 blocks available as an optional upgrade in 1969 and 1970. Obvious differences in the cast-iron blocks include 2- or 4-bolt mains and crankshaft stroke clearance on the 454-ci blocks. Other less noticeable differences include external oil cooler provisions over the oil filter boss and additional cooling passages in the deck of the block.

Block Identification

All tall deck truck blocks had the word "TRUCK" cast into the back of the block. All other production (non-GM Performance and performance aftermarket) big-blocks had the words "HI PER PASS" cast into the back of the block denoting a high-performance passenger car. Cast words below the front camshaft boss specify "PASS PERF" and "HI PER PASS." Both markings have been found on blocks with and without high-performance attributes. I've even seen "HI-PERF TRUCK PASS" cast into the back of a 454; so not all factory stampings tell the real story.

All standard deck blocks were considered high-performance, but these blocks had different power levels. Obviously, the 4-bolt main blocks were for higher power levels, and sometimes could be identified externally by two threaded holes for an external oil cooler above the oil filter location. This is not always the case though, and some two-bolt blocks had these provisions. In real-

Later model big-blocks have the distinguishing "GM" marking cast into the side of the block above the oil pan rail. The designation of "7.4L" next to the GM marking also gives the clue that this is a late-model block.

This picture shows the 4-model 454-ci block has cast 4-bolt main caps. Late-model GM Performance Parts blocks are available with steel main caps to provide superior strength for extreme performance.

ity, there are no definitive external markings specifying a 4-bolt main block. The only way to be completely sure a big-block is a 4-bolt block is to remove the timing cover to peek at the front main cap, or remove the oil pan. Even the casting numbers on the outside of the block for distinguishing attributes of the engine are not always correct to identify bore, stroke, deck height, application, year, or main cap configuration. You don't really know exactly what you have until you open up the engine and get your measuring tools out.

High-Performance Blocks

GM Performance cast-iron blocks feature 9.8-inch and 10.2-inch deck heights. GM also offers a new and improved ZL-1 aluminum standard deck height block that is based on original tooling. If you find one of these new GM engines, it will be easily identified as a new performance engine by the "GM" logo cast into the block or the lack of other "classic" cast markings. If you are looking to find a high-performance big-block to build and don't have to use a classic Mark IV, you can simply purchase a new GM block already equipped with billet main caps and other upgrades designed to hold the stresses of 1,000-plus horsepower.

Cylinder Heads

As you do with engine blocks, you also need to read cast-in numbers and denoted letters to identify the heads. Unlike the blocks, however, there is less guessing if the castings are what the numbers say they are and it's as simple as removing a valve cover in order to get the whole story. Visually, without running the

numbers, you can tell if the head is an oval or rectangle port. By running the numbers, you'll know the year of the head, the engine size from the factory, valve sizes, and the combustion chamber volume.

Early on, Chevrolet produced a few aluminum heads and these days they are extremely hard to find, so

All non-high-performance heads have the word "TRUCK" or "PASS" cast into the runners of the head to designate a truck or passenger car. These words are easily seen by removing the valve cover. The casting numbers in the heads are more reliable than the ones on blocks.

All high-performance heads had the term "HI-PERF" cast into the head. Here you also see the casting number. Checking these numbers lets you know what year they were made, what size engine they were on, cc size, and valve sizes.

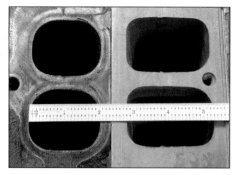

The "oval" port head is on the left and the "rectangle" port head is on the right. The oval port is 2-inches tall and the rectangular is nearly 2½-inches tall. The oval port head is more common on street engines because the smaller port allows for more low RPM power.

the information on these rare heads is nearly non-existent. These heads were available as an option on big-blocks, including L-88, L-89, and later LS-6 engines. In addition, these were standard equipment on ZL-1 aluminum engines. All aluminum factory heads available on production engines were a high-performance upgrade. Nowadays, the early aluminum heads are mainly sought after and used on rare vehicle restoration projects. Chevrolet is still producing aluminum big-block heads for the aftermarket and con-

Cylinder Head & Block Compatibility

Mark IV heads and Gen V blocks don't mix. The Gen V coolant passage design in the deck surface allows coolant to seep into the lifter valley when Mark IV heads are used, but Mark IV intake manifolds, camshafts, distributors, water pumps, and bellhousings work on the Gen V, VI, and VII engines. The Gen VI block coolant system was changed slightly, so Mark IV heads can be bolted onto it.

Cylinder Head & Piston Compatibility

Piston and head compatibility is not guaranteed. It does not always work to install closed chamber heads on an engine equipped with open-chamber-designed pistons or open-chamber heads on an engine with closed-chamber-designed pistons. Just because an open-chamber head has a larger combustion chamber does not mean there is enough room for a closed-chamber pop-up domed piston. Always check your parts compatibility before doing any work.

tinues to improve their designs for different applications.

Port Type

Big-block heads are referred to as rectangle and oval port types. The rectangle-port heads have huge intake ports that are designed to give maximum flow at high RPM, which makes them ideal for drag racing and other motorsports, which require a lot of top-end power. The oval port heads are more

common with street to high-performance applications because they give great low-RPM performance as well as mid-range and top-end power. All oval port and some rectangle port heads are labeled as "PASS" for passenger car and most rectangle-port heads are labeled as "HI-PERF." There's even a third and lesser-known port type referred to as "small" or "round" ports that came on late-model trucks. The truck head was labeled "TRUCK." They

Combustion chambers, from left to right: early closed-chamber, early open-chamber, and later open chamber. The far right chamber is found to be Chevrolet's cleanest burning and best flowing head.

are low on horsepower and high on torque, which makes them less desirable for most performance street applications, but they are great for towing applications.

Chamber Type

Open and closed combustion-chamber designs easily distinguish big-block heads from each other. The closed-chamber head's combustion chamber is small—doesn't open much more than the size of the valves, and just enough room for the spark plug. With the increased emissions standards attempting to clean up the offending "dirty" big-block, Chevrolet lowered the compression ratios and redesigned the combustion chamber. The lower-compression open-chamber design was designed to burn the fuel more evenly and create lower emissions. Inadvertently, the open-chamber made more power even with the lower compression. Chevrolet redesigned the open-chamber heads a couple of times, and each time they made more power. Open-chamber heads became the staple on Chevy big-blocks.

Spark Plugs

Over the years, Chevrolet big-block heads have used two different configurations of plugs. The type of plug you have can identify the era of your cylinder heads. All big-block heads use 14-mm spark plugs, but the seat type did change. The 1969 and earlier cast-iron heads, as well as all years of factory aluminum heads, use a "conventional" gasketed 3/4-inch reach, 13/16-inch hex plugs, and 1970 and up cast-iron heads used a tapered-seat "peanut" 5/8-inch hex spark plug.

Crankshaft

Chevy engineers did a great job using the same parts on many different engine combinations. The 366, 396, 402, 427, and 427 tall deck engines all used the 3.76-inch stroke crankshaft. The 454 and 502 use the 4.00-inch stroke crankshaft. The 496 Gen VII and the 572 Gen VI use a 4.375-inch stroke crankshaft.

Chevrolet installed nodular cast-iron and forged-steel crankshafts in its big-blocks. The nodular cast-iron crank was installed in its lower performance engines, such as two-barrel equipped 396s, 402s and 427s with horsepower under 335 as well as 1973 and later 454s. Higher performance engines and all pre-1973 454s came with a forged-steel crankshaft. The parting lines on the crankshaft between the journals identify the crankshaft as forged or cast. The cast crank has thin (usually less than 1/8-inch thick) parting lines left from the casting mold and the forged crank has a much wider (usually about 3/4-inch) parting line in comparison. Not all crankshafts, especially later model and non-GM cranks, have parting lines due to manufacturing process advancements.

The factory 454-ci and 502-ci engines are externally balanced. Thus, these engines don't have a crankshaft with internal counterweights to balance the rotating assembly. Therefore, a counterweighted harmonic damper on the front of the engine and a counterweighted flywheel or flex plate mounted on the rear of the engine keeps the rotating mass in balance. Conversely, the factory-equipped 366, 396, 402, 427, 496, and 572 engines are equipped with an internally balanced crankshaft. If you are attempting to quickly identify a big-block as a 454, 502, or other-sized engine, you can look for the distinguishing counterweight in the back of the harmonic damper. Keep in mind that this method isn't guaranteed to work, because someone could have installed an internally balanced 454 or 502 aftermarket crankshaft or the crank could have been modified to be internally balanced.

The parting line down the center easily distinguishes forged and cast crankshafts. A narrow parting line denotes a cast crankshaft (lower left) and a wider parting line (right side) identifies the stronger forged steel crankshaft.

 TECH TIP

Unique Camshaft Design

When the Mark IV big-block was first introduced in 1965, the oiling system pressurized the lifters by using an oil passage that fed past the rear cam journal. The camshaft had a groove in its rear journal as well as a groove and three oil passage holes in the rear cam bearing.

This design was only used for 1965 and 1966 and if you have one of these blocks, make sure you buy the correct cam bearings and get your machine shop to machine a 3/16-inch groove 7/64-inch deep in your new camshaft's rear journal or you'll have a disaster on your hands.

TOOLS

Unless you are MacGyver, it takes more than a hammer and some duct tape to build an engine. You need some basic hand tools, some specialty tools, and an engine stand. But the most important tools you have are not in your toolbox. They are your *life*, your *hands,* and your *eyes*. Treasure them and protect them.

There are some important safety aspects that you need to take into consideration for any engine rebuild. When working on or around your engine, there may be an accident or an unforeseeable occasion when your engine starts to fall toward the ground. *Be alert* when working around your engine. Every machinist has a horrific story to tell about someone maimed by an engine-building accident.

Engine Stand

If you were rebuilding a VW flat-four engine, you might not need an engine stand. A big-block Chevy is way too big and heavy to build on a workbench.

The engine stand you are looking for is a unit that is rated at least for 1,000 lbs. A complete big-block with iron heads weighs 600 to 700 lbs, depending on the accessories bolted to it. The big-block is a hefty chunk of iron and it puts a smack-down on the 750-lb-rated engine stands. Don't be cheap on this part of your project. It's not worth it. The best low-priced engine stand I've seen is the 1,500-lb Torin engine stand.

Engine Lifting

If you removed the engine from your car in the past, then you know it's a big task. You need an engine hoist or "cherry picker" to remove or install an engine in a vehicle. In the past, an engine hoist was a piece of equipment that was very large and expensive. Nowadays, you can purchase a much more compact bolt-together unit for a couple of hundred dollars. If buying one isn't an option, rent it for a day to pull the engine and move it to an engine stand then rent it again when you are ready to install the engine back in your vehicle.

Along with a cherry picker, I suggest using an engine-leveling device. Companies such as Trans-Dapt, offer

Don't take your chances with a three-wheeled engine stand. The big-block is a heavy engine. The best engine stand I've ever used is this 1,500-lb-rated brute made by Torin. I wouldn't use anything less. The front leg of this engine stand folds up for easy storage. It was modified with heavy-duty soft-tread casters in place of steel casters to protect my garage floor.

An engine hoist, also known as a cherry-picker, is one of those tools that you will either use twice or dozens of times. I use mine frequently and loan it to friends when they need it. I've had mine for 30 years and still use it to lift engines and other things when I don't feel like breaking my back.

No engine hoist should be without an engine tilter. This handy device allows you to tilt the engine and transmission at severe angles with a turn of the hand crank. It prevents the use of an unsafe single chain that requires you to rest the engine on your car in order to reposition the chain. Get out of the Stone Age and make installing and removing an engine a simple task.

There are a few different types of harmonic damper removal tools on the market. If you don't have one, you can rent one from some auto parts stores. This cheaper tool is the most common. Three puller bolts thread into the balancer, and the center shaft pushes against the outside of the crankshaft snout.

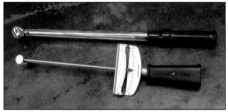

If you don't have a torque wrench you're definitely going to need one for this job. There are three types of torque wrenches: beam-style (analog), conventional (clicker), and dial-type (not shown). They each have their benefit application. Of the three, the conventional clicker torque wrench is the most commonly used by professionals.

To remove the connecting rod and piston assemblies, rotate the crankshaft many times. This special socket allows you to turn the crank with a 1/2-inch-drive ratchet If you don't have access to one of these sockets, you can thread the damper bolt back into the crankshaft with a stack of washers behind it, but this method only allows you to rotate the crank clockwise.

"engine tilters" that allow you to change the angle of the engine with the turn of a knob. With this tilter, it's possible to install an engine and its mated transmission with ease.

Basic Hand Tools

It's safe to assume that since you're reading this book you have a full set of basic hand tools, or at least know you are going to need some. You're going to need at least a 3/8-inch and 1/2-inch-drive ratchet and socket set with sockets ranging from 1/4 inch to 1 inch for the 3/8-inch drive, and 9/16 inch to 1 inch for the 1/2-inch-drive ratchet. You'll need a few different lengths of socket extensions, a spark plug socket, a decent 1/2-inch-drive torque wrench, combination wrenches ranging from 1/2 inch to 1 inch, assorted standard and Phillips screwdrivers, a couple of different types of pliers, a shot-filled rubber mallet and a ball-peen hammer. You'll also need small, medium, and large pry-bars, feeler gauges, an Allen wrench set, and a gasket scraper. This is the extent of the basics.

Best Tools for the Job

Basically, the best tools on the market wear the name Craftsman. They combine the best innovations, quality, finish, price, and warranty, and millions of mechanics and hobbyists know it. Craftsman tools last forever. I still use Craftsman tools handed down to me by my father 30 years ago. ASE Technician Lee Abel believes the same and wrote, "When I saw that my Grandfather made a living farming and maintained all of his equipment with Craftsman tools, I knew if I ever worked on cars I would be using a lot of Craftsman tools and I have for the last 20 plus years." Hobbyists and professional mechanics trust the integrity of Craftsman to get the job done.

Required Miscellaneous Tools

Engine-building tools that you will need include the following:

- Plastigage
- Spark plug feeler gauge or gapper
- A few drift punches
- Engine oil galley brush kit
- Harmonic damper removal and installation tool
- Dial caliper gauge
- Straight edge
- Manual valvespring compressor and tester
- Dial indicator
- Micrometers
- Piston ring compressor
- Ring squaring tool
- Oil pump pickup installer (if you are installing a stock pickup)
- Three-finger sprocket or gear puller
- Engine oil pump primer
- Handheld oil pump
- Flywheel turning handle
- Ring filer (if you are going to file-fit your piston rings)

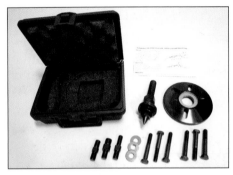

This damper removal kit is used for safe removal and proper installation of the damper. It comes with different bolts and adapters for more than just the big-block Chevrolet.

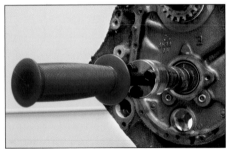

With this fancy handle offered by Goodson, you have more control and leverage to remove the camshaft. Bolt the handle to the camshaft and slowly/carefully pull the cam out of the block, without letting it drop onto the bearings. This is good practice for later when you re-install the cam during the rebuild. You can see that I have let the camshaft journals rest in the block on the bearings to adjust my grip. This is the only way the cam should rest in the block.

There are two distinctly different levels of precision measuring tools. Both of these calipers are used to take precise measurements. The top one from Goodson is stainless steel construction with a digital caliper and is accurate to .0005 inch. The bottom caliper is a fraction of the price and is nylon constructed without any accuracy listed, so it could be to only .001 inch or worse. Better accuracy is higher priced, so decide how precise you want to be.

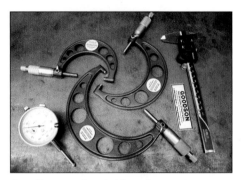

A caliper and outside micrometers are important precision tools to have at your disposal during the engine build process. If you don't have a caliper, you should get one to check depths and steps as well as inside and outside specs on projects. The outside micrometers allow ease of checking diameters of items your caliper can't slide over.

Some specialty tools, such as these from Goodson, are nice to have when building an engine by yourself. Some of the steps in this book use tools you don't absolutely have to own because you can have a machine shop perform some steps for you. The block "deck stand" for your dial indicator, precision straight edge, and dial bore gauge are nice to have for double-checking other people's work. If you are installing new rod bolts, you should be checking rod bolt stretch. The rod bolt stretch gauge (bottom) simplifies the process.

Specialty Tools

The depth and breadth of the rebuild will determine the list of specialty tools needed. ... tools, assuming you wil... machine shop ... machining and as... and pistons. Helpf... tools include:

- Camshaft in...
- Cylinder he... assembly c...
- Cylinder h...
- Rod bolt s...
- Hooked p... cotter pi...
- Scribe
- Number ...
- Crank ...

If you are building a high-performance engine, you should also pick up a camshaft degree wheel for degreeing up your camshaft.

Air Tools

... neces-... your ... em, but ... hat mat-... the assis-

... g air tools ... embly. Air ... essure than ... reak a bolt ... g assembly, ... y be used for ... threads and ... ld be done by ... ratchet, or

... are used to check ... and set critical ... 's important to use one ... h a magnetic base and extension a...m. This one had to be stuck to the metal bench to check the run-out on this valve because the head is aluminum, and the bench was a sturdy metal surface.

These specialty tools from Goodson are needed for you to perform some of the head assembly, and other work, by yourself. The valve-spring compressor is used for installing springs, locks, and keepers. The valvespring-height checker is used to correctly check valvespring installed height. The rotary files are for touching up the ridges and edges in the ports or for port matching the heads and intake manifold. On the right are a pair of cylinder head stands to elevate the heads for serviceability.

An important part of harnessing as much power as possible is to degree-in your camshaft. You can get separate parts or a whole kit, such as this one from Crane Cams. They make the process easy by supplying a precision degree wheel, dial indicator, special cylinder-head mount, piston-stop, pointer, and valve checking springs in a nice carrying case. With this kit, you can determine the accuracy of the cam grind, the dowel in the front of the cam, the keyway in the crankshaft, and the timing gears and chain.

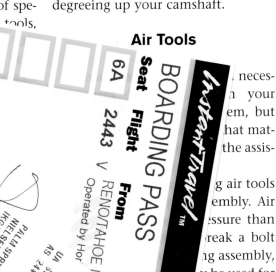

If you ... gaug... diam... tele... less... ac... in ... lo... th... pulling it out of the ... your outside micrometer or caliper ... read the width. Each tool has a slight plus-or-minus accuracy range. Using extra tools to read measurements can "stack" small inaccuracies, so be careful.

Supplies

In addition to tools, you also need some additional supplies during the process of rebuilding your big-block Chevy. Paper shop towels are a must. An engine builder pointed out that if you are wiping down your engine parts with polyester or cotton towels, and a stray thread gets into the engine, a thread could cause catastrophic failure. If you had used paper towels and a small stray piece of paper got left in the engine it would dissolve in the oil. This is the reason paper shop towels make sense.

It's a good idea to get some gloves to protect your skin from harsh and dangerous chemicals. Some chemicals that you will come into contact with while working on your engine are even known to cause cancer. Nitrile gloves work better than silicone work gloves because they do not break down as fast when subjected to harsh cleaners and solvents. If you're concerned that the gloves don't allow the same dexterity as bare hands, you probably haven't used form-fitting gloves. Avoid the cheap, one-size-fits-all multi-purpose gloves sold at your local hardware store.

Lubricants

Get yourself some camshaft installation lubricant. It helps prevent premature cam wear during cam break-in, before their surfaces have had a chance to "mate-in." Use a generous amount on the camshaft lobes before installation.

Engine assembly lube is different from camshaft lube. A lot of companies sell their own blend to help protect against wear during initial start-up, when oil might not be propagated through the oil galleries, even after using an oil pump primer to pre-lube the system.

The first 30 minutes is the most critical break-in period for flat tappet camshafts. Without the proper lubricant, you'll destroy your cam and lifters within minutes. Most V-8 push rod engines require more attention than ever during break-in because standard oil does not include critical elements, such as zinc and phosphorus, because of environmental laws. In addition, current production vehicles come equipped with roller cams or overhead cam engines, which do not require these critical elements for lubrication. Standard 30WT was the best lubricant to use for most of the 20th century, but not anymore. Now you need a bottle of special break-in additives from Comp Cams or break-in oil blended with the additives critical for ensuring that your camshaft and lifters have the lubricant they need. Joe Gibbs Racing Oil blends specific oil for this

Not all assembly lubes are created equal. All camshaft companies offer a suggested camshaft assembly lubricant. Here you can see Crane Cams and Edelbrock assembly lubricant for coating their valvetrain parts during engine assembly. Joe Gibbs Driven assembly grease lubricates parts and valvetrain components, including camshafts and flat-tappets in all Joe Gibbs Racing NASCAR racing engines. They wouldn't risk using inferior products on $70,000 racing engines or risk not finishing a race. Winning races is the team's number-one goal.

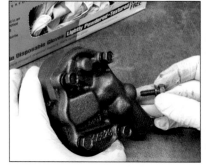

Wear nitrile work gloves to keep your skin protected from cancer-causing chemicals, such as cleaners and sealants. Unlike old silicone mechanics gloves, nitrile gloves are more chemical-resistant. These gloves work well and minimally restrict dexterity, but you need to get the correct size of glove to fit your hands. Good nitrile gloves are not one-size-fits-all.

Only use paper towels on internal parts. Professional engine builders don't use fabric rags to clean or wipe any part going into an engine. They know that small bits of fabric or threads can damage internal parts if they get into the oiling system because they don't break down in oil, but paper towel fibers do break down in oil.

specific need, called Break-In Oil (JGR BR). They also have Hot Rod Oil with the necessary additives not offered in standard off-the-shelf oil available today. These oils are blended with everything our hot rod engines need.

Engine Lubrication Options

If you're using JGR BR for break-in, use it for the first 500 miles and then switch to JGR Hot Rod Oil. If you're using the old conventional 30W oil for break-in method, add a bottle of Comp Cams break-in additive. After 5,000 miles, the rings will be seated and you can take your chances and switch to whatever protection-lacking newly regulated oil you choose.

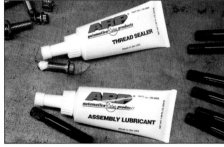

When it comes to sealing and lubricating threads, ARP (Automotive Racing Products) really knows what they are doing. They offer a specially blended Teflon sealant that lubricates and seals threads in applications—sealing out coolant, water, and gasoline. ARP assembly lubricant is a premium grade of moly mixed with rust inhibitors for engine bolt threads. Be sure to refer to the torque specs included with your bolts or the chart on page 150. for the correct spec when using ARP sealant or lubricant; stock torque specifications do not apply when using these products. Factory torque specs should only be followed if you're using 30W oil to lubricate threads.

Bolt Thread Lubricants and Sealers

You're going to need some thread sealant for sealing bolt threads, especially those that are associated with coolant passages and accessories. Many companies have their own blend of thread sealers. You'll also need some assembly lube or 30W engine oil for the bolt threads so you can get a more correct torque on your critical bolts like rod bolts, main bolts or studs, head bolts or studs, etc. ARP (Automotive Racing Products) sells thread sealants and thread lubricants that are specially blended for these specific applications. Using these products changes the amount of torque applied during installation.

Sealants

When it comes to keeping your engine sealed and preventing oil leaks, you have to rely on good gaskets and the correct sealants. There

An array of sealants, lubricants, and other chemicals is needed to build your engine, and Permatex is the number-one trusted company in the industry. For this build we used Ultra Black, No. 1 Form-A-Gasket, Anti-Seize, High-Tack Spray-A-Gasket, Blue and Red Threadlocker, Water Pump RTV, and Super 300 Form-A-Gasket (not shown).

are many sealants on the market and they are all meant for specific applications. For instance, you wouldn't want to use an adhesive where you need a sealant or vice versa. The correct sealants, according to Permatex and professional engine builders, are shown in each step of the book.

If you have an old opened tube of silicone sealer, please dispose of it properly.

For the most part, if you follow my suggestions for sealants you'll need these Permatex products:

- Ultra Black RTV Silicone Gasket Maker
- Permatex Form-A-Gasket Number 1 Sealant
- Super 300 Form-A-Gasket Sealant
- Permatex High-Tack Spray-A-Gasket
- Anti-Seize Lubricant
- Red Threadlocker
- Blue Threadlocker
- Water Pump and Thermostat RTV Silicone

Cleaning Equipment

I recommended that you clean your engine yourself before final assembly. You can trust your machine shop to perform cleaning duties, but the only way to ensure it's thoroughly done is to clean your engine parts one last time after the machine shop has hot-tanked everything. In order to clean your parts thoroughly you'll need a pressure washer, or access to some heavy-duty cleaner and some hot water with a little pressure behind it. If you can get a pressure washer, try to find one that allows you to add solvent or soap to a reservoir that mixes the cleaner with the hot water stream.

Oils Aren't What They Used to Be

With regulations imposed by the EPA, additives in oils that give proven anti-wear protection to engines, including big- and small-block Chevy engines, are being drastically reduced. Joe Gibbs Racing (JGR) is a racing company that blended their own racing oils for their racing cars. Other teams started purchasing oil from them and now it's a business. It's not like they were an oil company blending oil, they blended their own oil to protect their $70,000 racing engines on the track. Now everyone can benefit from JGR's hard work.

When asked about the difference in JGR Oils, Lake Speed Jr. said, "For years, enthusiasts have been using non-synthetic 30W as break-in oil for the first 3,000 miles, waiting for the rings to seat. They stuck with what worked in the past, which wasn't great." JGR's BR (Break-In) oil is not only formulated to properly lubricate flat tappet cams, it's also designed to seat piston rings in the first 200 miles, which is why it works great in roller cam applications too. JGR offers specifically blended oils for race cars and for hot rods. You can safely switch to their Hot Rod Oil after 500 miles.

Using regulated off-the-shelf oils in your newly rebuilt engine is taking a risk. These regulations help reduce emissions and protect emissions equipment but they don't properly lubricate flat-tappet engines or leave a protective lubricating film on critical parts for cold-start protection. JGR Oils protect engines better than any auto-parts store oil has done in the past, even before additives were taken out and regulated. You can protect and lubricate your street engine with oils designed by racers for racers, while reaping the benefits of their goal to win races and save money doing it.

Since 2007, flat tappet cams in hot rods have been going flat in record numbers because of the gradual reduction of specific additives (such as zinc to lubricate the cam and lifters) by the oil industry because of the EPA, automobile manufacturers, and the API (American Petroleum Institute). Choice of lubrication for pushrod engines like the big-block Chevy is important during break-in and afterwards. Joe Gibbs has us covered and offers synthetic Hot Rod Oil with higher levels of zinc and other additives than standard oils to continue protecting your lifters well after break-in.

Joe Gibbs Racing Oil is designed to protect their $70,000 racing engines. They offer a full line of designer petroleum, semi-synthetic, and full synthetic racing formula oils for specific racing applications.

For more than 50 years, builders have been using 30W non-synthetic oil for breaking in engines. Due to tightening of environmental regulations and changes in lubrication requirements for newer vehicles with roller camshafts and emissions control equipment, standard oils have dramatically reduced their zinc and phosphorus contents. Those additives are most important for lubricating flat tappets and rings, especially during the break-in period. Joe Gibbs Racing has specially formulated its Break-in Oil (BR) for the break-in period, so your engine is protected by a higher content of additives, which competing oil companies currently don't use.

REMOVAL AND TEAR DOWN

Well, you've either purchased an engine to rebuild for your project or your vehicle is equipped with a big-block that needs a rebuild. Either way, you've got this book and you are ready to dive into this project and get started.

Documentation

The first step in any project is to take pictures of all the hoses, wires, belts, and parts. Projects such as this

It's easy to get in a hurry and tear into a big project like this, but consider that you have to put all of this back together when you're done. The first step should always be to grab your camera and snap photos before tearing anything apart, especially if this is the first time you've pulled out an engine. Take detailed photos of wiring connections, vacuum hose connections, as well as specific locations of parts and brackets.

always take longer than anticipated, and there's nothing more frustrating than finishing your rebuild and not remembering how vacuum hoses or wires connected to your accessories. If you don't have a digital camera on hand, you can use the tried and true method of drawing a diagram on paper and labeling your hoses and wires with tape. When taking bolts off the engine, it's helpful to put them in separate resealable plastic bags and label them as to where they go. Take notes of how assemblies such as the throttle and other cables are attached to the vehicle.

Safety Warnings

There are many automotive-related injuries and deaths each year that are the results of unsafe work conditions and practices. Parts, equipment, and systems can fail, but most occurrences could have been prevented by simple compliance with routine safety precautions.

Jacking and Supporting

It is absolutely necessary to cautiously jack your car up and lower it onto jack stands, in order to take the weight of the car off the jack. A good friend was crushed to death

because he got under a truck that had been supported solely by a floor jack and the jack slipped. *Never* rely on a floor jack to support the weight of a vehicle. *Always* use multiple jack stands to support the weight of a vehicle. The jack stands should be placed under the frame in areas designated in your owner's manual. If you don't have one, you can probably find the information online or at a local shop.

*Use caution when jacking up your vehicle. Be aware of proper jacking locations on the chassis. **Never support your vehicle with a floor jack. Raise the vehicle and safely lower it down onto sturdy jack stands. Don't rely on the O-ring on a hydraulic ram to keep a vehicle from crushing you. Spend the extra time and money to save your life. These two stands were placed close enough together to allow for the cherry-picker legs to go around them.***

Always start by having your vehicle on a level surface. Use a pair of sturdy wheel chocks (one in front–one behind) on the same tire to keep your vehicle from rolling while jacking it up. I've seen people use 2 x 4-inch blocks, but in many cases they are too small to keep a tire from rolling.

Never rely on the transmission or emergency brake to keep a vehicle from rolling while you are working on it or under it. *Always* place a wheel chock in front of and behind at least one tire.

Driveshaft Removal

When removing the driveshaft, the transmission will no longer keep the car from rolling! So if your car is relying on the parking gear to keep from rolling off your jack stands, it's going to fall off them and crush you! If you are trying to keep a car from rolling, it should be relying on wheel chocks in front of and behind the tires. Even using only the emergency brake to keep the car from rolling is a safety hazard.

Most people who remove the engine also remove the transmission, so I'm including driveshaft removal in this section because there is a potential for a hazardous spill. In order to remove the driveshaft, you need to remove the four bolts holding the rear universal joint to the rear axle. Remove the rear of the shaft and wrap tape around the U-joint caps to keep them on the joint. If they fall off, all of the

needle bearings will probably fall out, and you'll have to put them all back, which can be a big chore.

Get your drain pan. Once you slide the yoke (connected to the front of the driveshaft) out of the transmission, a bunch of fluid will drain out. If you forget the drain pan and pull the yoke, the yoke's on you. There's nothing like a big pool of ancient gear oil or ATF on the ground, in your hair, and soaked into your clothes. Pull the drain pan and place the fluid in a separate container and take it to the engine-oil reclamation center as you did with the used engine oil. Then put the pan back under the end of the transmission, unless you have a spare yoke to plug into the back of the transmission to keep more fluid from spilling out upon engine removal.

Battery Safety

You need to disconnect the battery before you start your rebuild or do any electrical system work. First put on your safety glasses (older serviceable batteries have been known to explode if the battery has been degassing flammable gas in a confined

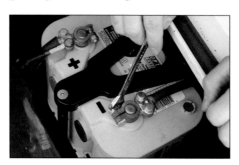

Disconnect your battery before removing any parts from the engine. Always remove the negative (ground) battery cable first and then the positive one. If you remove the positive cable first you run the risk of short-circuiting your electrical system if it happens to touch bare metal.

space and a spark ignites the gas), then remove the negative or "ground" cable from the battery, and then remove the positive battery cable from the battery. This procedure ensures that you don't accidentally "short out" your electrical system and burn your car to the ground.

Drain Fluids

So you don't get a surprise later on, drain the fluids from the engine. There is also a vital safety issue here. Make sure the engine has not been operating for at least an hour so hot coolant doesn't explode in your face and the fluids are cool enough not to injure you if they get on your skin.

Oil

Start with draining the oil. With the engine oil cool and your vehicle safely supported on jack stands, slide a drain pan under the engine. The drain pan should be able to hold six or seven quarts of oil. The larger the pan the better—I've drained an engine

Drain your old fluids into their own containers. Don't mix water/coolant with your oil-based fluids because it makes recycling them very tough. Place your oil filter upside down over your drain pan to drain as much oil from it as you can. Take the filter and your old used fluids to a recycling center in your town.

block that was filled with 12 quarts of oil and water due to a cracked block. Drain all your engine oil into designated oil containers and take them to your local engine oil recycler. While draining the oil into containers, look for signs of water and metal shavings that may be tell-tale signs of what to expect when rebuilding your engine. Most large auto parts store chains, oil-changing businesses, and city corporation yards have legal and "green" ways to cleanly dispose of old engine oil. If you have questions about recycling oil go to www.recycleoil.org.

Transmission Fluid

If your vehicle is equipped with an automatic transmission, loosen the transmission cooler lines and drain the fluid into your drain pan. Each transmission is full of fluid that should be drained or else you'll have a huge spill under your vehicle as soon as you tip the rear of the transmission down. The only way to keep fluid from pouring out is to plug the transmission with a spare tailshaft yoke. Using a plastic transmission plug does not always work. Tipping the transmission can put a lot of extra pressure on the plug and cause it to fly out and make a huge mess.

Power Steering

There are two ways to deal with the power steering fluid. You can drain it and add it in the container with the used transmission fluid. If you don't want to drain it, you can sometimes remove the power steering pump from the engine and safely secure the pump off to the side in the inner fender with bailing wire. You will still have enough room to remove the engine without draining the system.

Cooling System

Get a drain pan or bucket that will hold a few gallons of antifreeze and place it under the lower radiator hose. Remove the clamp from the lower hose and carefully break the hose free from the lower radiator port. If you pull too hard, you can break the radiator. Coolant hoses have a way of bonding to fittings and housings. The easiest way to remove any coolant hose without damaging the hose is to remove the clamp and use a cotter pin removal tool wedged between the hose and the water outlet. Wedge the tool around the circumference of the outlet, and it will break the hose free, making it much easier to remove. There are a few gallons of coolant above the hose you are removing, so remove it slowly or you will be taking a shower in the coolant. Letting the coolant dribble out is usually a much cleaner way to drain the system.

When you have drained the coolant from the system, remember that there will be a couple of quarts left in the engine and that coolant may spill out later when you least want it to.

Drain your coolant into its own containers and you can usually take it to the reclamation center along with your drained oil. Do not drain coolant into the street or onto the ground.

Air Conditioning

If your vehicle has air conditioning and you want to keep it, you can either loosen the compressor and tie it off to the side on the fender well to keep from having to deal with the Freon in the system or you can try to have an air conditioning repair service bring equipment to your car and

extract the Freon from your system. The easiest solution is to get slack in the hoses connected to the compressor and move it out of the way.

Fuel System

Disconnect your fuel line and plug the line to keep all the fuel in the tank from siphoning and emptying onto the ground and the engine compartment. Obviously fuel is flammable, so be careful when working around it and keep open flames and heat sources away from the area until you get the line plugged.

Wiring and Hoses

You can start disconnecting wiring connectors and vacuum hoses if you've made a diagram of the vacuum hose and wiring connections and disconnected the battery. Start by carefully removing the heater hoses and radiator hoses. Remove the vacuum lines and emissions hoses. Disconnect ground cables from the body and frame to the heads and block, as well as the wires from accessories like the alternator, ignition coil, and distributor. Remove additional fuel hose connections to the carburetor.

Distributor

Remove the spark plug wires and distributor. It takes a 9/16-inch wrench to remove the distributor clamp. Once you pull the distributor out, place a rag or paper towel over the hole in the intake manifold.

Belts

Loosen the alternator, power steering pump, and other accessories and pull the fan belts off the pulleys and set them aside for later inspection. If you aren't going to drain the A/C or power steering systems, you can unbolt their brackets now and tie them off to the side in the engine compartment. You can also remove the alternator and its brackets.

Spark Plugs

To make removing the exhaust manifolds easier, you need to remove the spark plugs from the heads. When removing the spark plugs, keep them in order by cylinder. They tell a story about what might have caused your big-block to be a candidate for a rebuild. A few signs are: a dry, light-brown to yellowish plug is usually a sign of normal conditions; a black, sooty plug is a sign of running rich; the center electrode and the porcelain around it are eaten or chipped away and a dark to black color usually means severe detonation from bad timing and/or cheap crappy gas with too low of an octane number; and, a wet oily plug is a sign of oil getting into the combustion chamber through a leaky intake manifold gasket or failing piston rings.

Don't throw the plugs away because you may need them later to keep debris from getting into the cylinders.

1 Unbolt Torque Converter

Before you unbolt the transmission from the engine, it's a good idea to unbolt the torque converter. Using a screwdriver to keep the flex-plate from spinning or a special flywheel tool (step 6) you can unbolt the three converter bolts. Then gently pry the converter away from the flex plate. It should move 1/4 inch away from the plate. When removing the transmission from the engine or moving it around the garage, the converter will now be loose so be careful not to tip the transmission or the converter will slide off the input shaft and land on your foot and make a big mess. It's a good idea to secure the converter to the transmission as soon as possible with a strap or bracket to retain it.

2 Remove Distributor

Now the engine is on the stand and it's time to start disassembly. If you were simply removing the intake manifold to replace the gasket, you would want to mark the location of the rotor on the distributor body. Because we are rebuilding this engine completely, the distributor and rotor location/ relationship are not important at this point. Simply remove the clamp at the base of the distributor and pull it out.

Exhaust

With the car safely on jack stands, get under the car and remove the bolts on the flange of your exhaust manifolds or, if your vehicle has headers, unbolt the flanges from the exhaust pipes. These bolts can be stubborn, so squirt a liberal amount of penetrant lubricant on the nuts and threads. Exhaust manifold studs usually require special attention and sometimes you can spray the backside of the stud on the exhaust manifold. Let this sit for a little bit and try again. If you can safely heat them with a torch, this may loosen the corroded threads. If they just won't come out, it's time for extra force with the ratchet; go ahead and snap them off and you can install new studs later. Make sure the pipes don't fall down on your head. Some bailing wire should keep the exhaust pipes off the ground or out of your way.

3 Remove Exhaust Manifolds

Before removing the exhaust manifolds from the heads, it's a good idea to remove all the exhaust nuts and studs. The bolts and nuts are usually baked and rusted into oblivion and need some assistance. Soak all points of the manifold bolts (even on the backside of the stud, if there's access) with your favorite penetrating lubricant before starting.

Sometimes the nut spins some, and then locks again. In this case use more penetrant lube, then tighten the nut again and loosen it again. It usually comes loose by going back and forth. If the nuts don't turn but the stud does, don't worry. If nothing budges, try some more penetrant lube. If that doesn't work, you may need to force the nut and break the stud. If the stud breaks and you're using these manifolds again you must drill out the broken stud and replace it.

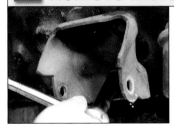

To safely remove the exhaust manifolds, remove all bolts except for two; leave one on each end. The cast exhaust manifolds weigh about 13 lbs, so it's a good idea to support the manifold with one hand and remove the bolts with the other hand. Each manifold is fastened to the block with eight bolts. Remove these bolts with a 9/16-inch socket.

While you are under the car, you may as well remove the wires connected to the starter. Don't forget to take a picture of the wires on the starter solenoid or at least make a mental note as to their orientation. Remove the starter. If it's a stock starter, it weighs about 20 pounds, so support it when removing the last bolt.

If your car has headers, there's a good chance you can't lift the engine out of the compartment until you remove them. If you have exhaust manifolds, you can sometimes leave them on until the engine is out of the car. Remove the oil dipstick located between cylinders number-4 and 6 by unbolting the tab that mounts to the exhaust bolt. Now you can remove the manifolds or headers. Most passenger-side headers will drop out the bottom without issue. The driver-side header is usually a tight fit and requires hanging the header up inside the engine compartment with some rope or bailing wire once removing all the bolts. After the engine is out, you can remove the header and don't forget to do this in reverse when re-installing the engine or you will be installing the engine twice.

4 Remove Motor Mounts

Remove the engine mounts from both sides of the block. Some mounts are side-specific; of those, some have "RH" or "LH" stamped on them and some don't. Keep track of which side they come off so they can be re-installed correctly. They are held on with three 9/16-inch bolts per side.

Carburetor

Remove the throttle cable or rod, return springs, and transmission detent or throttle-valve (TV) cable from the carburetor. Remove the carb and cover the open intake manifold plenum.

Use Special Tool

5 Remove Fuel Line

If your engine isn't a carbureted model, you can skip this step. Before removing the two mounting bolts for the fuel pump, remove the fuel hard-line that transfers fuel to the carburetor. Use a special "line" wrench to keep the fitting from getting damaged.

Transmissions

You can pull the engine and transmission out as one unit or you can separate the engine from the transmission. This book only covers removing both the engine and transmission as one unit.

Since you are following the steps, I probably don't need to mention that you should have already removed the driveshaft from the car and have heeded the suggestions and safety warnings on doing so.

If your vehicle has a standard transmission with mechanical clutch linkage, you need to remove the Z-bar linkage and any other bracketry or springs connecting the engine to the car. Remove the shifter and linkage from the transmission. Take a picture and keep the shift linkage from moving around and getting out of adjustment during this whole process.

If you have an automatic transmission, you need to disconnect the transmission lines. Most of these lines run from the passenger side of the transmission to the cooler inside the radiator. Remove the shift cable and any electrical plugs from the transmission.

Support the rear of the transmission with a floor jack, so you can remove the transmission mount and transmission crossmember. Without lowering the transmission too much, place a jackstand or sturdy support under the transmission in place of the transmission mount. In some cases, you simply remove the bolts holding the transmission mount to the crossmember and let the brace hold the transmission up.

Pulling Engine

You can pull the engine and transmission out as one unit or you can separate the engine from the transmission. This book only covers removing both the engine and transmission as one unit.

Some vehicles require removal of the radiator and/or removing the water pump and lower pulley on the harmonic damper from the engine before you can

Now you have your engine out of the vehicle and it's ready for disassembly. Lower the engine to the ground or place it on blocks before working around it, so that it doesn't fall on your toes. Placing it on the ground also keeps the engine from moving while you work on it, until you can put it on your engine stand.

lift the engine out. If you pull the water pump now, know that some trapped coolant will pour out upon removal.

Get your engine hoist into position with the hook and chain so it clears the top of the carburetor or remove the carb altogether. The job of removing the engine is made so simple with an "engine tilter." Using a chain is old news; it works but it can be a big, dangerous hassle. In turn, it's unsafe for pulling the engine and transmission out as one unit because of the chain placement and necessary tilting of the engine to get it out of the engine compartment.

Place all four engine tilter chains on the engine. If your valve cover is close to your brake booster or wiper motor, you may need to remove the driver's side valve cover or wiper motor or both. Place a drain pan under the back of the transmission because, once you move the engine or tilt it, a bunch of fluid will shoot out of the tailshaft. Make one last sweep to make sure there's nothing connecting the engine or transmission to the car. Remove the nuts on the two long bolts holding the engine mounts to the "frame stands" on the frame. Using the engine hoist, lift the engine just a touch so you can pull the two long bolts out of the engine mounts. Once you have the two long bolts removed you should be free to lift the engine out of the vehicle. Use the engine tilter to your advantage by changing the lifting center of gravity forward and backward to get the engine and transmission up and out.

Once the engine is out you can set the assembly on the ground and separate the engine and transmission. If it's an automatic transmission, you need to remove the three bolts that attach the torque converter to the flex-plate. If it's a standard transmission, you simply remove the transmission and then the bellhousing. Remove the flywheel or flex-plate from the crankshaft.

With those removed from the engine, you are ready to put the engine on your sturdy engine stand. Now you're ready to continue the disassembly.

6 Remove Flywheel or Flexplate

Remove the flywheel or flexplate before you put your engine on the stand. The flywheel turning tool seen in the top of the image is more effective and safer than using a screwdriver to lock the flywheel for bolt removal and turning the plate into different positions. It's safer to perform this step with the engine resting on the ground, rather than a couple of feet in the air.

7 Bolt Engine Stand to Block

While the engine is still on the ground, attach the engine stand head to the bellhousing area of the block. The head typically has four adjustable arms. Adjust the arms to locate the head post a couple of inches above the crankshaft centerline, if possible. This helps balance the load and makes turning the engine easier.

Tear Down Long Block

8 Remove Fuel Pump

When you loosen the two bolts from the fuel pump flange, it will have some pressure because the fuel pump rod is slightly compressed. Tilt the fuel pump as shown and lift up and out.

9 Remove Fuel Pump Plug

To remove the fuel pump pushrod, use a 5/16-inch Allen wrench to remove the plug below the pump mounting surface. I've also seen them as square drive plugs. Expect some trapped oil to spill out when the plug is removed. The fuel pump pushrod should slide out at the same time. If you are going to re-install the pushrod, make sure to protect it when storing it with other parts.

Documentation Required

10 Remove Accessories

Remove other accessories such as the alternator, air conditioning compressor, smog pump, and power steering pump. Most of these accessories can be removed with 9/16-inch and 5/8-inch wrenches. You should know if the air compressor is working and holding a charge before you remove it from the engine compartment. Smog pumps are subjected to constant heat and are notorious for wearing out, so replacement may be inevitable. When all these parts have been removed, inspect them for wear. You may want to replace or rebuild your alternator, if you spin the pulley and hear a metallic sound from the bearings or if it drags. A leaky seal on the power steering pump is obvious. Place all these accessories in a box or inside large plastic bags to keep your garage clean and to keep dust and debris from inside them while you rebuild your engine.

Documentation Required

11 Organize Fasteners

If you are going to use these accessories again it's a good idea to keep all bolts in labeled bags or you end up with a huge bucket or valve cover filled with hardware like the one shown in the background. If a shim is used to space out an accessory, mention it in your notes.

13 Disconnect Water Temperature Sender

Depending on the model and year of the car the engine came from, the water temp sender is located in the left or right head. This one is located on the left head. These are stubborn, so you should apply some penetrant lube. A box end wrench and a hard rubber mallet persuader broke this switch free.

Important!

15 Drain and Recycle Oil

If your engine still has oil in it, unscrew the drain plug and drain the oil into a bucket. Remove the oil filter and drain it into the oil bucket while you're at it. Depending on the area you live in, you can safely get rid of this oil at a local repair shop or oil-recycling center. For more info and to help find oil recyclers in your area, you can visit www.recycleoil.org and follow their links.

Professional Mechanic Tip

12 Disconnect Hoses PRO TIP

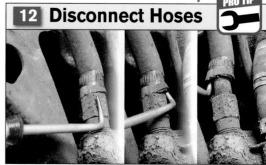

PRO TIP *If you have inspected your hoses and they are in good shape, here's a tip on how to save them. Get a nice cotter pin puller and carefully insert it under the lip of the hose. Run the puller around the fitting to the left and to the right. The hose should break free from the fitting and slide off with a couple wiggles of the hose.*

14 Take Out Water Jacket Plugs

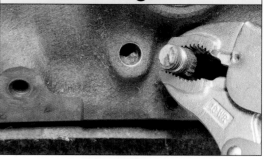

The water jacket plugs in the block are located at the center of the bottom of the block above the oil pan rail. There's one on each side of the block. Using penetrant lube and a six-point socket doesn't always work on these. The six-point rounded the heads, so a dead-blow hammer and a pair of locking pliers or Vice-Grip pliers were used to finish the job.

The water gallery plug in the head opposite the water temp switch is a bigger challenge. Breaking one of these free requires a few doses of penetrant lube. The factory plugs have a 1/2-inch-square drive indentation. With some luck and persuasion, this plug came out with a 1/2-inch-drive ratchet.

16 Remove Front and Rear Oil Gallery Plugs

Typically, this is the location of the oil-pressure line or switch tapped in for a gauge, but this one came out of a motor home so the switch was located near the front (as seen in the right photo), so this port was capped off. Remove the front and rear oil gallery plugs, fittings, or senders.

17 Disconnect and Label Wires, Lines and Hoses

Make sure you have followed the step to record all connected hoses or taken detailed pictures, so you can reconnect them later. Remove all connected hoses, lines, wires, choke accessories, and then remove the carburetor. If you tip the carburetor on its side or upside down, be careful because excess fuel will pour out.

18 Remove Carburetor

While removing the carburetor, the choke rod was disconnected, but the choke hold-down screw was not ready to come out because the head had stripped out. The outer choke shell is simply pressed on, which made it easy to remove in order to gain access to one of the intake manifold bolts. The choke housing screw needs to be drilled out in order to get it off the intake manifold.

The big-block has one distinct bolt and bolt boss located atop the center of the intake ports on all four corners of the intake manifold. The bosses are large enough to require stamped steel valve covers to have reliefs cut into them.

19 Remove Valve Cover

To remove the intake manifold it was necessary to unbolt one valve cover to give room. You can remove both valve covers but it's not required; one is fine for now.

20 Remove All Intake Manifold Bolts

Back out all 16 bolts with a ratchet and 9/16-inch socket. With all the intake manifold bolts removed you are ready to remove it, but it's not likely to budge. Some prying around the intake-to-head surface (but not on a bolt boss) is customary, but it is safer to keep the prying between the block-to-intake manifold surfaces.

Important!

21 Lifting and Removing Intake Manifold

The stock cast-iron intake manifold weighs 42 lbs, and an aluminum intake weighs about 20 lbs. Make sure you position yourself so that you don't strain your back while lifting it. To get a good grip on the intake, you can insert a couple fingers in the distributor hole and in the water jacket below the thermostat housing. Lifting the intake by the center carburetor ports does not give you as much control or leverage.

I plan to completely rebuild the engine, so I did not bother to clean all the dirt and debris from on top of the intake manifold before I removed it. This debris fell into the lifter gallery and intake ports. Excess water trapped in the water jackets also fell into the lifter gallery.

22 Spin Out Spark Plugs

Spark plug condition indicates the condition of the cylinder. If water pours out of the spark plug hole, you may have a cracked cylinder wall or the engine was simply sitting out in the rain without an air cleaner.

Critical Inspection

23 Inspect Valvetrain for Wear Pattern

During the life of valvetrain parts, they get specific wear patterns. These patterns are like fingerprints and need to be kept in order. One lifter "wears" into a specific lobe on the cam and a pushrod wears into the specific lifter, and so on. If you plan on reusing the rocker arms, pushrods, lifters, or the camshaft while rebuilding the engine, you need to take them out in order and put them back in order. I used my Goodson valvetrain organizer tray to keep all the parts in order while removing them.

Important!

24 Pull Out Lifters

There are a few ways to remove the lifters. In most cases you can simply pull the lifters out by hand. If you can't, grab them with pliers and pull them out. If you plan on using the cam and lifters again you should get a hooked tool like an O-ring remover or a cotter pin puller, hook the inside ridge of the lifter (the gap in the snap ring groove), and pull upward.

If a lifter is stuck in its bore and won't lift upward, do not force it! A lifter can be badly damaged and have a ridge worn in it (known as a mushroomed lifter) at the bottom, causing it to hang up on the lifter bore. Pull the lifter up as far as it will go, without forcing it, and put a tie strap around it to keep it elevated. After removing the camshaft in a later step, cut the tie strap and drop the lifter out through the bottom of the lifter bore. If you don't raise the lifter, the camshaft won't slide out of the block. If you forcibly pull the lifter upward, you will damage the lifter bore and it will require expensive machine work to sleeve the bore.

25 Remove Cylinder Heads

Important!

> To keep the head from falling to the floor or onto your foot while breaking the head loose from the block, loosen all 16 bolts and remove all but the two bolts at the front and rear of the head, directly below the valve cover bolting surface. These two bolts should be left threaded into the block two or three full turns. This prevents the head from falling off the block when it breaks loose in the next step. For extra muscle needed to remove the bolts, I started with a 5/8-inch socket on a 1/2-inch-drive breaker bar and moved on to a 1/2-inch-drive ratchet.

26 Remove Cylinder Heads from Cylinder Block

By sticking a hammer handle or a strong piece of wood into the intake port and giving a few quick pulls, you should be able to break the head loose from the block. If that doesn't work, check to make sure you got all the bolts off (except for the two loose bolts you left in the head for safety). Try the wood again.

Professional Mechanic Tip

> If the wooden handle doesn't work, check to make sure you got all but the two bolts off (very critical before any more force is applied in this manner). There are two non-critical areas you can give a lightly applied pry to separate the head from the block. Do not *under any circumstance* pry on a mating surface or drive a bar between the head and the block.

Safety Step

> After the head is loose from the deck surface but still resting on the dowel pins, and remove the two bolts you left threaded into the block. If the head is not resting on the dowel pins and you remove the two bolts, the head can slide off the block and fall on your foot or other part of your body. Each cast-iron head weighs 74 lbs (aluminum heads weigh about 41 lbs) and can cause major bodily harm. An easy way to lift the head off the block is to put a few fingers into intake ports number-7 and 5 while you put a couple fingers into exhaust port number-1. Remember, the head is heavy; be sure to not strain your back. If you need help, call a strong friend.

27 Unbolt Oil Pan

Remove all but two of the twenty 1/2-inch bolts from the oil pan with a ratchet and 1/2-inch socket. Don't forget about removing the two smaller bolts at the front of the pan. Leave one bolt loose near the center of the pan on the left side and one on the right side. Use your wide-blade gasket scraper tool to break the pan loose from the gasket. Pull the last two bolts from the pan. Some excess oil will still be in the bottom of the pan, so be sure not to dump it onto your floor. Pour the oil into your bucket of drained oil.

28 Rotate Engine and Drain Fluids

With the heads off the block it is easier to rotate the engine on the engine stand. If you don't have a handy drain tray designed for your engine stand, lay some rags or a floorpan on the floor under your engine stand. Excess water, oil, and debris will pour out of the block because it's almost impossible to remove it without all the plugs removed and a lot of effort. The engine will also drip for a few days—make that weeks—after turning it over.

29 Rotate Engine for Removing Bottom End

Now it's safe to rotate the engine over so you can start removing the bottom end. Carefully and slowly rotate the block in order to reduce the risk of injury if the block or engine stand becomes unstable. This also helps control the mess described in the previous step.

30 Remove Oil Pump Pickup

If you are going to install a new oil pump (strongly recommended), use the original oil pump pickup. This is the best time to remove it because it's still bolted to the engine. If the pickup is braised or welded to the pump you can use a cut-off wheel to break it free.

You can use an old screwdriver or dull chisel to tap the pickup off the oil pump. Sometimes it helps to use your hand to nudge the pickup to turn it clockwise and counter-clockwise in the pump to initially help it break free. If you are going to replace the pump, pickup and oil pan, don't waste your time on this step.

31 Remove Oil Pump

A single bolt holds the oil pump onto the rear main cap and is removed with a 5/8-inch wrench. With a little bump, the pump should break loose. Lift the pump straight up. The oil pump driveshaft should still be attached. The stock shaft has a nylon bushing to keep the two shafts locked together. The bushing is very brittle and may break during disassembly and should be replaced anyway.

Important!

32 Remove Damper From Crankshaft

Remove the bolt with a 1/2-inch-drive ratchet and 3/4-inch socket. Following the instructions included with the puller, install the plate, threaded shaft, and three damper bolts. Be sure the damper bolts are installed evenly; otherwise, the puller pulls the damper off at an angle, which damages the tool and the damper. Apply anti-seize lubricant to the main puller shaft to ease removal. Using one wrench to hold the main shaft in place and another to turn the nut on the shaft, the tool pulls the damper off the crankshaft snout.

The beauty of this tool is that it threads into the crankshaft snout. When the damper comes loose from the crank, it doesn't fall on the floor or your foot because it's still attached to the crank.

33 Take Off Timing Cover

Remove all 10 bolts from the timing cover with a 1/4-inch-drive ratchet and 7/16-inch socket. Wedge your gasket scraper or wide-blade screwdriver between the block face and the top lip of the timing cover and pry it loose from the seal.

Professional Mechanic Tip

34 Remove the Camshaft

 There are a few ways to remove the camshaft. You can purchase a nice handle from Goodson. Or you can save your money, take your chances, and use the upper timing gear to pull the cam. First, remove the three bolts holding the timing gear to the camshaft with a 3/8-inch-drive ratchet and a 1/2-inch socket. Remove the timing gear from the cam, remove the timing chain, and re-install the gear by installing the bolts by hand. Push in on the bottom of the gear and pull on the top of the gear to produce leverage while gently twisting and pulling the cam out of the block. If you are rebuilding the entire engine, you will replace the cam bearings and you can use this careful removal process as practice for when you are installing the new cam. Caution: If the cam falls on the bearings, it can damage them. The camshaft has many sharp edges and the bearings are very soft. The camshaft has five bearing journals. While removing it, you can rest the cam when the journals are interfaced with the bearing surfaces to get a better grip or leverage on it. Do not rest the cam lobes on the bearings.

Notation Required

35 Rotate Crankshaft for Access to Rod Bolts

Be sure your hands and tools are not on the rotating parts. Using a ratchet or breaker bar with your crankshaft socket, rotate the crankshaft so that connecting rods number-1 and 2 are on top. This allows access to their rod bolts and caps in order to ease their removal.

36 Number the Rods

Before removing the rods, make sure you number them by using a number stamp or a center punch with the number of times correlating with the cylinder number. If the rods are numbered already, make sure they are all correct. In some cases the rods have been replaced and the numbers won't match, or you have multiples. For instance, you may have two of number-5 and no number-7. Number the mains "1" through "5" (starting at the front as number-1) while you are at it.

37 Loosen Connecting Rod Nuts

Loosen the connecting rod nuts with a 1/2-inch-drive ratchet and a 9/16-inch socket until they are flush with the tip of the rod bolt. Use a dead-blow hammer or a hammer and a piece of wood to strike the nut. If you strike the bolt threads without the nut, you could mushroom the threads or damage your hammer; the threaded nut protects both. When the rod cap breaks loose from the rod, remove the cap and cap bearing.

Professional Mechanic Tip, Important!

38 Properly Protect Crankshafts

 To protect the crankshaft during the next couple of steps, get some bolt protectors or some 3/8-inch rubber hose and slide it over the threads. Then rotate the crankshaft to position the rod journal directly in-line with the cylinder bore of the piston you are removing. Make sure it is lined up so the connecting rod and its bolts do not touch the bottom edges of the cylinder during removal.

Important!

39 Remove Rods and Pistons

With the rod lined up with the cylinder, place a wooden dowel (about 20 inches long) down into the cylinder on the backside of the piston dome. Place your hand under the piston, so it doesn't fall on the floor, while lightly striking the dowel to drive the piston and rod assembly out of the bore. While placing your hand under the piston, place something soft under your engine to safely catch the piston as it is driven out. Cement floors damage piston and rod assemblies.

40 Use Block Reamer to Remove Pistons

If your engine has a deep ridge just below the top of the bore, it may keep the piston from coming out of the bore. You may need to purchase a ridge reamer to remove the ridge. If you remove too much material (easy to do), you either have to replace the block or have a sleeve installed. Either way, it's an expensive mistake to make. If the ridge isn't too deep (less than .0020 inch) you can drive the piston out with more force, which can break the rings but save the block. Or, you can simply have the machine shop remove the pistons safely.

Professional Mechanic Tip, Use Special Tool

41 Remove Rod and Piston Assemblies

The safest way to remove the rod and piston is to pick up a Wildman Products rod guide. It's made of a heavy-duty plastic material that won't damage the crankshaft. One end fits over the rod bolts to protect the crank. The other end has a flat surface for applying force to drive the piston and rod out of the bore.

In most cases, you only need to smack the top with the palm of your hand. If the ridge mentioned in the previous step is present, you may need to apply more force than the rod guide will take, so follow the previous step.

Important!

42 Take Precautions to Prevent Rod and Piston Damage

When the piston is forced out of the bore, you should place your hand under it to catch it. If you let it fall, the crankshaft will stop the rod guide and the rod bolts will slip out of the guide. The piston will crash to the floor, damaging the assembly.

43 Reinstall Bearings, Caps and Nuts on Connecting Rods

When you are done removing the first rod, put the bearings, cap, and nuts back on the rod. The good way to keep all your parts organized is to label them or, even better, keep your engine parts in order with an internal engine organizer, such as one from Goodson Tools. This keeps all the parts in order so you can inspect them and identify problems for a specific cylinder—more on that in the next chapter.

44 Remove Main Caps

If you didn't already, number the mains "1" through "5," starting with the front main as number-1. Remove the main bolts with a 13/16-inch 6-point socket. The caps are designed to fit tightly in their registers, so it may take a tap from a hard rubber or plastic hammer to get them loose. The rear main is usually harder to remove, so thread a main bolt into the oil pump bolt hole and lightly tap it with your soft hammer. As with the rods, keep the bolts and bearing halves together.

Important!

45 Lift Crankshaft from Block

Lift the crankshaft straight up from the block. If you tip it too much front to rear, you can severely damage the crank. However, it may require some wiggling. Be careful, the crank weighs approximately 75 lbs, so get assistance lifting it if necessary. Some of the bearing halves may still be stuck to the crank. Remove them and keep them in order before they fall off and get mixed up. Put the block halves with the corresponding main caps.

46 Remove the Freeze Plugs

Use a large, blunt (not sharp) punch and hammer to drive the plug into the block. The cylinder walls are close behind the plug; reposition the punch if the plug stops moving so you don't risk cracking a cylinder. You may need a coat hanger to get the plug to a point where you can grab it with pliers to pull it out of the block. If the plug won't easily return to its hole, try a different hole.

47 Remove Oil Gallery and Coolant Passage Plugs

If the oil gallery and coolant passage plugs won't budge with a punch, hammer, and wrench, you may need to have your machine shop remove the plugs. Remove the plugs that you can, but don't waste too much time trying to do so. The machine shop knows how to get them out quickly. If you can get to it, try to also get the oil gallery plug from the back of the block.

48 | Remove Valve Retainers

Place the head on a piece of wood. Place a socket over the valve retainer and give the socket a good rap with a brass or dead-blow hammer. This breaks the retainer free from the valve locks and allows you to compress the valvespring.

49 | Remove Valve Locks

Use the valvespring compressor to compress the spring far enough to remove the valve locks. If it requires too much force, the locks are still stuck in the retainers; try the previous step again. Compress the spring almost completely. Pull the two lock halves with a pick or magnetic tool.

! Stock replacement valvetrain components are not designed to take the abuse of performance driving conditions. Here, the retainers failed, which allowed the lock to pull through, and the valve to drop and have a fight with the piston. There were no winners. When the locks fail or start to fail, they dig into the valve stem and leave a ridge (see arrow).

Important! **!**

50 | Remove Valves

If the valve does not freely slide out of the valve guide, don't force it because you could severely damage the valve guide. There may be a ridge as shown in the previous photo on the locks area; if so, you need to file it down. Turn the valve from the bottom to ease this process.

INSPECTION

Before you start purchasing parts, find out what needs to be replaced and what can be used again. Not everyone is going to replace everything in the engine, so if you are replacing all the internal parts for new ones, you can skim through this chapter to pick up some knowledge and move on to the next chapter. If you are purchasing used parts to replace the ones coming out of your engine, you can use this chapter to assist you in making good purchases.

This crankshaft has seen better days. It came out of a racing engine that lost its dry-sump oil-pump drive belt, and the driver completed a lap before pulling into the pits. The dark discoloration was caused by the heat, created by friction and the lack of oil pressure. The heat caused extreme fatigue and, as a result, this crank is a piece of junk.

Critical Inspection

1 Inspect Bearings

The bearings tell a lot about what your engine has been through. With normal wear, the bearing wear should be fairly uniform from front to rear. Uniform brass material exposed is common, but these bearing shells show brass spots, which are from debris trapped under bearings before assembly. Tiny debris can make a big difference. Slight scoring or gouging in the bearing surface is usually caused by loose debris making its way past the filter and into the bearings. Deep tears in the top layer and dark coloring is usually caused by lack of oil pressure. Stamping on the backside tells you if your engine may have been rebuilt before; Delco or Moraine stamps are a good sign of rebuilding. If your journals don't have a ".010-inch," ".020-inch," etc., stamp, they are most likely still stock size. A ".010-inch" stamp on a main bearing means it's for a .010-inch undersized crank journal.

2 Inspect Intake Manifold

If you are going to use your original cast-iron intake manifold, inspect it for cracks in the carb mounting flange and intake ports. If your engine has a short water pump check, make sure the alternator boss in the front is in good shape. Check the water jacket ports and thermostat housing mounting boss and threads for severe rust and erosion.

3 Remove Oil Splash Shield

Do not skip this step if you're going to use your cast-iron intake. During a rebuild, always remove the oil splash shield that keeps oil from splashing on the hot EGR crossover from under the intake. The amount of hard carbon deposits under the shield depends on the mileage of the engine. Clean the intake in a hot tank or pressure wash only; do not sand blast because the media can get trapped and damage the engine later.

4 Replace Intake Manifold Rivets

Replace the rivets with small Allen-head screws. Tap the holes that hold the shield in place, then install the screws with a drop of Red Loctite to keep them from coming loose and falling onto the rotating assembly.

Visual Inspection

Your engine is disassembled and you are ready to start the visual inspection. Wear patterns and defects in the parts tell a story of what's been going on inside the engine and why it's being rebuilt. Different types of failures leave different types of damage. There are all types of failures including: loss of oil pressure; foreign objects entering into the intake manifold; internal parts failure due to over-revving or using parts not designed for your driving style; overheating; freezing; and, head gasket failure.

Each type of failure requires a different repair. If your engine suffered

If you plan on using the same camshaft and lifters in your rebuild, you have to keep them in order so you can put them back in the engine the same way they came out. The cam and lifters "wear" to each other, so this order is critical. Each cam lobe face should be flat and their measurements should all match. The lifter faces should all be completely flat and smooth, unlike the lifters shown here. If you have a hydraulic non-roller lifter cam, set each lifter on a flat wooden surface, push a pushrod into the cup, and make sure each of the lifters compress under an equal amount of pressure. If your cam or just one of your lifters doesn't pass the inspection, you must replace the cam and lifters.

from a head gasket failure or if you suspect it, there are some tell-tale signs to look for. When a head gasket fails, the water escaping the coolant passage or compression leaking out of the combustion chamber can cause pathways or grooves in the head gasket surface of the block and heads. These pathways are typically found between two cylinders or between a coolant passage and one cylinder. If these pathways exist, the block and head can be resurfaced to eliminate the groove. Machining these surfaces can lead to intake manifold fitment and piston-to-valve clearance problems. The machine shop will make a determination on fixing this problem or if other components need to be sourced.

Inspect the parts and follow the clues they leave in order to approach repairing the engine or rebuilding it. Every engine and part has a different story to tell.

This big-block has a pretty serious ridge worn in the cylinder bore. This can be done over many thousands of miles, from constantly racing the engine when it's cold (engine wear decreases as the temperature increases), and insufficient lubrication. This ridge can make it tough to remove the pistons from the cylinders. Boring the block is necessary to make the cylinder true again, if there's enough material left to bore.

5 Verify Pushrod Trueness

Check a pushrod for straightness by rolling it across a flat surface, preferably a piece of glass. A slight bend will be obvious as you roll it. Replace any pushrod that is not completely straight. If you are going to use your original pushrods, you need to keep them in order and put them back with the correct cylinder. Visually inspect the rocker arm for abnormal wear in the fulcrum socket; the rocker tip should be smooth, not grooved like the tip of this rocker.

Critical Inspection, Important!

6 Inspect Block for Cracks

Inspect for visible cracks over the entire surface of the block including the cylinder walls. The machine shop does a more precise inspection if you opt to have them leak check and Magnaflux the block and heads. Your inspection could save you money if you detect a bad block. Carefully inspect your lifter bores with a light and your finger to make sure the surfaces are free of burs and grooves. Check the deck surface around the cylinders for possible grooves caused by failed head gaskets. Glance at the threads to make sure they aren't stripped. Make sure there aren't any chunks of block missing around the transmission mounting holes and starter.

Block

Inspecting your parts is an important step. If you find visual damage on your parts before going to the machine shop, you can save yourself some money by not paying them to do the same thing. The damage that's harder to find, like fractures or small cracks, will be caught at the machine shop. If you see a crack in your block on any surface other than the cylinder, you should consider replacing it unless it's a numbers-matching block on a rare car. In the case of saving a severely cracked block, you should contact your machine shop and determine your options. Saving a rare block after it has been cracked from rotating parts failure or from a frozen cooling system is a dying art. Most machine shops don't do more than sleeve them. A crack in a cylinder is repairable as long as the crack hasn't traveled into the main cap web or too far up to the deck surface.

7 Check the Block for Sleeves and Other Problems

 *A sleeve doesn't necessarily mean that the block is junk. This block has a sleeve installed. Closer inspection showed signs of coolant leaking into the crankcase at the base of the sleeve and that a small crack was present. It's obvious; a good shop did not do this work. This sleeve would need to be machined out and replaced. After weighing the cost of repairing it, this block was discarded.*

 *The main caps should fit tightly in the block registers. If you have a dial bore gauge, you can re-install the main caps and check for out-of-round main bores from excess stress caused by detonation. Also run that gauge in the cylinder bores for out-of-round bores. The machined boss on the face of the block behind the cam sprocket should be smooth. If it's different, the timing chain set uses a bearing plate (shown). Check for chips on the web at the bottom of the cylinder bores usually caused by a previous failure or by knocking the rods into the block upon disassembly.*

8 Replace or Rebuild Oil Pump Pickup

It's typical to replace the oil pump but to reuse the oil pump pickup. If you are going to reuse the pump, it needs to be rebuilt (see Chapter 8 sidebar, "Oil Pump Checking and Modifying"). The oil pump pickup has a screen on the underside and it should be in good shape. If the pickup is mangled in any way, replace it. If the pickup has been welded to the pump, you should consider replacing both because you have no assurance the person who did the welding didn't damage the oil pump in the process. The oil pump mounting surface on the rear main cap should be smooth and the oil pump should fit tight in the two dowel pins.

Check the block for wear and cracks in the cylinders. If the cylinders don't appear to have any significant wear, you probably don't need to waste much time looking for cracks. If you notice a ridge about a quarter inch below the deck surface, such as the one seen in this chapter, your block should go under some close scrutiny to determine if it can be bored far enough to eliminate the ridge. If the cylinders do have significant wear, the machine shop will need to determine the fate of the block.

Heads

Once your heads are disassembled, you will have a clear picture of their condition. When removing the valves, you know if they had a ridge you needed to file down and might have noticed if they felt loose in the guides when you took them out. Give the entire casting a once over and look for visible defects, which include worn valve guides, damaged threads, deterioration around the coolant passages, chunks of material missing, or cracks in any part of the casting.

If you see cracks or divots in the head castings' combustion chamber area, your engine might have stopped working because a foreign object made its way into the cylinder or a valve was dropped. I've seen a carburetor base-plate screw fall into an engine and cause three bent intake valves, one bent exhaust valve, a damaged head, a cracked block, and a collapsed piston. The screw bounced around to three different cylinders before getting past one valve completely where the real carnage took place. I'm sharing this to relay that damage in one cylinder can also mean that other cylinders should be checked for problems.

Professional Mechanic Tip

9 Inspect and Clean the Head Gasket Surface

Clean the head gasket surface so you can inspect it. Don't gouge the surface. At a slight angle, lightly scrape the surface with a razor blade scraper (this is a good method for all gasket surfaces). Check for divots or grooves leading away from the combustion chambers (caused by head gasket failure); if present, the head and the block may need resurfacing.

10 Inspect Valves

If you had to file a valve to remove it from the head, you should replace the valve and the locks. Build-up of carbon on the backside of the valve is a sign of oil getting into the intake port by way of a worn valve guide or a leaky gasket under the intake manifold. The valve on the left shows signs of "peppering" on the sealing surface because the seats are original; they have not been upgraded for use with unleaded fuels.

Crankshaft

Get your micrometer out and start checking the journals of the crankshaft. Check for any deep scratches and to see if the crankshaft has already been ground too far. The size of the rod journals should not be less than 2.17 inches and the main journals should not be less than 2.72 inches. If they are, consult your crank grinder. After all is said and done with the crankshaft machining, you don't want to use it if it has been ground more than .030 inch from original; it's not reliable enough to use. If you notice dark spots on the journals or if one journal is noticeably darker than the others, it's possible a bearing failure caused that journal to soak up some extreme heat and should be replaced.

Precision Measurement

11 Check the Crankshaft

A few quick checks indicate the condition of your crankshaft. The crank key should be a tight fit in the keyway. There should not be a deep groove in the journal where the rear main seal rides. The thrust flange on the crank should be flat and smooth to the touch. Check the size of the crankshaft journals with your micrometer. Dark spots or deep scoring on the journals are bad signs. If your crank is more than .030 inch undersize or if your crank doesn't pass these initial inspections, you need to start shopping for a new one.

Improper balancer installation could have damaged the threads in the front of the cranks, so check these threads. Also check the threads in the flange on the back of the cranks where the flywheel or flexplate mount. If your crank has one, remove the pilot shaft bushing and install a new one later if you have a manual-transmission-equipped vehicle.

12 Check Flex-plate for Damage

The flex-plate should be free of cracks. They typically crack around the area that bolts to the crank. The flywheel friction surfaces should not have deep stress cracks. Sometimes you can resurface a flywheel and save it; if not, get a new one. Your flex-plate or flywheel should be inspected for missing or chipped teeth; replace it if you find any. These are slightly chipped and could cause problems in the future.

Critical Inspection

13 Inspect Pistons

Make sure the pistons don't have any excessive skirt wear or cracks, including around the wrist pin. The piston rings shouldn't be locked into their grooves. If they are, and carbon build-up is not the cause, it's possible the piston needs to be replaced. Clean the carbon out of the grooves and check fit again. The face of the piston should be free of holes, gouges, and marks that look like pools of molten aluminum. The rods should not be bent or twisted. They should not be severely discolored around the bearing end. If your engine was rebuilt, make sure the rods are number stamped "1" through "8." If your pistons or rods don't pass, you can simply replace the ones you need and have them matched to the good parts.

Rods

Replace connecting rods that show signs of being bent or twisted. A bent rod is not always apparent upon visual inspection. Uneven wear patterns on the piston is a sign of possible problems with the connecting rod it's attached to. The machine shop needs to make more in-depth inspections of them when they are reconditioning them. As with the crank, if your connecting rods have a darker bearing end than the wrist pin end or one rod is visibly darker than the others, it's possible that a bearing failed and it severely overheated the rod and could have fatigued it to the point where replacement is necessary.

The crankshaft has a lot of force when the engine is running. When a part fails, severe damage happens in a hurry. This rod bolt came loose due to improper torque or it wasn't stretched properly upon installation.

Harmonic Damper

Inspect the harmonic damper for visible cracks in the keyway or any part, a worn-out seal between the hub and the outer ring, and a groove in the hub where the seal in the timing cover meets the damper hub. Any cracks in the metal or a worn band between the hub and ring are signs that you need to replace the damper. A groove worked in by the timing cover seal can be fixed with a repair sleeve.

Critical Inspection

14 Inspect Harmonic Dampers

Harmonic dampers are wearable items. Check your damper's rubber ring between the hub and outer ring. If the rubber shows signs of cracks, distortion, or misalignment, it's time to replace it. When they fail, the outer ring can slip on the hub causing the timing mark to move and also cause bearing-damaging vibrations.

15 Harmonic Damper Repair

The seal in the timing cover can wear a groove in the harmonic damper. Victor-Reinz makes a repair sleeve that simply presses over the hub and turns a leaky damper into a useable unit.

Machine shops typically have many engines apart at the same time that yours is in their possession. Use a number stamp like these. These are used for numbering rods. Use these, a center punch, or an engraving tool to distinctively mark all the parts you plan to take to the machine shop so there are no accidentally swapped parts while they are out of your hands. Mark the rods on the flat surface near the rod bolt.

SELECTING PARTS

Plan to succeed. To build a strong-running engine, you're going to need a plan and you should put it together before you hop on the Internet or crack open a catalog to start getting parts for your engine rebuild. There's an old saying, "If you fail to plan, you plan to fail." This book is written with the intent of success, not failure. In this chapter we'll go through the steps of managing the parts for netting success with your rebuild.

Got Performance?

The first step in the plan is figuring out what you are going to do with the car. Are you going to drive the car like your grandparents: slow, steady, and not always in the correct lane? Are you only interested in using your stump-pulling torque to tow around your sand toys? Do you want to add extra power to run down the quarter-mile? Are there any twisty open-track excursions in the future? You need to build your engine to suit your needs. Be realistic about your intent.

There are many parts available that work best in specific applications. For instance, you wouldn't put an Edelbrock Victor Jr. intake on a tow vehicle, and you wouldn't typically put 13:1-compression pistons in your daily driver. It's not a bad idea to overbuild the engine a little bit, but you should stick to a realistic plan. To get the most out of your hard-earned money, read through the chapter to help you make some educated decisions on what parts to buy.

The various build types to consider are: stock, towing, street and off-road, road course, and drag strip.

Aftermarket Blocks

When the engines exceed 650 hp, many top engine builders said they prefer to upgrade to aftermarket engine blocks like GM Performance

---

TECH TIP

DynoSim Software

You can develop the best plan and still make some bad choices. ProRacing Sim engine simulation software saves you from making costly and unnecessary build-up mistakes. They started out with the well-known simulation "Desktop Dyno" and have been improving upon this great tool since its introduction years ago.

The ProRacing SimT DynoSim Advanced Engine Simulation with ProToolsT was the software used to plan the 496 in this book. Within 20 minutes of reading the manual and loading the software, I was entering engine specs. It wasn't much longer and I had all my num-bers in place and was running the simulation.

For more information about DynoSim, visit ProRacing Sim, LLC, at: www.ProRacingSim.com. To find out more about Dynomation-5, visit Motion Software at: www.MotionSoftware.com.

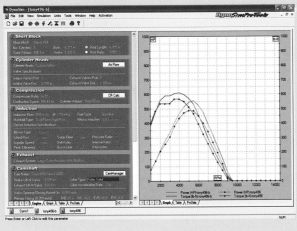

If you don't feel like using a stock block, you can upgrade to stronger performance blocks cast in iron or aluminum from manufacturers such as GM Performance Parts, World Products, Dart, and Donovan. Top engine builders said they prefer upgrading from the stock Mark IV block when the HP level exceeds 650.

Parts, World Products, Donovan, and Dart. They said upgrading to 4-bolt main caps, which are stronger than the stock cast-iron caps, helps the strength of the Mark IV block. They also said they prefer the aftermarket blocks because they come with taller decks and bigger bores, suitable for building monster big-block engines for their customers. The old adage, "bigger is always better," certainly rings true for racing applications. Aftermarket blocks have been re-designed with better options than the Mark IV, including priority main oiling systems, blind-tapped head bolt bosses, standard four-bolt mains (minimum of Nodular iron caps), enlarged water jackets, thicker wall castings, intake valley head bolt bosses, etc. Most of the aftermarket blocks also accommodate all stock components such as starters, mechanical fuel pumps, oil filters, etc.

If your engine produces more than 550 hp and revs more than 6,000 rpm, you should consider upgrading your stock cast-iron main caps to high-strength ductile steel, such as these Milodon 4-bolt main caps. The Milodon cap (gold) is larger and stronger than the stock 2-bolt cap. Machining is required to upgrade to new main caps.

Main Cap Conversion

You may consider upgrading the main caps of your two-bolt main block if you are going to build your big-block to put out over 550 hp or the engine will have a redline over 6,000 rpm. Even the factory four-bolt blocks with cast main caps could benefit from upgrading to high-strength ductile aftermarket caps. Milodon and a few other companies offer conversion kits that replace the three center main caps. You typically replace the three caps and not the front or rear main caps because most of the flex in the crank happens in the middle of it. You can purchase the other caps separately if you feel the need to replace them.

Bearings

Even though the rotating engine parts (the cam, connecting rods, and crankshaft) ride on the oil between the component and bearing surface, that doesn't mean you shouldn't use high-quality bearings. There are different quality bearings available. The most recognized bearing manufacturer in OEM and the aftermarket is MAHLE Clevite Inc. When purchasing your bearings, you should be aware that there are different bearings for different applications. The Clevite 77 P-Series (rod bearing CB743P) non-chamfered bearing is more suited for stock and lower revving engines. If you are building a high-performance engine, you should use Clevite 77 H-Series (rod bearing CB743H) bearings because they have enlarged chamfered sides for crankshafts with larger radius bearing surfaces and are made with a hardened steel backing for higher loads and increased revs. Running P-Series bearings on a performance radius crank spells disaster because the larger radius interferes with the side of the bearing and this causes bearing failure, so consult your machinist and/or the manufacturer of your crankshaft. There is also an

To clear up a myth, oil siphoning isn't a problem with big-blocks, unless you are revving your engine beyond 10,000 rpm. Anything less than that and you're fine. Extra oil from a high-volume or high-pressure oil pump combats any possible oiling issues. Even GM cross-drills its performance big-block cranks, so there can be no serious problems by doing so. Both the stock crank (on the right) and the Eagle crankshaft (on the left) have the usual oiling passage (see yellow wire), but the Eagle is cross-drilled (see blue wire).

M-Series bearing offered, but that's for some specific applications. The most common Clevite 77 bearings are the P- or H-Series. Talk to your engine machinist for professional advice for your application.

Coated Bearings

Coating technology companies offer pre-coated bearings or you can send your bearings to an experienced coater. Engine builder and racer Paul Caselas says, "Get the coated bearings. It's cheap insurance!" Clevite offers their TriArmor coating on their H-Series bearing line. Its coating is a low-friction PTFE/polymer moly/graphite treatment that adds extra protection and lubricity on the surface of the bearing. It's extra protection for your engine at startup and if it ever experiences momentary oil starvation.

Rotating Assembly

Crankshafts

Cast and forged-steel are the two types of crankshafts available. Of those two types, the forged crankshaft is the stronger of the two. There are stock and performance crankshafts available for both types. Chevy installed forged crankshafts in their performance engines; all other engines received the standard cast crankshafts. Aftermarket companies rate their cast crankshafts from 500 to 700 hp and their forged cranks to upwards of 1,500 hp.

Among the factory and aftermarket crankshafts, there are internal and external balance units. History shows that the Chevy 366 to 427 big-blocks were internally balanced, so they use zero-balance flywheels and harmonic balancers. The 454 and 502 engines are externally balanced, so it's necessary to use a special

counterweighted flywheel and harmonic balancer. Machinists and builders have expressed their dislike of the external balance design. Most said if given the choice in high-performance applications, they would spend the extra money to convert from an external balance crank to an internally balanced unit. Otherwise, they would buy a performance crank, like the ones offered by Eagle Specialty Products, which is initially cast or forged as an internally balanced unit. The process of changing external to internal balance is

accomplished by drilling out the counterweight, welding heavy Mallory-metal into those holes, and typically costs a few hundred dollars.

Chevy changed the design of the rear main seal in 1991, from the trusty two-piece to the one-piece. With this change came a newly designed rear section of the crankshaft, which is easily identified. The flywheel mounting face on the one-piece rear main seal crankshaft is a perfectly machined circular hub, and the same surface on the two-piece main seal crank is a notched and misshaped flange. If

Here are two cranks, a stock one on the right and an Eagle internally balanced (note the larger counterweights) forged crankshaft on the left. Extra money won't be spent welding heavy metal into this crank to internally balance it. Internally balanced cranks have less stress because they don't have counterweighted dampers and flywheels hanging on the ends (especially on the front snout). This is the best way to go on high-revving high-performance engines.

If you're replacing your crank, rods, and pistons, you can purchase all of them separately or you can purchase them all together as a rotating assembly kit, which includes those parts along with rings and bearings. These types of combined rotating assemblies, from reputable companies such as Eagle and Scat, are nice because they come with the correct, good-quality parts and take some research off your list of projects. Unless you are comfortable with your measuring tools and inspection skills, you should stay away from buying these parts separately from swap meets and from local private parties. Even if a crankshaft measures out beautifully with a micrometer, that doesn't mean it's a good crank. There's no way your eyes can see .030 inch of runout. This 496 project receives an Eagle Specialty Products rotating kit, which includes heavy-duty high-performance parts that match the power potential of the engine.

you have a block utilizing a one-piece rear main seal, but you want to run a two-piece seal-style crankshaft, a few companies offer adapter ring kits. After talking with crankshaft and seal manufacturers, along with a couple of engine builders, I got mixed feedback on whether the one- or two-piece seal was a better design. The majority opinion was that both were good, but the one-piece design was better.

The aftermarket crankshaft companies have made some changes to crankshaft design, which further convolute your crankshaft choices. Did you notice I didn't report that they made "improvements?" They changed the oiling design in the crankshaft. The new design is referred to as "cross-drilled oiling" and the original design is still referred to as "standard oiling," There have been some half-truths circulating around the engine building industry on cross-drilled crankshafts. Some builders don't use them because it's been printed that this design siphons the oil from the system at high RPM. World-renowned racecar engine building company Reher-Morrison did tests years ago that proved siphoning occurred above 10,000 rpm. If you were building a big-block Chevy that will be revved that high, you probably wouldn't be reading this book. For all intents and purposes, cross-drilled crankshafts should be considered for all applications destined to turn less than 10,000 rpm.

Displacement Choices

The engine's displacement (cubic inch size) is determined by your bore and stroke. Displacement formula:

.7854 x Bore x Bore x Stroke x 8
(number of cylinders) = CID

Unlike in the old days, there are numerous cubic inch displacement (CID) options available with the introduction aftermarket blocks, stroker cranks, and pistons. Now the sizes range from 366 to infinity and beyond...well, at least 632 ci, and they keep getting bigger. You can change your displacement on an engine by putting a different-sized stroke crank in it. You can take a 396 or 402 block (that came with a 3.76-inch stroke crank) and put a 454 4-inch-stroke crank in it, but it's not easy. Your machine shop will have to clearance the block to make it fit, and you will need some special stroker pistons and possibly a stroker-relieved oil pan. You may decide a more cost-effective way would be to just get a 454 block and put all that extra cash into a set of heads or something else. Although... stroker big-block Chevy engines make unreal torque numbers on the dyno.

The better you arm yourself with knowledge about the differences of available crankshafts, the easier it will be for you to make an educated decision for your application. Before making your decision on a crankshaft for your engine, don't forget to take your plan for the vehicle into consideration. If it's a stock rebuild, the cast crank is more than adequate. If you plan on driving the car like you just stole it, you should opt for a forged crank. Even though companies list their crank ratings in HP numbers, RPM and load ratings should also be considered. When it comes to the crank, rods, and pistons, it's a good general rule to over-build rather than undercut the foundation of your engine. You wouldn't build a skyscraper on a wooden foundation. The stock 3/8-inch bolt-equipped connecting rods

and stock cast crankshaft is good up to 500 hp, as long as you keep the RPM under 6,000. Any level over that, and you should seriously consider upgrading to an aftermarket crankshaft and rods.

Rods

Connecting rods are the important link between the crankshaft and piston. If you are doing a stock rebuild and the stock rods are in good shape, they will be fine for your application. If your engine is going to be used for anything other than basic street driving, you should upgrade the rod bolts to some aftermarket bolts, such as ARP. You'll need to get the rods resized after replacing the rod bolts, but it's worth it because half of the time (during the rebuild process) you'll have to get the rods resized anyway.

Stock connecting rods come in two versions: standard duty, and high-performance. The 3/8-inch rod bolts easily distinguish standard-duty connecting rods, while 7/16-inch rod bolts identify the high-performance rods. The performance rods are also beefier on the larger journal end.

In the old days, if you wanted to replace your rods with better ones you would have to scour the swap meets for good factory rods or spend a fortune to buy some performance rods. Now there are enough performance companies producing different levels of performance rods that you can find a good set to fit any budget.

Aftermarket rods come in two different configurations: I-Beam, and H-Beam. Depending on the manufacturer and the materials they use on their rods, the strength/horsepower ratings vary. The I-Beam version resembles the stock rod, but it is beefier around the journal area and along the beam. The H-Beam rod is significantly different. The most obvious difference is the beam shape. Besides design improvements, both types of aftermarket rods gain extra strength by utilizing heavy-duty (typically ARP) rod bolts. For instance, Eagle's ratings for its H-Beam rod jumps from 850 to a 1,200-hp rating just by changing the rod bolts. There are also aluminum connecting rods on the market but they are for full-tilt drag racing applications and should not be used for any other application.

Pistons

Caution: You need to consider what type of heads you will use *before* purchasing pistons. Pistons for open-chamber and closed-chamber cylinder heads have differently shaped domes and can lead to major interference when used with the wrong head. Check for footnotes and specifications before making any purchases, especially when working with pistons for compression ratios greater than 10.5:1.

In the history of big-blocks, GM has equipped its engines with hypereutectic or cast-aluminum pistons on light-duty applications (starting in the early 1990s), and forged pistons on its high-performance engines. Any of these three types will do fine in a stock application. A step toward performance would be hypereutectic pistons. They feature high-silicon content, which reduces thermal expansion from heat. This allows for tighter clearance to the cylinder wall for reduced emissions as well as increased economy and power. The factory hypereutectic pistons don't generally survive under the pressures

Your piston choice should depend on your application. The first major consideration when purchasing pistons is the type of cylinder head you are using. Closed-chamber heads require closed-chamber-designed pistons and vice-versa. Without taking closed-chamber or open-chamber head configurations into consideration, it's likely to end up with a disastrous combination. If you're building a stock replacement engine of 325 hp or less, you can install some cast pistons and the engine will work great. The next step up is KB Performance hypereutectic pistons. These are great for stock engines and performance engines. When you get into serious performance levels or if you're running nitrous, a supercharger, or a turbo, you need to consider spending the extra dough on some forged pistons.

of nitrous-oxide assisted, supercharged, or turbocharged applications, but with advancing technologies the aftermarket piston manufacturers have been improving upon them. The best piston for all performance, especially at power levels over 400 hp, has always been the forged piston.

Damper and Flywheel

The first and most important item to address about harmonic dampers is that there are two differ-

All intake manifolds are designed for specific applications determined by the cam, heads, and other engine and drivetrain parts. A good general rule is that dual-plane (identified by the divided plenum) intakes offer better low-end torque with an optimum operating range typically from idle to 6,500 rpm. A single-plane (identified by a single open plenum) offers better top-end power, performing best in the neighborhood of 3,500 to 7,500 rpm.

ent dampers on the big-block Chevy. If you get the wrong damper on an engine, you can damage the bearings real fast. The two types are: a zero-balance version for the internally balanced big-block, and a counterweighted version for the externally balanced big-block.

For factory applications and GM crate engines (Gen IV, V, and VI), the 366, 396, 402, 427, and 572 engines are internally balanced. The 454 and 502 engines (both use the factory 4.00-inch-stroke crank) are externally balanced. With the introduction of internally balanced 4.00-inch-stroke aftermarket crankshafts you could potentially have or build an internally balanced 454 or 502. From the outside of the engine, if the engine doesn't have a flywheel or damper attached, it is virtually impossible to distinguish between the internally or externally balanced big-block without researching the block casting numbers. The externally balanced damper and flywheel have extra counterweights on them and these are easy to identify from under the vehicle. The easiest part to identify is the extra weight on the backside of the harmonic balancer.

If during your rebuild you switch from an external to an internal balance crankshaft, or vice versa, make sure you get the correct flywheel and damper to go with it. This is very important: Using the incorrect flywheel and/or damper on the wrong crankshaft can cause severe engine vibration and destroy the bearings in a short time.

There are a few different types of harmonic dampers on the market. A stock engine works great with a stock replacement damper, which is made of a cast-iron hub and cast-iron outer inertia ringer separated by an elastomer band. The cast-iron ring can fatigue and fly apart if it's used in high-stress and high-revving conditions. If you plan on racing your car on a regular basis, you should purchase an SFI-approved damper. The SFI unit is made from a machined, billet-steel hub and external ring separated by an elastomer ring for increased strength. The SFI rating is a racing specification for durability and strength standards required by racing associations.

The flywheel or flexplate for your application should also be considered. The SFI rating required on dampers is also required on flywheels and flexplates. For clarification, a flywheel is what you would have your clutch bolted to in a manual transmission application and a flexplate is what you would have a torque converter bolted to in an automatic transmission application. If you are building a mild daily driver engine, you need a standard-duty flexplate or flywheel. When you step up and start building your engine to pound out more than 400 hp, you should invest in heavier-duty equipment. The SFI-rated units are built from stronger materials and are designed to take more abuse without flying apart when they are put to the

Damper not Balancer

Just about every car guy knows what a harmonic balancer is. Unfortunately, many of us have been taught wrong. Brian Clarke, President of BHJ Products and Dynamics Inc., set the record straight. He stated, "In this industry we are re-educating people. They're called dampers. That's their job. They dampen, not balance." When I thought about it, his statements made sense. They are sometimes counterweighted for balancing the rotating assembly, but their main job is to dampen vibration and harmonics.

How does the damper work? The engine runs because sequences of combustion push the pistons, rods, and journals of the crankshaft down. That downward motion on the journal sends a shock through the crank because there is a split second before the next cylinder fires and does the same thing. The force pushes down on the crank, then it snaps back before another section of the crank is put through the same motions and keeps on going through these cycles eight times per revolution. These cycles cause the crank to twist from one end to the other. The twisting motion sends harmonics and vibrations through the crankshaft. Without the damper to reduce these forces the engine would quickly shake itself into a pile of broken parts.

This is a cutaway SFI-rated damper. The SFI rules require the outer ring to be made of forged steel, and it has to be locked in place, so it can't fly off if the elastomer ring fails. The orange flange keeps it from moving backward. A large ring clip on the backside keeps the outer ring from sliding forward. This outer ring remains in the hub; in case the elastomer band fails, the outer ring will not fly off the hub. The hub may be steel or aluminum, depending on application.

If your engine is internally balanced, you need a non-counterweighted damper (left), If it's externally balanced you need a counterweighted version. Be sure you get the correct flywheel or flexplate to handle balancing duties on the other end of the crankshaft.

test in high-performance applications. The last thing you need is a chunk of your flywheel flying off your engine at 6,000 rpm and tearing your foot off. This is one of those areas of your build where it's a good idea to over build your engine for your intended application.

Induction

This is an area where your engine plan is really going to be necessary. If you get an intake manifold that doesn't work with your heads, you're going to run into big problems.

Chevy made two intake manifold and head configurations: oval-port, and rectangle-port. You can't mix rectangle-port heads with a set of oval-port heads or vice versa.

The oval-port intake and head design makes more power at a lower RPM range than the rectangle port versions. The oval-port design is found on most truck and passenger car applications producing less than 375 hp from the factory. The rectangle-port design was used on high-performance factory application engines, typically producing 375 hp or more.

Intake Manifold

Your choice of an intake manifold is completely decided by your plan, addressed in the beginning of this chapter. The first thing you have to take into consideration is the height of the manifold. If you are installing your big-block in a car with a stock or flat hood, you are limited to a few select low-rise intake manifolds. If you are willing to modify your hood or install a scooped hood, you can opt for a high-rise manifold. In some cases you may be stuck with a factory intake manifold.

Each intake manifold has an operating RPM range. If you fail to match the intake with the range of the camshaft and your application, you will be disappointed with the end result of all the time and money you spent to get there.

Even the factory cast-iron intake manifolds have an operating range, albeit very low-performance. The typical low-rise factory cast-iron intakes provide an operating range from idle to 5,500 rpm, but they take a long time to get there. Chevy also produced some high-rise cast-iron intake manifolds back in the day. Except for the fact that their heavy weight robbed power, they were decent performers. Chevrolet also produced high-rise aluminum intake manifolds for their high-performance engines.

Cast-iron intake manifolds retain heat, and as they get heat soaked, they heat up the air and fuel going into the engine. Colder air-fuel mixture getting into the combustion chamber makes more power because the lower temperature allows the mixture to be denser and burn better. Aluminum intake manifolds don't soak up and retain the heat like cast-iron, so they are better for performance and they are about half the weight. Losing 35 lbs off the weight of your car is worth extra power.

Aftermarket intake manifolds are readily available from many manufacturers, such as Edelbrock, Holley, and Weiand. These are available with operating ranges of: idle–5,500, 1,500–6,500, 2,500–6,500, 3,500–7,500, and 3,500–8,500 rpm. The first two RPM ranges are probably best suited for your everyday or typical street-driven carbureted cars. Switching to electronic fuel injection (EFI) changes the drivability of the specific design

of an intake manifold because of fuel injector placement and computer-controlled fuel distribution. (That's an entirely different book.)

Intake manifolds come in two different types. A divider running down the center of the carb breaks the dual-plane intake manifold into two sections. Its design forces the left half of the carb to feed four cylinders while the right half of the carb feeds the other four cylinders. The dual-plane intake manifold is closer to the factory-designed intake and is better suited for stock to moderate performance levels because its design allows for more low-end performance and efficiency.

A single-plane intake manifold is completely open under the carb, which allows the fuel to feed all eight cylinders at the same time. High velocity is required to produce optimal power. These are better suited for higher RPM applications because they don't get into their power range until 2,500 rpm or higher. Those numbers don't work great on daily drivers, tow vehicles, or four-wheel-drive applications.

Heads

Chevy has produced a lot of different configurations of heads for different applications. Along with oval or rectangle port heads, there are also the open- and closed-chamber head designs. Open or closed refers to the combustion chamber configuration. Closed-chamber means the head has a small combustion chamber and open-chamber means the combustion chamber is larger, as seen on page 12. Be careful when changing heads or pistons when rebuilding your engine. You can't always mix pop-up pistons on closed-chamber heads.

Combustion chambers are all different sizes. They are measured in cubic centimeters (cc), which is the physical amount of volume of chamber. The size of your combustion chamber and the face configuration of your piston determine the compression ratio of your engine. Not all open-chamber heads have the same size combustion chamber.

Factory

If you are building your engine on a budget, the factory cast-iron heads work well for most applications. There are many heads to choose from, including open- and closed-chamber heads and oval- and rectangle-port configurations. The best factory head for your build-up depends on your application. If you are building a truck for towing, you are better off using oval-port heads. If you are building a street car with performance in mind, you may be better off with some early to mid 70s open-chamber "smog" oval-port heads because these provide better breathing and good low-end RPM power. For high-performance applications, stay away from "truck" heads. Truck heads have the smallest intake ports that are so small they are more round than oval and are matched with small valves. These heads are only good for low-RPM towing applications. If you are building a high-performance drag strip warrior, you might be better off using a pair of open-chamber rectangle-port heads. The factory also produced some aluminum rectangle-port heads back in the 60s and 70s for muscle cars.

All factory heads can be improved upon. If you want some extra performance from your heads, you can unshroud the valves to increase airflow around the entire valve instead of just one side as the factory left them. For more power, you can increase the size of the intake valve only. You can also upsize the exhaust. These performance upgrades can add up in the machine shop, so get an estimate first and check to make sure it doesn't make sense for you to simply purchase a new set of aftermarket heads.

There is also power to be had in factory cast-iron heads by porting and polishing them. Read up on the procedures of porting your own heads. There are books on the market that get into detail on the right and wrong way to do these upgrades to your heads in your own garage. If you don't do your homework ahead of time, you can make some serious mistakes in a hurry. If you have reservations, most machine shops offer good porting services or can point you in the direction of a good shop that can.

Aftermarket

Since the mid 1990s, market demand and advances in casting technologies have created a skyrocketing increase in the aftermarket head offerings. Before that, it was hard to find a good assortment of aftermarket oval-port closed-chamber heads with oversized valves. The belief was that if you were buying aftermarket heads, you should buy 119-cc rectangle-port heads or probably just stick to factory heads. As mentioned earlier in this section, make sure you are buying heads that work well with your pistons. If you have pop-up piston domes, you can't run closed-chamber heads. The piston can destroy the head and/or valves. Check the cc of the head and make sure you don't make a serious mistake. For instance, if you have flat-top pistons pumping

10.0:1 with 96.4-cc heads, buy the best heads you can. However, if you install a 124-cc head rather than a 96.4-cc head, you may think you increased power but, instead, you just dropped your compression ratio to less than 8.5:1. Remember what I said about planning? You have to do your homework. If you have doubts or questions, ask a professional.

Cast Iron

Even though more companies are casting aluminum heads, there is still a large market for cast-iron big-block Chevy heads. World and RHS list their cast-iron heads as their entry-level performance heads and their aluminum heads are the next step in performance. The cast-iron heads are no slouches when it comes to performance gains. You can purchase cast-iron heads from a few different manufacturers such as RHS, World, and Dart.

Aluminum

With technological advances in aluminum casting, there are a lot of aluminum heads available in the aftermarket. With Edelbrock, AFR, World, RHS, Dart, Brodix, and others offering the full range of performance levels and configurations of heads, you can find a head that best suits your application. If you can't find a head you aren't looking hard enough.

If you install cast-iron and aluminum heads of the same compression ratio, the cast-iron heads will make more power because they retain heat. Aluminum heads allow you to run more compression than cast-iron ones because the aluminum dissipates heat faster than iron heads, which lowers the chance of detonation. Along with increasable compression, the aluminum heads weigh 680 lbs less than the cast-iron heads. This provides more power to move your car.

Edelbrock has been known for years as a street head manufacturer and has head offerings ranging from street to high-end Big Chief racing heads for 1,500-plus-hp Top Sportsman racing. If you buy bare heads, beware of valve stem size. For instance, some heads, including stock heads, come with 3/8-inch-diameter stems. Some manufacturers choose to use 11/32-inch-diameter stems to promote flow and reduce valve weight. If you mix 11/32-inch valves with 3/8-inch retainers and locks, the first ignition of your engine will be a disaster.

Incompatibility Warning!

Mark IV heads are a direct bolt-on for big-blocks built before the 1991 model year. In the 1991 model year, GM started producing the Gen V Big Block, which had a redesigned coolant system called a "parallel flow" design. This new cooling system changed the block and head castings so that the block and heads cannot be interchanged. The Gen VI block was redesigned so that the Mark IV heads could be bolted on with the right head gaskets. The part numbers have changed because of design changes, so it's best to contact your parts store to get the latest design. The Gen VI block can be easily identified by its six-bolt plastic-front timing cover. The later "Gen" heads don't work on the Mark IV block. In the past, a few companies have offered adapter bushings and gaskets to allow interchangeability, but none have stood the test of time. Big problems arise because the coolant passages can easily leak into the lifter valley.

Valvetrain

There are entire books to educate you on valvetrain and camshaft selection so I will not provide exhaustive explanation in this section.

The valvetrain is made up of all the parts that operate the movement of the valves. The order of parts is: timing chain, camshaft, lifters, pushrods, rocker arms, and valves, which are controlled by the springs, retainers, and locks. All these parts work in unison to keep the piston and valve from having a fight, in which nobody wins. The strength of these parts should not be taken lightly in high-performance applications.

Upgrading one part sometimes shows the weakness of other parts. If you upgrade the springs for a slightly modified or high-performance engine, you may be asking too much of the retainers and locks, and they may fail. Take all parts into consideration when building a performance engine because one set of components must be compatible with another, otherwise you may suffer an engine failure. Consult your machine shop or speed shop if you have questions about what parts you should upgrade. At the same time, consider spending your hard-earned money on parts that fit your application and budget.

Incompatibility Warning!

A unique oil system design was made for 1965–1966 big-blocks. This oil system feeds the lifters by traveling up through a groove in the rear cam bearing and in the rear camshaft journal. If the camshaft and cam bearings are grooved, this is a 1965–1966 system, and you better make sure you get new cam bearings. The oil was fed through three holes in the rear cam bearing. The 1967 and later blocks

Be very careful with early big-blocks. If you have a 1965–1966 engine, your engine has an early oiling system gallery design. This system uses a groove in the rear cam journal and a grooved rear cam bearing with three oil feed holes to supply oil to the lifters. If you don't get the correct replacement parts, you'll have a disaster on your hands.

only require a single hole in the rear cam bearing. While finding a cam for your 1965–1966 engine may be difficult, a machine shop can cut a 3/16-inch groove that's 7/64-inch deep around the center of the rear cam journal. The groove in the bearing doesn't provide enough of a passage to allow for proper oil supply to the lifters, so the groove in the cam is necessary.

Camshaft Selection

Selecting a camshaft can be a daunting task if you're trying to pick one on your own. The cam companies have included detailed descriptions of camshafts in their catalogs and on their websites to make the process easier. Some companies have cam and lifter kits designed for use with intake manifolds and engines of a specific power range. If you're searching for a camshaft tailored to your driving style and the sum of the parts on your engine, you can either consult professionals at your local speed shop or call the cam company. The cam manufacturers have experienced tech personnel who can help you choose a cam that suits your gear ratio, transmission type, intake, carb, heads, compression ratio, and a bunch of other factors. They'll be able to give you qualified professional advice on running a hydraulic or solid flat tappet cam or a hydraulic or solid roller cam to best suit your application. Their job is to help you be pleased with your engine build.

The choice between flat tappet and roller cams is completely up to your application and your pocketbook. Flat tappet cams have been working fine in stock big-blocks since 1965. Roller cams are more exotic and well suited for any performance, but especially ones that rev to more than 5,500 rpm. The roller hydraulic cams have been used in Chevy production engines for many years, providing great performance and reliability. The roller tip allows some stock engines to run trouble-free up to a few hundred thousand miles, while the friction from most flat tappet cams causes signs of serious wear after 100,000 miles. Flat tappet cams are more than enough for most applications, so spend your money wisely.

Lifters

Your choice of lifters should be determined by your camshaft selection. There are hydraulic and solid flat tappets and roller versions of both. You can't run a flat tappet on a roller cam or vice versa. Solid flat tappets can't be used on hydraulic flat tappet camshafts or vice versa because of the incompatibility of design and materials used. I've heard of using

solid roller lifters on hydraulic roller cams, but it's not suggested due to aggressive cam-lobe profiles.

Lifter technology has advanced a lot in the last 30 years. The roller lifter is at the forefront of those advances. Roller lifters have received much needed attention in the effort to reduce power-robbing friction and increase valvetrain life. The introduction of hydraulic roller lifters has changed the way people look at a roller valvetrain.

For so many years enthusiasts have avoided using solid roller or flat tappet cams on the street because they think it necessitates adjusting their valves all the time. Times have changed and so have valvetrain accessories. In the past, solid lifters would get out of adjustment because of the absence of stud girdles and locking rocker arm adjustment nuts. Valvetrain materials in general were not as good as they are today. Solid lifters still need to be adjusted but a lot less frequently than the myth suggests. The bigger drawback of solid lifters is that they produce more valvetrain noise than hydraulics do.

Pushrods

Standard duty big-blocks have been equipped with 5/16-inch- and 3/8-inch-diameter pushrods, depending on year and application. GM only installed the huge 7/16-inch-diameter pushrods on their performance engines.

Replace any 5/16-inch pushrods with 3/8-inch pushrods when rebuilding a big-block that's going to be exposed to performance driving with RPM reaching near 6,000. Only severe-duty high-output big-blocks should consider the tree-trunk-like 7/16-inch pushrods.

Pushrods must be made of hardened steel because the canted valve orientation of big-blocks requires pushrod guide plates. Any non-hardened pushrods are too soft and get chewed up by the guide plates.

Aftermarket companies sell specific pushrod lengths for the big-block. In a perfect world of engine building, you could use exactly what the catalog calls for. Unfortunately, the world is not perfect. Pushrod length changes if the block has been decked, the heads have been shaved, or you are installing all new aftermarket parts. Purchasing pushrods at the start of the build is just asking for trouble. It would be great to have them on your workbench when you get to that step, but you may have to return them for a different-length set. There are two tools on the market to assist you in checking for correct pushrod length: a pushrod length checker, and a pair of adjustable pushrods (the intake pushrod is shorter than the exhaust and requires two different tools). To be precise, you should take your measurements after installing the cam and lifters in the block with assembled heads bolted on the block with the head gaskets in place. This will ensure the proper length measurement.

Rocker Arms

For stock applications, you can use stock rocker arms. As soon as you increase the lift on your camshaft, the rocker arms should be upgraded. A stock rocker has a slot at the base that allows it to pivot on the rocker stud by using its fulcrum ball. Increased valve lift tries to pivot the rocker more than the slot is cut for. There are just as many pounds of leverage at the rocker arm as at the valve spring (447 lbs for the 496 project engine). When there's binding, a stock-sized slot in the rocker (the weakest part) fails. Either the stud snaps off in the head or the rocker arm snaps at the base around the slot.

Long-Slot Rocker Arms

To use larger lift cams and stock-style stamped steel rocker arms, many companies offer rocker arms called long-slot rocker arms. The slot in the base is longer to eliminate bind when used on higher lift camshafts, hence the term "long slot." Crane suggests using long-slot rockers for camshafts ranging from stock lift to .560 inch and their extra-long-slot rocker arms for applications over that.

Roller-Tip Rocker Arms

Typically, performance enthusiasts upgrade to a roller-tipped stamped-steel rocker arm from the long-slot stamped rocker arm. These roller-tipped rockers have a longer slot already designed into the body. The roller on the tip reduces friction by rolling on the tip of the valve stem. This reduced friction is usually good for a good gain of a few horsepower.

True Roller Rockers

The next upgrade in rocker arms is the true or full-roller rocker. It has a roller at the tip like the previously mentioned rocker arm, but is not hampered by the design of the stock fulcrum it has to pivot on. The true roller rocker has a body that rides on needle bearings that reduce friction over stock-style fulcrum. The rocker's rollerized pivot points offer greater reduction in side-loading the valve into the valve guide, for less guide wear and increased power.

Shaft Rockers

If you are building a brutal, high-performance big-block and cost is not an issue, you can't do better than shaft-mounted rockers because the location of the shaft fully maximizes rocker geometry. Crane Cam's shaft-mounted rocker arms use a unique "Quick Lift" geometry by placing the pushrod seat location lower in the rocker body than other brands and increase the advertised rocker ratio a full .1 higher during initial opening. So a rocker advertised at 1.7:1 rocker ratio will act as a 1.8:1 ratio for the first .300 inch of valve opening, then reduce to the advertised 1.7:1 until

the valve returns to within .300 inch of the seat when the ratio increases again. This Quick-Lift increases power by allowing flow into the combustion chamber sooner to maximize cylinder pressure. The design also works on the exhaust valves, allowing spent gases to exit from the chamber faster. This geometry is much like changing to a more aggressive camshaft profile without changing the operational cam duration. Crane's shaft-mounted rockers also utilize a unique low-friction polymer-matrix bearing on a specially treated oversized 5/8-inch shaft for reduced friction and increased durability.

Valvesprings

The valvesprings should be replaced during the course of every rebuild, unless your springs have less than 10,000 miles on them, even if it's a stock rebuild. I only state that because stock replacement springs do not cost much and they are cheap insurance. Valvesprings take serious abuse and weaken from harmonics and heat produced in the valvetrain. A broken spring will lead to a cam failure in a hurry.

The 402 is going to be running an Edelbrock Performer camshaft with a higher-than-factory lift of .500 inch. It's not aggressive by any means, but we're going to replace the rockers with "long-slot" stamped steel rockers to eliminate rocker arm bind up to .560-inch lift.

Our performance 496 engine is going to see more than 6,000 rpm on the rollercam with more than 450 lbs of seat pressure, so stamped rockers are out of the question. We could have upgraded to Crane Cams Gold Race roller rockers, but we decided to go exotic and install shaft roller rockers. The highly polished surface indicates that they have been treated to the Mikronite process.

All aftermarket camshafts have suggested valvesprings to use in conjunction with them. If you are upgrading your camshaft for a performance application, you need to read the information that comes with it. It's possible to use some power-upgrade camshafts with stock-height valve springs. A camshaft with higher lift than stock requires a valvespring with the proper compressed height. If you run a stock spring on a high-lift camshaft, the spring could bind before the cam is at full lift. If this happens, the valvetrain will destroy itself in an instant.

Spring pressures and rates are important, too. You can wipe out the cam if your chosen cam and lifter combination is incompatible, and if the combination is installed with too much spring pressure and increased friction load. If the spring pressure is not high enough, the engine can experience valve float before peak RPM. Spring pressures are measured as seat pressure (uncompressed) and open pressure (compressed). The

Be realistic and purchase parts to the level of power you plan on putting to the pavement. These Crane Cams' titanium retainers and locks meet the level of performance we plan on achieving with the 496 project engine. According to the dyno software, the engine should produce 641 hp and 680 ft-lbs of torque. Consult your local speed shop or the Crane Cams tech line for what parts work the best for your application.

spring rate is determined by the amount of pressure required to compress it. Conventional valve springs have the same outside diameter from top to bottom and are rated linearly. For instance, a linear rated spring of 400 in-lb would take 400 pounds to compress it 1 inch and 200 pounds to compress it 1/2 inch. Beehive valvesprings have a progressive rate; a 400 in-lb beehive spring would take 400 pounds to compress it 1 inch, but it may only take 165 pounds to compress it 1/2 inch. Because the beehive spring diameter is smaller at the retainer end, the retainer and keeper is smaller, which reduces valvetrain weight. Also, they are not subject to the same damaging harmonics as conventional springs. With those benefits, the beehive spring is great in some, but not all, applications due to its progressive spring rate.

If you have questions about your application that can't be answered by the catalog or website, call the tech line at the camshaft manufacturer. They are always willing to get you what you need to have a good experience with their products. Before calling, make sure you have the specs on your camshaft and engine readily available.

Retainers and Locks

Don't skimp on retainers and locks. Stock retainers and locks are not designed for performance use. The piston and the valve get acquainted really fast when these parts fail. If you're building a stock engine, inspect your current retainers and locks for signs of wear. Consider replacing them with new stock replacements, if possible. If you're building an engine with more than 375 hp, you should be upgrading

these valvetrain parts. Purchase the best ones your application requires.

Guide Plates

Depending on what year big-block Chevy you are working on, your engine could have 5/16-, 3/8-, or 7/16-inch pushrods and size-corresponding guide plates. Unless you are going to install shaft rockers on your big-block, you're going to need guide plates. There's a good chance you're working on an engine with perfectly good guide plates. There are only three reasons for replacing your guide plates: you are building a new engine; you are rebuilding an engine with damaged/worn-out ones; or, you are upgrading the size of your pushrods. Just about every valvetrain manufacturer sells new guide plates, but most only offer 3/8-inch and 7/16-inch versions.

Timing Chain or Gear Drive

Some older low performance big-blocks had single-row chains mixed with gears with nylon teeth. In the past, some racers have found success with using standard single-row factory timing sets. Nowadays the most-common timing chain upgrade is to install a double-roller setup. If you are going to spend time to dial-in your cam for extra power, you might as well buy a true double-roller timing set with multiple crankshaft keyways. Timing sets are available with hard-set timing and some have an adjustable cam sprocket. These timing sets, such as the Hex-A-Just chain set from Edelbrock, allow timing adjustments of plus or minus six degrees without removing the lower sprocket from the crank for adjustment. The adjustment is in the adjustable offset bushing on the cam sprocket.

Crane Cams/Mikronite

When Crane Cams was founded in 1953, Harvey Crane, Jr.'s, goal was to repeatably manufacture precision camshafts. Since its inception, Crane Cams has grown from a small office in the corner of a machine shop to a huge multi-million-dollar company. Crane has always been at the forefront of technology when it came to processes and production of their high-quality valve-train components.

In 2006, Mikronite Technologies, a company that has refined a revolutionary surface-finishing process, acquired the ever growing and advancing Crane Cams. This process is so intense and advanced that Mikronite has performed this procedure on ceramics and plastics for aerospace and medical fields. The process can be used on most high-friction auto parts, such as ring and pinion gears, camshafts, lifters, bearing races, transmission parts, etc. Second parties have conducted multiple tests to find unbiased comparisons between unprocessed parts and Mikronite-processed parts. One of the tests ran a 409-ci LS1-powered 1998 Camaro, equipped with a 4.10:1 gearset in a Ford 9-inch rear differential, on the dyno with an unprocessed ring and pin-

The rocker on the left has been through the Mikronite process. As you can see, the process not only polished the surface but it also rounded off some of the harsh ridges produced by the stamping process that produced the rockers.

ion. After installing a processed ring and pinion, the Camaro picked up 7 rear-wheel horsepower and 8.6 ft-lbs of torque. The differential temperature during the tests was 30 degrees cooler on the Mikronite-processed gears. These results were similar to results from tests performed by the same facility on another vehicle.

There are great possibilities for gaining power from reduced friction on car parts. The Crane Cams acquisition gives Mikronite an avenue for expansion in the automotive market. They've also already started applying their process to materials in other sectors. Their process has been used to polish diamonds into ball bearings, treat human-implantable blood pumps, and aerospace aircraft turbine blades, to name a few.

With Mikronite breaking into the automotive industry, there will be some major changes for Crane Cams and their customers in the years to come.

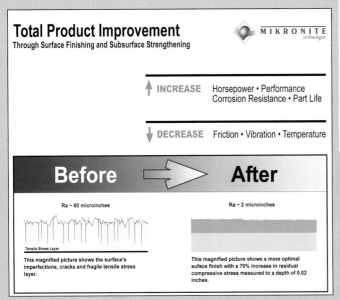

Total Product Improvement
Through Surface Finishing and Subsurface Strengthening

MIKRONITE *technologies*

↑ INCREASE Horsepower • Performance
Corrosion Resistance • Part Life

↓ DECREASE Friction • Vibration • Temperature

Before ➡ **After**

Ra ~ 60 microinches

Ra ~ 2 microinches

Tensile Stress Layer

This magnified picture shows the surface's imperfections, cracks and fragile tensile stress layer.

This magnified picture shows a more optimal suface finish with a 70% increase in residual compressive stress measured to a depth of 0.02 inches.

On the left is a magnification of an unprocessed metal surface, and on the right is the processed surface. The processed surface is stronger and extremely smooth, which drastically reduces friction and vibration.

The Mikronite process increases the strength of the parts by polishing the surface imperfections, reducing stress-risers. The surface is so smooth that friction and power-robbing heat is greatly reduced. This process can be applied to high-friction auto parts, such as camshafts, lifters, gears, pinions, bearing races, etc.

Cam timing is as important to the engine as the flux capacitor is to time travel (remember Back to the Future*). Get yourself a good quality double-roller timing chain set. The timing sets are shown from left to right. The Edelbrock Performer-Link double-roller is pictured on the left. Edelbrock Hex-A-Just features an adjustable true double-roller. These multiple adjustments can be performed with a turn of the hex adjuster and one of the three keyways to choose from. The Milodon gear drive with single fixed-idler in the cover and the drive are turned over so you can see the gears. The front access cover comes off for easy timing changes without removing the entire timing cover to do so. Gear drives allow for use of 100 percent of the cam's available power at all times because all chains have some play, which causes slight timing changes during operation. This type allows for setting up as noisy or quiet. Quiet is preferred by most.*

Gear drives are an option if you want to do away with the timing chain and have the most precise timing without the possibility of chain stretch. They come in two types. There is a fixed-idler type with a single idler attached to the timing cover (like the Milodon gear drive) or a non-fixed idler that has two idlers connected by two bars that float between the cam and crank sprockets. Milodon's fixed-idler system can be set up as quiet or noisy while being installed. The non-fixed type can usually be purchased as noisy or quiet systems, but if you don't like the noise of a jet engine running without oil, you should buy a quiet gear drive. Some non-fixed gear drives require a little machine work to install them and some drop right in, so check with the manufacturer before purchasing. The drawback to gear drive, especially the noisy ones, is their interference with knock sensors on computer-controlled engines.

Oiling System

Your moving parts don't ride on bearing surfaces; they ride on a thin layer of oil. Getting oil from the pan to the bearing surfaces is priority one. Oil pumps should be purchased for your engine according to the application. Bearing clearance set by your machine shop and planned operating RPM should be the deciding factors. Tighter bearing clearances on stock engines don't require as much volume to keep the pressure high. Due to increased bearing loads and heat, high-performance engines have higher operating-bearing clearance. Increased clearance means that

Stock oil pump driveshafts have a nylon bushing joining the shaft to the pump drive. These get brittle and can fail in performance applications. In every rebuild, it is suggested that you replace the driveshaft with a performance driveshaft that has a steel collar pinned to the shaft like this Melling replacement shaft.

it takes more volume to keep the same pressure in the engine because more oil is escaping out of the larger clearance. The higher projected RPM will demand more volume to keep the pressure up since the rod journal travels on a circle around the cranks axis. The higher the RPM, the more centrifugal force pulls oil out of the rod journal. Consider that, compared to the center of the crankshaft, the outside edge of the cranks rod journal is spinning about 15-mph faster at 1,000 rpm and by 6,500 rpm the journal is reaching speeds of 100-mph

Melling is the biggest name in oil pumps. They also make a lot of other internal engine parts. The stock engine is getting a Melling oil pump, oil pickup, and pump driveshaft to go with the stock oil pan.

faster. That force pulls a lot of oil out of the system. If you are building a high-performance big-block, you should be installing a high-volume oil pump. If you are building a stock engine, you should consider replacing your oil pump with a stock replacement pump.

Pump Shaft

The camshaft indirectly drives the oil pump. The camshaft drives the distributor, which turns the oil pump shaft. The stock oil pump driveshaft has a nylon collar that centers the shaft on the top of the oil pump. The nylon collar can become brittle with age. For extra insurance, especially on high-performance applications, most engine builders ditch the stock shaft and collar. They suggest replacing the stock setup with a heavy-duty shaft with a steel collar because they hold up better when subjected to the stresses from moving more volume and heavier oils than the factory intended.

When installing a Milodon oil pan on a previously built engine, we used a Melling pump and Milodon pan and pickup. We found that Milodon pans and pickups work best with its own pumps. Oil pump manufacturers don't have a "standard" and in order for Milodon to ensure its pickups fit its pans, the company designed their products to work with their pumps. On that project, the pan had to be modified to fit. The new 496 project receives a Milodon pump and pickup to go with the new pan.

Oil Pans

The oil pan is a seriously overlooked part. It's very common to not consider the oil pan when building an engine. The stock oil pan will work for stock, moderate street/racing/off-road, and mild open-track driving. Higher levels require more specific oil control and purpose-built pans. More acceleration, deceleration, and cornering g-forces move the oil away from the oil pump pickup. Don't allow the oil pump to starve, or your bearings will be very upset. Manufacturers like Milodon

Oil pans hold the engine's life-blood, the oil. If you're building a performance engine, you should install a pan that controls the oil for your application. Most performance pans have oil control "trap doors" that open and close to keep oil trapped around the oil pickup. If you're building a stroker engine, you need extra clearance for connecting rods in the pan-rail area. Other oil control parts include windage trays, pan baffles, and crankshaft scrapers (these remove residual oil from the crankshaft, but don't touch the crank or rods).

have a full line of oil pans that cover your street, drag race, circle track, road race, and off-road applications. Many Milodon pans are notched for 454s being stroked with a 4.250-inch crankshaft and they are zinc plated for protection against the elements.

Windage Tray

Uncontrolled oil flow in the oil pan can rob power from the engine. Milodon has tested their windage trays on 400-hp engines, and its louvered windage trays have been shown to add about 12 hp while its Diamond Stripper can add up to 25 hp. Installing a windage tray helps control oil in the pan during hard braking, acceleration, and cornering. Milodon's Diamond Stripper has a specially angled mesh screen. Oil flying off the crank (outer crankshaft counterweight speed can reach approximately 240 mph at 6500 rpm) passes through the screen, and it also controls the oil from splashing back up into the crankshaft.

Gaskets

Technology has come a long way since the big-block first rolled off the assembly line. Some gaskets on the market for Mark IV engines have been made with little change since the 1960s. For instance, you can still purchase cork oil pan gaskets with rubber end seals. I will admit that the cork composition has changed to improve its sealing abilities since then, but you can upgrade to Fel-Pro late-model one-piece silicone-rubber oil pan gaskets with a solid steel core, crush-proof bolt shims, and anti-stick treatment for easy removal. These gaskets just make sense.

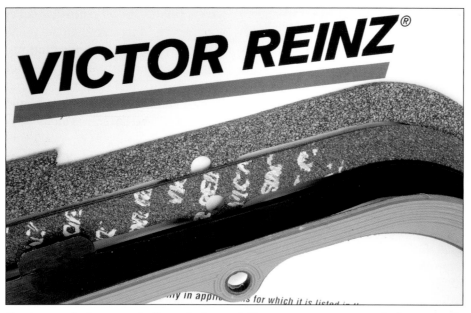

Engine gaskets are not all created equal. Every company seems to have good gasket designs. Most of the gaskets installed in this book are Victor Reinz brand. The valve cover gaskets shown demonstrate different materials available: (top to bottom) cork, cork with steel-core, rubber, and rubber with steel-core, which is the best design that money can buy. The easiest oil pan gasket to install is the one-piece gasket because there are no over-lapping joints; they are reusable and they require very little sealer. For Mark IV engines, you can't beat the Fel-Pro one-piece oil pan gasket. When it comes to intake gaskets, steel core gaskets are for cast-iron intakes and paper-type gaskets are for aluminum intakes.

Head Gaskets

Make sure you get the right gaskets for your application. Each version (Mark IV and Gen V, VI, and VII) of the big-block requires different gaskets. The timing cover, oil pan, and intake gaskets are easy to identify as being wrong when you get ready to install them. The head gaskets are not easy to identify as wrong and will cause you a lot of overheating problems if you install the wrong ones for your application.

There are two different types of big-block coolant flow systems: series and parallel. The water in the "series flow" system is designed to flow from the water pumped into the front of the block, around the cylinders, and to the back of the block. At this point,

it flows up through two large holes in the head gasket into the two corresponding holes in the head. Then, the hot coolant flows to the front of the head where it's forced up into the intake manifold and thermostat.

The water in the "parallel flow" system gets pumped into the front of the block and around the cylinders and ports in the head gasket between each cylinder. This allows coolant to flow up into the head as well as one small port in the back of the block. In other words, the parallel flow system flows coolant evenly up into the head from the entire deck surface, from front to rear. All the coolant travels to the front of the head where it flows into the intake manifold and thermostat.

Don't make the mistake of installing a Gen V, VI, or VII head gasket with a small rear port on an early Mark IV block. The Mark IV's (depending on the year) deck surface doesn't have the ports between the cylinders, and it relies on the two large rear passages for all of its flow. The late-model gasket with one small rear port seriously restricts the coolant flow and causes overheating problems that will plague your engine until the gasket is replaced.

Both the series flow and parallel flow cooling systems work well. Some engine builders have found a slight advantage to the parallel because it cools the engine a little more evenly than the series flow does, but it's not worth the trouble of trying to convert a series flow to a parallel flow.

You will face cooling problems from installing the wrong head gasket, but you can have a few other problems as well. The gasket could be the wrong material for your application. For instance, steel shim gaskets are almost always used only on cast-iron-headed applications while composite-type head gaskets can be used with cast-iron and aluminum heads. Solid copper head gaskets are supposed to be used in conjunction with stainless steel O-rings, which require machining O-ring grooves in the block, and are not suggested for street use. Proper cylinder bore size and gasket thickness is also important when picking your new head gaskets. Fel-Pro also has a full line of head gaskets for your big-block. Check with your machine shop for the best head gasket for your application.

Fasteners

Using the correct bolts and nuts to assemble your engine is as important as adding oil to your engine before start-up. I've seen engines with cylinder heads held on by Grade 5 hardware store bolts. There are plenty of different levels of quality bolts available on the market for your engine.

Stock

If you are building a stock engine, you can get away with reusing most of the original bolts. However, since you are spending the time to rebuild your engine, you may want to consider replacing critical bolts like rod bolts, main bolts, and head bolts. Victor Reinz and Fel-Pro sell stock replacement bolts if you don't want to upgrade to aftermarket bolts.

Aftermarket

Because you are going to spend some good money to rebuild your engine, you should consider replacing your critical bolts with aftermarket bolts to protect your investment. There are different levels of aftermarket bolts available. If you are on a budget, you can find great aftermarket bolts available from companies such as Mr. Gasket and Milodon. Both companies offer bolts for just about every need on your engine. ARP fasteners cost more than stock, but this brand is chosen by more engine builders than any other available fastener.

There are different types of bolts available for most applications. The most common bolts are hex-head bolts, which are identified by their 6 points. Although less common, 12 point bolts are the choice of some engine builders because, in tight spaces, you can reposition a 12-point combination wrench on the head with a smaller turn of the wrench.

Studs vs. Bolts

Which is better, studs or bolts?

Studs are the best way to go, whenever possible. When you torque a bolt, it twists into the threaded hole, which causes two different forces (twisting and clamping) to get to the proper torque. A stud is installed in relaxed mode, only threaded finger tight. When you torque a nut on a stud, all the clamping force is on a single axis for a better and more precise torque. This also saves the threads in the block by only pulling in one direction when the threads are fully engaged. It's recommended to use main studs because they reduce cap walk and fretting, which can spell disaster for bearings, especially on high-performance applications. If you're going to use studs in critical places such as the mains and heads, you need to purchase them before machining is done. As you just read, the clamping force is different between studs and bolts. The studs change the way the main caps fit the block, so the main alignment should be checked with the studs installed. Head studs are much better than head bolts, but sometimes they make extra work because they don't allow for removal of the head (while the engine is installed in the car) without removing the studs first.

Cooling System

Don't overlook your cooling system during the course of your engine rebuild. The wearing parts of a cooling system consist of the water pump and thermostat. Don't overlook the hoses. They should be checked for swelling and/or surface cracks and possibly replaced before installing your newly rebuilt engine. You should take the vehicle's radiator to be checked and flushed while the engine is out of the car, so you can start with a completely fresh cooling system.

Water Pump

During tear down you identified your water pump as good or bad. If it was bad, you should replace it. If you plan on upgrading the performance output of your big-block, you should look into installing an aftermarket high-flow water pump. Aftermarket performance pumps are available in cast iron and aluminum. Aluminum pumps are higher priced, but they don't retain as much heat and they weigh less. As I mention throughout this book, you get what you pay for.

If you're installing a mechanical fuel pump, you need a fuel pump pushrod. The stock ones are solid steel; so to reduce reciprocating weight, you can install a lightweight unit from ARP. The fuel pump should match your application. If you're building a performance engine, you can upgrade from a stock pump to a higher flow-capacity pump, such as this one from Edelbrock (left). To reduce power-robbing friction in the engine, you can simply install an electric fuel pump, such as this Barry Grant model (right), accompanied by a fuel-pressure regulator.

Thermostat

As a cheap insurance policy, you should think about replacing your thermostat. You could go through the trouble of sticking your original thermostat in a beaker of water while using a thermometer to make sure it is opening at the proper temp (typically stamped in the housing) and that it closes when it's cold. Or, you could just save yourself the hassle and buy a new Mr. Gasket or Stant unit. Thermostats come rated for specific temperatures. The most common are rated 160, 180, and 190 degrees. A general rule is to use a 180-degree unit. In drag racing applications, some guys leave the thermostat out or install restrictor plates in place of the thermostat. Drag racing has short bursts of intense power and heat, so they can get away without using a thermostat. Run a thermostat if your car will be driven more than a quarter mile at a time. Without a thermostat, your car will take much longer to warm up on the street. A colder operating temperature increases the wear of parts like piston rings and cylinder walls. Wear decreases substantially when the operating temp is higher than 140 degrees. A good operating range for performance and drivability is between 180 and 195 degrees.

Cooling System Accessories

Don't overlook replacing old, corroded, and possibly failing coolant plugs, fittings, and the thermostat housing. You must run fresh coolant through the system at all times or else parts start to deteriorate from exposure to the elements. Thermostat housings deteriorate and cause pinholes in the casting, or they can be over-torqued and start to leak. Consider replacing them with new parts so you know these parts won't cause

an unforeseen overheating problem down the road. These fittings and housings come in many forms. The most cost-effective ones you can buy are available from Mr. Gasket. These are typically chrome-plated steel and can survive the elements better than some other brands. If you want plugs or fittings (factory style or aftermarket) that will never give you a hassle or rust (internally or externally), you should look into stainless-steel fittings from Performance Stainless Steel. They also offer stainless-steel thermostat housings that stand up to the harsh elements like no other housings on the market.

Fuel System

You've got to have fuel if you want fire. Getting the right amount of fuel is the most important part. Too much fuel can wash past the piston rings and contaminate the oil, which, in extreme conditions, can cause bearing failure. Too little fuel can cause catastrophic meltdown of your pistons under the right conditions. Pick your fuel system with care.

Mechanical Pump

The stock mechanical pump bolts to the mounting pad on the passenger side of the engine on carburetor-equipped Gen IV (and limited numbers of V and VI) blocks. Fuel pumps are different for each application due to space constraints, along with fuel and smog requirements. The standard performance stock engine doesn't require high volumes of fuel to be supplied to the carburetor. When you step up the performance level or you are working on a high-output big-block, you will need a higher-output pump. Companies such as Edelbrock offer mechanical fuel pumps for power lev-

els up to 550 hp that pump 110 gph (gallons per hour) and operate at a pressure suitable for a carburetor without a separate regulator. For racers who continue using a mechanical pump beyond the 550-hp rating, Edelbrock sells a Victor-series pump that feeds 130 gph at 13 to 14 psi. However, this is too much pressure for the needle and seat of a carburetor, so this pump requires a separate fuel-pressure regulator to limit the pressure being fed to the carb until the demand increases.

Electric

There are reasons to run electric fuel pumps: You may be running fuel injection, or you may simply prefer to not have your engine pumping its own fuel. Whatever your reason, make sure you are getting sufficient fuel. Electric fuel pump manufacturers require installing the fuel pump as close (within 12 inches, typically) to the tank as possible. A fuel line up to the carb on every big-block should be at least 3/8 inch in diameter, or as big as 5/8 inch, depending on the power output. If you don't get enough fuel to the engine you'll run the risk of running lean enough to cause piston damage.

Pushrod

The stock fuel pump pushrod is a solid piece of steel actuated by a lobe on the camshaft. At high RPM, the weight of the pushrod can cause the pump arm to stay compressed and the engine will run out of fuel. If you still want to run a mechanical fuel pump pushrod you can get a lightweight version from many manufacturers. It is typically a hollow rod with hardened ends. Note: A fuel pump pushrod will wipe out a roller cam due to material incompatibility.

MACHINE SHOPS

Get to know your local machine shop. From talking with the guys at the counter, you can tell a lot about their business practices. Here Bob Gromm of Gromm Racing Heads and Engine Machine explains what kind of magic he can work on cylinder heads. After the initial visit, I could tell he really knew what he was doing with performance engines and that cutting corners is not his business practice, so he received our head and balancing business.

Selecting a machine shop is a decision that must be carefully made. After all, the performance, reliability, and longevity of your Chevy big-block depend on it. To illustrate the differences in the three most common types of machine shops you will find, I will be using letters to differentiate make-believe shops. A great shop will be referred to as "Shop G" and a bad shop will be "Shop X."

If you are going to rebuild your big-block, you're going to need to find a machine shop. Search your area by looking in the phone book, get on the Internet and search for it, and/or ask around. There are two things you need to know before contacting a machine shop. First off, you need to

know what you plan to do with the engine ahead of time. Are you building your engine to be stock, a mild performer, or a serious powerhouse? A shop that builds stock engines on a regular basis might be a great place to have your stock or a mild street engine built; however, if you are building a high-end rat you may need to find a different shop. High-performance engines are machined with different bearing clearances due to the high loads and excessive heat for that application (I'll address that in a later section).

Second, the cost of good machine work is not cheap, and, oddly, the cost of questionable machine work is about the same. The

difference is not just in the overall cost of the job. Both shops may charge the same for an align bore but when it comes to boring the cylinders, Shop G may charge $400 to bore your cylinders, and Shop X may only charge $300 for boring your cylinders. Often, the step Shop X is leaving out is the torque plate. The torque plate is an important step left out by the shops you want to avoid, but Shop G uses it and has to charge for the time it takes to install it and remove it. By the end of the whole job, Shop G is going to be more expensive than Shop X but you will get a better and longer lasting engine by going with Shop G.

After you find a machine shop that seems promising, talk to the machinist about their services and costs. If you are building a high-performance engine, ask the proprietor if they build many high-performance engines. If not, then you should continue your search because you need to select an engine builder that builds Chevy big-blocks to the level of performance you're seeking. Appearance isn't everything. Just because a shop looks like a grease pit doesn't mean they do poor work. On the flip side, a clean shop doesn't mean they turn out great work. If you get a good feeling about the shop, it's a good idea to get a few references. Check with previous customers to see if they were satisfied with the work done to their engines.

At this point, there are a few items to take into consideration. People run machines and people make mistakes. Tolerances that are merely the thickness of a human hair can be the difference between a great engine and a boat anchor. Every machine shop is bound to have a few customers who have had a bad experience and then some people have a bad experience wherever they go, so it's your job to find a machine shop by reading between the lines and using your people skills. Most machinists are into precision and this is the career they chose because precision is all they know. If you do have a problem at the end of the job, you are more likely to get help and better service if you keep cool and treat them with the same respect you like to be treated with. They are human just like you.

Good luck with making the correct decision. Be patient and choose wisely.

Pre-Machine-Shop Planning

You need a good picture of what you want and a detailed build-up plan before heading to the machine shop because services can add up fast and it's easy to spend a ton of money in a hurry. Follow along with the list of machine shop services and identify the ones you need, the ones you can perform yourself, and the ones you don't need. Because you bought this book, you're going to save yourself a big chunk of change by assembling the long block by yourself or you're going to at least be educated about the big-block Chevy and know how it ticks.

Machine to Application Requirements

Are you building your engine for drag racing, street driving, off-roading, or road racing? There are certain machine shop services you need for each application and some you do not. For instance, if you are building a street or off-road engine, you may not need to convert to 4-bolt racing caps, mill your piston domes, or internally balance your externally balanced rotating assembly. If you're planning on revving your engine over 6,000 rpm often, a main cap upgrade is a good idea because it provides improved strength and reliability. A good machine shop will spend a few minutes going over the list of services they offer and won't sell you stuff you don't need, but they will rely on you to tell them exactly what you are going to do with the engine.

Pre-Machine-Shop Tasks

These are steps you don't have to perform to have a good running engine. They are additional steps you can take to further enhance your engine project. These steps leave metal particles in the block so they should be performed before your engine goes to the machine shop, where more debris will get into the engine and oil galleries. When all the grinding and machining is finished you'll have to clean the entire block inside and out before assembly.

Professional Inspection

When you are done with your preliminary inspection you should have the machine shop perform more in-depth checks for defects you can't find without a lot of training and the right tools. Some engines run perfectly fine with more cracks than you can shake a stick at. I've personally seen an engine turning 12s in the quarter-mile with multiple cracks in the crank, three cracked pistons, and multiple cracks in the heads. The cracks weren't discovered until some piston noise prompted a rebuild. It only takes one crack in the right component, in the right spot, for catastrophic failure.

To find cracks, the surface is lightly covered with iron particles. Magnetizing the component reveals the crack because the iron particles are drawn to the crack. Magnaflux calls this a "magnetic leak."

A machine shop employee, Tim Walker, said, "In the last six months of work, I haven't disassembled one

1 Remove Casting Flash

Before sending the engine to the machine shop, spend a few minutes cleaning up the stress risers (casting flash) on the block and the casting flash in the lifter valley. It's not likely a crack will start in the area around the oil filter or other external surfaces, but it only took a few minutes to grind the flash down.

2 | Smooth Front of Block

A lot of time was spent smoothing the rough finish on the front of the block with grinding heads from a head porting kit. It really stands out in the engine compartment and in the long run it's really easy to keep clean. It was too much work to smooth the entire block, so only the front was done. When it comes to performance, if you smoothed the lifter valley in the engine with this same method the oil could return to the pan much faster.

3 | Grinding

The smoothing head slipped a couple of times. If you try this technique, be careful not to slip and hit a critical surface like the head surface. This timing cover seal surface is not a critical surface, so it won't be a problem. I suggest having a head installed on the engine while doing this, to ensure you don't slip and damage the deck surface.

4 | Radius Oil Port

There are sharp edges in the oil passage entrance going into the block above the oil filter. A race engine builder recommended knocking down the harsh edges and making the entrance more gradual for less restrictive oil flow. Do this before the block goes to hot tank.

5 | Prepare Lifter Valley Screen Kit

The lifter valley was prepped for installing a lifter valley screen kit, such as this one from Milodon. Using the screen as a template, the correct areas where epoxy will be applied were slightly roughed up, so the epoxy has a better surface to adhere to. Installation of the kit is located on page 114.

engine without [finding] a crack in one of its components." The machine shop will find any crack in your engine when they Magnaflux the components.

Machine Shop Services

Each component of the engine is manufactured with precision. Years of heating and cooling along with extreme driving and weather conditions can cause precise parts to shift and distort. This movement can cause leaks, bearing tolerances to change, and engine failure. Your machine shop is in business to get your engine back to the precision instrument it once was.

I've listed some of the more critical machine shop services in this chapter. I have covered a few services in less depth than others due to space constraints. If you want to learn more about machine shop services, read *The Step-By-Step Guide to Engine Blueprinting*, by Rick Voegelin.

Block

The engine block is like the foundation of a building. It needs to be straight and true, otherwise everything put on top of it isn't going to be worth a darn. Unless your machine shop makes your engine block the perfect foundation for your engine build, you might as well throw all the money you spend on parts into the garbage.

Bore/Honing Plates

Good machine shops use a boring/honing plate when boring the block. Some machine shops skip this step because using it takes extra time and costs more money. If a machine shop quotes a cheaper price for

Aftermarket Heads

In the past, if you wanted better flow and really high performance from your heads, you had to modify your stock heads with tried-and-true porting techniques and accept the expense of increasing valve size. When aftermarket big-block cylinder heads hit the market, they were expensive but were better than stock configurations because of the gain in performance. By the end of the 1990s, the market had changed and there were multiple cast-iron and aluminum heads that were more affordably priced for performance enthusiasts. Edelbrock is one of those companies increasing the availability of heads for big-blocks with the four different performance levels obtained with their Performer, RPM, Victor Jr., and Victor heads. The levels of power range from mild-performance street engines to full-race big-inch competition big-blocks with more than 800-hp potential.

When it comes to installing aftermarket heads, you assume full responsibility for the parts as soon as you bolt them on your engine and get it running. No matter whose aftermarket heads you are installing, it's in your best interest to carefully scrutinize the heads by performing disassembly and full inspection of parts and their clearances, even if the heads are listed as "bolt-on" items. Also check the concentricity of the valve and valve seats. They should be within .002 inch to ensure the valves, seats, and guides run for many years without issue.

In some cases you can spend just a couple of minutes performing modifications to greatly increase performance on aftermarket heads. For instance, these Edelbrock heads have been CNC ported, but to keep the cost down for you, the shop elects not to spend additional time fine-tuning the heads inside areas that are harder to reach. The area in particular is the curve around the pushrod tunnels inside the intake runners. The edge is a little sharp and could easily be softened for a smoother transition with just a few minutes of work with a porting bit. Warning: Don't get crazy with the porting and port through the wall into the pushrod tunnel! This area is really delicate and you could easily introduce a serious leak by porting just a little too much. This goes for any area on any cylinder heads.

Before performing any modifications on cylinder heads, remove all the valves and springs. The lip on the tip of the valve damages the valve seals if you pull the valves though them. If your heads already have the valve seals installed, leave the valves in the head and thoroughly clean them before running them on the engine. Debris can easily get caught in the springs. If you don't pull the valves, at least pull the springs, shims, retainers, and locks off and keep them in order in a valvetrain organizer or use a large piece of paper with the number of the cylinder clearly marked on it. Perform all grinding away from your engine-building area and any parts you want to keep clean. Thoroughly clean any debris out of the head before reassembling it.

These ARP studs are stronger than stock and were lubricated with ARP moly assembly lube, so they were torqued to 58 ft-lbs. If one rocker stud is loose it will ruin your day. If it came off, it could possibly ruin your camshaft and lifter because the rocker keeps the lifter pressed against the cam to keep the lifter rotating in its bore, and possibly pull the thread out of the cylinder head on its way out.

The valves in these Edelbrock heads are +.100-inch longer than standard valves and required .060-inch-thick hardened valvespring locators to protect the valvepocket and raise the spring in the pocket. These are combined with specific locks to drop the retainer low enough to fit the springs required for the camshaft on the 496 project.

Always use head bolt washers when installing aluminum heads because they help evenly distribute the torque load across the entire head. The washers also prevent false torque readings, galling, and cracking of the head bolt bosses. Lubricate the underside of the head bolt flanges and the washers with assembly lube or 30W oil to ensure proper torque during assembly.

machine work than others, usually there's something that they are not doing. Most likely, they are leaving out an important step.

Bore

The cylinder bores must be enlarged in order to repair worn or damaged walls and the pistons have to be replaced with corresponding sizes. The boring is also performed in order to install oversized pistons when upgrading for increased performance.

Machine Hone

When the cylinder bores are not going to get a big bore, and a significant taper is present, the machine shop uses a machine hone to remove it. This hone removes a significant amount of material and oversized pistons and rings are necessary.

Flex-Type Hone

The machine shop can simply use a flex-type hone in the cylinders if your bores pass inspection and don't have excessive taper or need to be bored oversize in order to rebuild the engine. This process refinishes the proper crosshatch to the cylinder walls without changing the shape of the bore. This is done so a new set of piston rings can seat in the cylinders properly to keep compression in the combustion chamber and oil in the lower crankcase.

Line-Hone or Line-Bore Mains

The bearing bore must be straight (less than .001-inch runout) or else your main bearings will wear excessively or fail. Your machine shop will determine if you need an

Precision Measurement

6 Check Deck Trueness

Use a precision straight edge and a feeler gauge to check the condition of the block deck. Surface irregularities more than .003 inch need to be machined flat. A quick check can be done with a light on one side of the bar, while looking to see if light can be seen under the straight edge. If you can see light, you need your feeler gauge.

7 | Block Overbore

The 454 is getting bored .060-inch over, then it is honed to get the correct cylinder surface so the rings can seal properly. Note: This shop uses a plate that is torqued to the block while it's being honed. This plate mimics the distortion of the heads installed on the block. Goodson states that this distortion can be as much as .004 inch when you use one. Not all shops take this step when honing or boring a block; find one that does.

Cam Bearing Install

The cam bearings need to be replaced every time you perform a complete rebuild of an engine. In the cam removal stage (including Chapters 1 and 5), I said that it is imperative to not damage the bearings. That was meant to save the cam if you planned to use it again or to protect you if you were using this book for assistance in simply replacing the camshaft. Plus, being careful with the bearings is good practice when you go to install the cam during the assembly process.

During the time your engine is at the machine shop, the cam bearings will get damaged. First, the chemicals in the hot tank will eat the surface layer off the bearings so they won't be usable anymore. Second, there will be many chips and debris in the oil galleries that the cam bearings can help trap in the oil system—it would be a bad idea to leave them in. Third, some of the machine work your engine is going to go through will require the bearings to be removed anyway.

There are only a few steps I suggest having the machine shop perform because of the special tools and experience required to do the job right. Removing and replacing the cam bearings is one of them. You may be determined to do this job yourself, and it's good for you to have knowledge of all the steps even if you don't do them yourself, so I will give a general overview of the process.

Installing cam bearings is not an easy task, and it requires a special installation tool. Unless you plan to build more than a dozen engines in your lifetime, it doesn't make sense to purchase a cam bearing installation tool. Your machine shop installs cam bearings all the time, so they can do it quickly and won't charge a lot to do it.

Sometimes the cam bearings have small burrs or nicks on the inner beveled edge, which can catch the cam bearing journals during cam installation. Using a knife, lightly drag the knife-edge over the nick. Don't cut into the bearing. Drag the knife-edge away from the direction of the blade. Don't scratch the bearing surface; only knock down the burrs on the very edge of the inner chamfer.

8 Line Honing Block

In order to line-bore a block, material is taken off the parting line surface of the main cap, and then the line-bore can be performed without moving the crankshaft centerline closer to the camshaft centerline. Line-honing removes material from the cap and the main saddles in the block.

In order to get the proper line-hone, this "dummy" oil pump boss is torqued to the rear main cap. Now any stress on the cap from bolting on an oil pump will not throw off the line-hone.

To ensure proper bearing positioning front to rear, you should scribe the block with lines showing bearing location before removing the old bearings.

To prevent distortion to the bearings by the tool's arbor during installation, take your bearing scraper and chamfer the front and rear edges of the bearing.

Big-block camshaft journals are all the same diameter, but the bearing bores in the block are different sizes. Your cam bearings have specific positions listed on the included directions. Check all the bores in the block and compare them to the outside diameter of the cam bearings. If they don't match, it's possible your block has previously been machined to repair a damaged cam-bearing bore and you may need to purchase special oversized bearings.

When installing the cam bearings, make sure you line up the bearing oil-feed holes in the block with the corresponding holes in the bearings or else you'll destroy your camshaft and engine.

After installing a couple of cam bearings, clean them and lightly lubricate them. Get your camshaft out and carefully install it in the bearings to confirm that it doesn't bind. After installing every bearing, lubricate the bearings and test fit the camshaft to confirm the cam bearings are properly aligned. If the camshaft binds more with the installation of each bearing, you need to confirm your camshaft is not bent. If it's straight, the cam bearing bores are not aligned properly.

The front cam bearing edge should line up with the inner edge of the chamfer on the front of the block's cam boss.

The rear cam bearing should not protrude into the counterbore for the rear core plug at the back of the block.

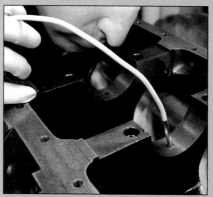

The oiling holes in the block and the holes in the cam bearings must line up or else the oil can't get to the camshaft and you'll have some serious engine failure. Use a small inspection light to confirm the alignment by shining it through the main bearing oil gallery holes in the block.

The camshaft journals are all the same size, but the bearing bores in the block are not. Each bearing has a specific location by position and outside diameter.

align-bore or align-hone, depending on the condition of the main bearing bore. To perform either task, material must be removed from the main cap surface that meets the block. The align-bore can be adjusted to remove less material from the block half of the main bearing bore, which is the preferred method. Line-honing the block removes an equal amount of material from the block and cap. Removing material from the block will position the crankshaft centerline closer to the camshaft, which can produce more slack in the timing chain, tighten clearance on timing gear drives, reduce piston deck height clearance, and increase compression ratio and piston-to-valve clearance.

Sleeve Block

This service is used when your engine suffered a catastrophic event that damaged a cylinder wall and it won't take a larger over-bore. This is usually cheaper than replacing the block with a used or new one. Some people look down on sleeves, but aluminum blocks all run them and they perform great. When installed correctly, they are stronger than a cast-iron cylinder wall.

Install Cam Bearings

Cam bearings require special tools to install them. This is a service that I suggest you leave to the machine shop.

File Fit Rings

If you are performing a standard or performance rebuild that uses pre-fit rings, you don't need to do more than check them for proper ring gaps. Performance rings also come as file-fit rings. The rings have to be filed down in order to get the correct gap.

Main Cap Upgrade

Upgrading main caps is tedious work and most machine shops don't do it because it takes a lot of time and it's expensive for a customer. The shop has to fit the new caps to your original registers in the block and then line-bore it.

Stroker Clearance

When installing a crankshaft that has a larger stroke than what the block was designed for, you have to clearance the lower block web around the bottom of the cylinders and the oil pan rail. A 4.25-inch-stroke crank fits almost any 454 block without clearancing.

O-Rings

Engines with extreme cylinder pressures need O-rings fitted to the block or heads. To do this, a small groove is machined in the surface of the head or the block to capture a stainless steel or copper wire ring that seals the cylinder of an engine producing a 12:1 or more compression ratio. This is also a modification used on supercharged and turbocharged engines because of the high head and block pressures produced under high boost.

Heads

Your engine won't breathe well or hold good compression without a proper valve job or a flat head gasket surface. Without compression you can't make power. Valve guides keep

Professional Mechanic Tip

9 Converting to 4-Bolt Main Bearing Caps

If you are going to be pumping more than 550 hp, you should consider upgrading any two-bolt block to 4-bolt main caps. The 496 project got a set of Milodon splayed, 4-bolt ductile steel main caps. The two outer bolts are angled to attach to the stronger outer main web and also stop "cap-walk" (movement of the main cap under extreme loads).

10 Checking 4-Bolt Main Bearing Caps

Rick Santos of S&S Automotive (36 NHRA National Champion wins) checks his work after performing the necessary machine work to install the 4-bolt main caps on the 496 project engine. After drilling and tapping the splayed outer bolts on this machine, the block was moved to the line-boring machine.

the valves operating smoothly and the valve springs keep them opening and closing when you want them to.

In order to have combustion in the chamber, you need compression. If a valve doesn't seal against its seat, it won't hold any pressure. Brand new heads out of the box aren't even as close as you'd like them to be. Your machine shop can check your old heads and determine if you need to replace any parts. In some cases you may need to replace valve seats, guides, and valves.

Rotating Assembly

The rotating assembly is made up of the pistons, rods, crank, flywheel, and harmonic damper. The rotating assembly is made up of the fastest-moving parts in your entire engine. The tolerances on these parts are just as critical as the block that holds them. If you are building a high-performance engine that revs more than 6,000 rpm on a regular basis, you should consider balancing all those fast-moving parts.

Grind Crank

Often a journal on a crankshaft is worn or damaged too much to be repaired by polishing. The machine shop grinds the journal surface down to start with a fresh surface.

Polish Crank

If the crankshaft journals aren't scuffed, damaged, or worn too badly, the machine shop can polish them to a smooth, useable finish without the expense of grinding the crank.

Balance

If you are going to drive your big-block with a heavy foot (and you probably are), you should consider having the rotating assembly balanced. At the speed that these parts travel, it's good to have all the pistons and rods weigh the same. The crank should be smoothly spinning around in the block too. If the balance is off, it can have a distinct vibration that increases as the RPM

Precision Measurement

11 Measure Valve Seat Accuracy

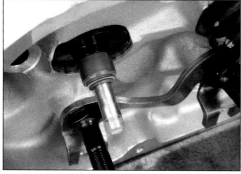

If the valve isn't round or the seat isn't centered on the valve guide, the valve won't be able to keep the compression in the combustion chamber. If the valve is as much as .003 inch off center with the valve seat, the guide will be damaged and chances of valve failure are increased drastically as the spec increases. All these specs need to be precise.

12 Install Press-On Valve Seals

If the machine shop is installing press-on-type valve seals, have them make sure they fit the heads but do not install them yet; you or your shop can install them later. They can only be installed over the valve one time, and (in the next chapter) you need to remove the valve to check clearances. The valve stem toward the tip is sharp and tends to damage the seal. If the shop installs the seals, you can carefully slide a clear plastic sleeve over the valve with some lubrication and push it down into the seal to save the seal lip, and then slowly pull the valve out. Do not try to pull the sleeve through the valve guide. Call your shop for this sleeve. To reinstall the valve, push the sleeve into the seal and then install the valve. The valve lock groove cuts or damages the seal, so it should never come in direct contact with it.

13 Relieve Wall Around Valve

The wall behind the valve is very restrictive to flow. The wall around this valve has been relieved so more air can flow around all sides of the valve. If the gases can't get in or out fast enough, the performance is hampered.

Weights are fastened to the crank to simulate connecting rods, and then it's spun at a few hundred rpm (differs for each application) to check the balance. This determines if weight needs to be added or removed from the counterweights for a perfect balance.

14 Converting to an Internally Balanced Crankshaft

In order to convert an externally balanced crank into an internally balanced crank, heavy metal ingots of Mallory metal have to be welded into the counterweights. This crankshaft had some serious weight gain.

Professional Mechanic Tip **PRO TIP**

15 Balance Components

PRO TIP Components advertised as "balanced" are only within a gram or two of each other. These Eagle kit components are closer than most other manufacturer's kits, so more precise balancing is always possible. A precision scale is used to weigh the pistons, rods, and pins. Each is weighed separately, and then material is carefully removed from the heavier components until each assembly is within less than a gram of each other. Better shops weigh each half of the rod with a rod-hanging device such as this; that way each end of the rod is balanced correctly. The image on the far right shows the rod hanging level on roller bearings to ensure exact weight is produced and the setup is repeatable for each rod.

Precision Measurement

16 Check Connecting Rods for Straightness

The rods were checked for straightness then material is taken off the rod cap at the parting line. After new ARP rod bolts are installed, the rods are torqued to spec and resized to the correct rod bearing diameter. Here, two rods are on the shaft at the same time, so they can be held together to help ensure the straightness of the bore. Then they are put on the Sunnen Precision Gage and rotated to ensure the bore is true.

goes up. This vibration can shorten the life of the bearings, depending on how far balance is off. In order to balance the rotating assembly, the machine shop needs to have your crankshaft, flywheel, harmonic damper, pistons, and rods.

Assemble Rods and Pistons

It's wise to have the machine shop install your pistons on your rods unless your rods and pistons have full-floating wrist pins. You can assemble full-floating wrist pins in your garage.

Intake Manifold and Head Fitment

Not all big-block intake manifolds are the same. The factory intake manifold mating-surface angles and head surfaces are critical, and as such, those surface angles must be maintained. Those critical angles change when you add aftermarket heads and intake manifold and machine-shop services, such as resurfacing (or shaving) the heads or decking the block. If the intake manifold does not match up to the heads

correctly, you will have problems with vacuum and coolant-passage leaks that you won't be able to see until it's too late. Check these angles by placing the intake manifold in place between the heads without the gasket in place. Get out your feeler gauges and check to see how close the angles are. Verify that there is a gap at the top and the bottom of the intake-to-head mating surfaces. If they are within 1.2 degrees, you will be all right; any more than that and you should be concerned. You need to note your findings and take your intake manifold to the machine shop to have them cut a new angle on the intake manifold.

Also check to make sure the intake manifold does not rest on the top rail of the block surface before the manifold touches the heads. If it rests on the block without touching the head surface, the machine shop needs to machine that surface. When you get the intake back from the machine shop, check the fitment again. Once it fits correctly, degrease and clean the mating surfaces, put the gaskets in some place dry (without any sealers), and place

the intake manifold on the engine. Now check to make sure all intake manifold bolts thread into the heads. If they don't, you may need to get out your rotary tool and clearance the holes a little so the bolts will fit. With the gaskets in place, check to make sure there is a gap between the front and back top rails of the block where the intake does not have a paper gasket. If there isn't a gap, you need machining done to fix the problem.

General Machine Shop Services

A high-quality general or full-service machine shop is capable of many more precision operations than the ones that I will reference here. Due to the necessary limits in the scope of this book, I am citing the procedures and services that pertain most to your big-block Chevy rebuild.

Disassemble

If you followed through with all the previous steps in the book, you performed the disassembly on your

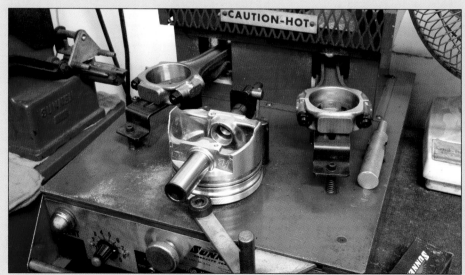

The machine shop can easily assemble the rods and pistons for you. The connecting rod heater heats up the pin end of the rod to enlarge the bore without weakening or damaging it, and then installs the piston and wrist pin with ease. If pressing the wrist pins at home without a rod heater and good knowledge of the process, you can gall the rod bushing and pin. When the rod cools, the wrist pin locks in place.

own. If you didn't, then the machine shop offers this as a service.

Remove and Replace Plugs

This service comes in handy because some plugs are extremely difficult to remove or require a special tool that you may not want to purchase. It usually takes a shop some time to remove stubborn plugs so it typically charges for this service. I personally remove all the plugs that I can and have them take out the last few stubborn plugs in the oil galley system and the heads.

Clean and Sonic Clean

Most machine shops offer washing and blasting services for blocks, heads, intake manifolds, and other parts. Large industrial pressure-washing cabinets are used to wash the components with extremely hot detergent, which performs a deep cleaning. Some parts, such as engine block and heads, can be cleaned in a media blasting cabinet that allows the shop to get grime and carbon buildup that the hot wash won't touch. For a thorough job, every part and plug needs to be removed before the shop starts cleaning. Some shops skip the step of cleaning out the oil galleries at this point, so it's a good idea to ask them to make sure they do it.

The sonic clean is a newer process that uses high-frequency sound waves and soapy water to deep-clean debris that normally sticks to the block. This supposedly removes debris that was left over in the block—debris that was originally locked into the castings. It's environmentally friendly and performs a deeper clean than any other method available. Jewelers have been using this method to clean delicate jewelry

17 Machining Considerations   *Important!*

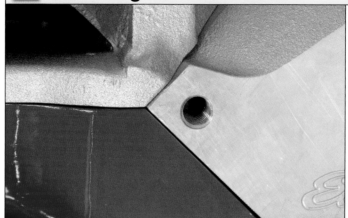

Machining the block and head surface can change the angles for the intake manifold. If these angles are off 1/2 degree, you can have problems with intake manifold gaskets not sealing, which can lead to running problems that are a headache to diagnose. If these surfaces don't match, you need the machine shop to mill the intake manifold to match the gasket surface.

18 Remove Oil Gallery Plugs

Oil gallery plugs tend to be the most stubborn plugs to remove during disassembly. The machine shop used these tools to remove the plugs by driving them into the plug and turning them with a wrench; a couple had to be drilled to use the next size up to remove it. Some plugs are stubborn and require heat and sometimes they have to be completely drilled out. Beware; if you don't specify to remove all of them, some machine shops cut corners on this step. Without removing all of them, there's no way to thoroughly clean the oil passages with years of dirt and debris.

and watches for many years, now machine shops are also using this method, only on a larger scale.

Prep and Magnaflux

As I noted previously, the Magnaflux process also reveals cracks because the iron particles are drawn to the crack, whether it is part of a pressurized system or not. A shop will also perform a pressure test to check for leaks or cracks in the coolant system. The machine shop bolts special adapter plates to the block and heads and pressurizes them for a few minutes. If they find a leak, then they can address it by welding or using some industrial epoxy. Pressure testing the block is especially important when clearancing for a stroker crankshaft because the lower web is close to the coolant passages.

Important!

19 Check Straightness of Deck

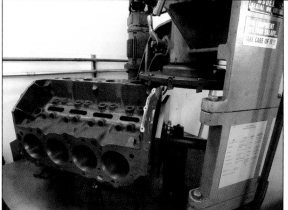

The deck can be flat but not square with the crank. The machine shop should check this for you. Here, the 496 deck was machined flat because it had been uneven. It's bolted to a BHJ fixture to ensure the deck is machined true. The heads should also be checked to make sure they are true.

Professional Mechanic Tip

20 Chase the Threads

In order to get proper torque on your bolts, the threads have to be cleaned. This service is available at the machine shop. They chase all the threads in the block, then clean them. You can save money and do it yourself at home, but don't try it with a regular tap. This ARP tap is designed specifically for cleaning threads. A regular tap is larger and removes important thread material. This also shows you (or the machine shop) if a thread is damaged and needs to be repaired with a thread insert.

21 Thread Cleaning Tips

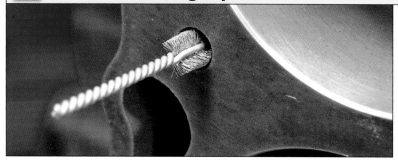

Meticulous shops take extra steps to chase the threads with a small brush installed on a drill to ream every bolt hole. These thread treatments make sure the bolts have clean threads and bolt torques are consistent.

Milling

The head gasket surfaces on the block and heads need to be completely flat and be the same distance from the centerline of the main journals. Symmetry is key and therefore both heads have to be machined by precisely the same amount. As a result, if the surface on one head is warped or damaged and needs to be machined, the other head must be machined to the same specification. The same goes for the deck surface on the block. If one head or deck is surfaced more than the other side, it will cause uneven compression ratios and strange running conditions.

Thread Clean and Repair

Cleaning and checking all the threads in a block is a time consuming step, so most machine shops charge for this service. First they run a special tap designed for cleaning debris and straightening threads (not for removing block material), and then they run a small metal cleaning brush into the threads to basically clean what the tap may have left behind. This service also allows them to find any threads that may need to be repaired with a threaded insert.

CLEANING

Obviously, an engine that has experienced parts failure will have some extra debris trapped in oil galleries and tight crevices, but it's amazing how much debris and deposits can be found inside of an engine block that has been leading a normal life and has not suffered a parts failure. Depending on what kind of oil or lubrication additives were used, the engine could have a protective layer of oil that is tough to get off the internal surfaces.

No matter what's in or on the internal engine passages and surfaces, you have to remove everything before going to the next chapter. Any debris left behind inevitably finds its way into your bearings or between the piston and the cylinder wall. Once there, these particles will wreak havoc on all the parts you have spent so much time and money installing on your big-block.

This nasty debris is a combination of shavings from the machine shop, abrasive media from bead blasting, casting sand, rust from inside the coolant passages, dust, lint, hair, dirt, and other debris from around your shop or garage.

Safety First!

This chapter is all about cleaning with solvents and using high-pressure air and water. This means there will be a lot of flying debris and chemicals, so you need to protect your eyes with some wraparound safety glasses and/or a face shield. Pulling cleaning brushes out of oil passages may send metal and debris flying your way, so keep your eye protection on during this entire process. Take precautions to protect your skin and hands by wearing a long-sleeved shirt and long pants as well as nitrile work gloves.

When cleaning your engine, don't use toxic, ultra-powerful, or highly flammable solvents. Don't use gasoline as a cleaner. Use off-the-shelf, safe automotive cleaning solvents. Most solvents stain and damage the surface of your driveway, so properly protect the cement surfaces and spend some extra care to keep your mess to a minimum.

You'll be removing dirt and grime from the engine during the cleaning process. Try to keep this grime contained with a drain pan under the engine and clean it up when you're finished and properly dispose of oily debris by using environmentally friendly methods.

Simply blowing air into the oil galleries and wiping bores does not clean them enough, so you need an engine brush kit like this one from Goodson. This kit comes with 10 different heavy-duty purpose-built engine brushes for cleaning out the engine block and parts. The long brushes are just what you need to clean the oil passages that run the length of the block.

Tools and Cleaning Items

In order to clean using the following instructions, you need some simple but specific tools and supplies. Round up degreasing solvent, powdered laundry detergent, plenty of white rags, and paper shop towels. Find a good cleaning area outside, where you can spray the engine with water and solvents, and make sure you have a good water source nearby with cold (and hot, if possible) water access.

Engine Cleaning Brushes

You'll need an entire engine cleaning brush kit from Goodson, Eastwood, or Moroso. The Goodson standard engine brush kit comes with 10 different-sized brushes, specifically designed for cleaning engine blocks and all of its oil galleries. Using general-purpose brushes for cleaning your engine is not a good idea because their performance isn't nearly as good as purpose-built brushes and may leave bristles or remnants of the brush in critical spaces.

Chemical Dip Cleaner

It's a good idea to have a bucket of carburetor and parts chemical dip around the garage for cleaning small parts and bolts. The most popular one on the market is Chem-Dip Carburetor and Parts Cleaner by Berryman Products. These buckets have a fast-acting cleaning solution that strips everything off carburetors and small parts, but isn't corrosive to metal parts and comes with a dipping basket. Some area's laws restrict chemicals like this, but Berryman has a VOC compliant Chem-Dip for these areas.

Your machine shop can clean your small parts and bolts for you but they are going to dump all your nicely bagged parts into one bin and clean them all at once, so if you want to clean them yourself and keep them organized, your best solution is a Chem-Dip.

Compressed Air

You could suffer through cleaning your engine without having an air compressor on hand, but, since the engine will start to rust within a couple seconds (yes, seconds!) after cleaning the oil residue off, compressed air is better for parts and makes the task much easier and faster. You'll be working against the clock to clean the block, get it dry, and apply rust inhibitor. Compressed air is your friend in this task. There are also many tight areas, bolt holes, and oil passages that you need to get debris, water, and cleaner out of that will make compressed air worthwhile. If you don't have an air compressor, try to rent one or borrow one for this stage of the project.

Pressure Washer

Pressurized water spray really helps perform cleaning tasks because the extra pressure breaks debris off the rough cast surfaces in the tightest of areas and oil passages in the block. A pressure washer with a siphon for adding cleaning solution to the pressurized blast is particularly useful. They are relatively inexpensive at your local hardware depot, or you can rent one.

Cleaning Area

You'll need an area where you can clean your engine without kicking up a bunch of extra debris from the environment. A great area to clean your engine is on a concrete driveway or a patio area. You can safely wheel out your engine on the engine stand and blow debris and cleaning solutions on the surrounding areas without concern. Wet down the ground around your chosen area to keep airborne debris to a minimum during this process.

Critical Cleaning Details

Rust is your worst enemy during cleaning. Rust will appear within a couple of seconds, especially on the cylinder walls, as the water starts to dry after cleaning the oils off the engine block. For the life of your engine, it's critical that you keep rust from forming on the cylinder walls because a rusty cylinder wall leads to piston and piston ring damage. Your job of keeping the block from rusting is something to take seriously. Don't let the engine dry during the cleaning process.

Here are a few tricks to reduce (but not by much) the speed with which rust starts to form during this process: mix an overly concentrated soapy solution to wash the surfaces because the thicker residue of the soap slows the rusting process; hot and soapy water cleans best but the heat of the water speeds up the evaporation process and rusting process, so using warm water is better. When getting to the final stage of rinsing the block, keep the block wet with cold water to give you slightly more time before evaporation takes its toll; and, have a helper start coating the cylinders (especially the cylinders!) and other machined block surfaces with rust inhibitor or oil as soon as you are done washing the block— while you are using the compressed air to dry the block.

If you just received your engine from a high-quality machine shop, there's a good chance they have already performed a preliminary cleaning of the block, but this does not exempt you from having to clean the block thoroughly. Machine shops only perform thorough cleaning when they are performing the assembly. They leave the detailed cleaning for you.

When it comes to cleaning your engine for pre-assembly or final assembly, you have to follow all the cleaning steps in this chapter. Don't skip this cleaning step before performing pre-assembly because you won't be happy if some debris enters and destroys your engine. Remember, you can have a metal shaving fall out of an oil passage in the block or crankshaft and damage a bearing while rotating the parts, have a chunk of grit fall onto the camshaft and gouge the face of the lifter or a cam lobe when dialing in the camshaft, or have damaging debris come into contact with any other moving part. You can sometimes get away with performing a slightly less tedious cleaning on your parts, but make sure you clean out all the oil passages in the block and crank with extreme care, whether you're performing pre-assembly or final assembly cleaning.

Step-by-Step Engine Cleaning Process

1 Cleaning Supplies

Important!

Don't skip the cleaning step before performing the pre-assembly tasks, or you'll be sorry when undetected shavings or debris destroy your brand-new bearings. If you're at this point in the process, then all the machine work, grinding, and scraping is done. Get all your supplies before starting the cleaning. Once you start cleaning, you can't stop until you're done or you'll have to start over. Your supplies should include 5 or 6 gallons of solvent, hot and cold water access, powdered laundry soap, a 5-gallon bucket, a few rolls of heavy-duty shop towels, a lot of white shop rags, an engine cleaning brush kit, wire and stiff-bristle nylon handbrushes, compressed air with nozzle, rust inhibitor (WD-40), large engine bags, and a quart of automatic transmission fluid. During this process you need your eye protection, nitrile gloves, and some long-sleeved work clothes to help protect your arms from solvents. The engine is easier to clean if it's on your engine stand rather than lying on the ground because debris won't transfer back onto the block.

2 Rough Clean

Start with the block in the upright position on the stand and blast the entire block surface, bolt holes, oil passages, and water jackets with the compressed air to break debris loose. For the most effective air blasting, rotate the block 90 degrees and blast the block again, turn the block another 90 degrees and blast, and then 90 degrees again and blast again. This ensures that gravity assists in the cleaning process. Using your hand brushes and solvent, scrub the entire block, making sure to not work on the bearing surfaces or the cylinder bores during this step. Make sure not to scratch the cam bearings with your wire brush, if they have already been installed. Our pressure washer has a siphon hose that allows us to cover the block with a solvent bath as well as blast away the surface dirt. Watch the block closely, keeping it wet until you are ready to dry it entirely. A dose of solvent helps keep the block wet. Keep scrubbing. Turn the block upside down and spray pressurized water into the water jackets through the deck and freeze plug holes to flush out the coolant system.

3 Brushing Passages

Beware! When spraying air, water, and solvent into holes, debris and fluid travel back at your face at high speed; so make sure you are wearing eye protection. For best results from your small passage brushes, there are good techniques to follow. Work on one gallery or port at a time until it's clean before moving to the next one. Shove the brush into the port you're working on and rotate the brush as if you're threading the brush into the gallery. This helps draw the debris toward you and out of the port. Plunge the brush in and out a few times, then pull it out and clean the brush with fresh solvent. Use your sprayer to flush the hole with solvent, then follow up with compressed air, and then spray with solvent again. Work the clean brush in the hole again and repeat until the brush comes out clean, then move on to the next bolt hole, water port, or oil passage.

4 Clean Passages

You're going to be amazed at how much debris comes out of the oil passages in the block. Use the right size and length brushes for each passage. The brush should be slightly larger in diameter than the oil gallery so they can actually clean the passage. The longer brushes are for running the longer oil galleries and coolant passages that run the length of the block. Don't forget to brush the main bearing galleries, the rear main feed gallery, the lifter galleries, lifter bores, fuel pump pushrod hole, and oil return ports.

Professional Mechanic Tip

5 Initial Cylinder Clean

It's finally time to initially clean the cylinders to remove metal particles, grindstone, and stone-binder embedded in the cylinders during the machining processes. Before starting, remember that the cylinder walls are machined to promote piston ring sealing; they are highly susceptible to rusting within a couple of seconds of drying after removing oil/rust inhibitor from them. Keeping them oiled after cleaning is very important. Work on one bore at a time. First wipe the bore with a solvent-soaked rag. Then scrub the bore with your large bristle brush. The brush should be rotated and the bore should be scrubbed up and down to follow the crosshatch pattern. Repeat the scrub with a solvent-soaked rag. Periodically switch to a clean white rag with solvent. To check for dirt transfer and when the dirt is almost gone, spray the cylinder with rust inhibitor and move to the next bore.

6 Wash With Soap and Water

Now mix about 4 gallons of warm (not hot) water with the concentrated soap solution (about 1 cup per gallon of water). Without washing the cylinder walls, wash the block with soapy water with your brushes or spray the block and passages with your siphon pressure washer. Rotate the block during this process so gravity can help you clean. Apply rust inhibitor and let the block dry without rust inhibitor (especially the cylinders); otherwise it starts to rust right away.

7 Scrub the Surfaces

While washing with the soapy water solution, get your brushes and gallery bristle brushes and start scrubbing every surface, bore, gallery, and bolt hole. Use a stiff wire brush on all rough-cast surfaces inside the lifter valley and lower crankcase to break loose seriously embedded debris. Continue washing and scrubbing on the soap solution until you are sure that you have washed away all the dirt and debris.

Important!

8 Initial Cylinder Cleaning and Inspection

Inspect your handywork after spraying the soapy solution off the engine with straight cool water out of your pressure washer or hose. Spray the engine surfaces, and especially the cylinder bores, with rust inhibitor. When the block is safe from rusting, carefully use your clean, bare fingers to inspect all the corners and crevices by poking them and feeling for loose debris and grit. If you feel anything that didn't get washed off or your hands start getting dirty, go back to step 6 and repeat the cleaning process.

9 Prepare for Pre-Assembly

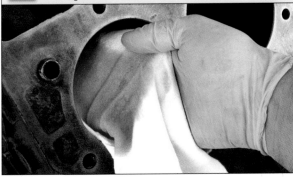

If you're cleaning your engine for final assembly, go ahead and skip ahead to step 10. If you're cleaning in order to perform pre-assembly steps in Chapter 8 and your engine has passed the previous inspection step, you're ready to: 1) blow off extra moisture and rust inhibitor with your compressed air; 2) thoroughly wipe the cylinders with clean oiled rags; 3) spray a final coat of rust inhibitor on the block surfaces; and, 4) place a new engine bag over your engine to keep debris out. But don't seal the bag for at least 12 hours, to allow any moisture to evaporate. Then skip ahead to step 14.

10 Final Cylinder Clean

Important!

Important Warning: *Only work on one cylinder at a time in this step and don't let them dry out while working on them. If they dry, rust forms quickly, causing the rings to get damaged and not seat properly during break-in. Scrub the bore with cool soapy water solution using the large round brush. When it's completely free of dirt, quickly wash it with straight water, spray it with rust inhibitor, and then move on to the next step.*

11 Last Block Rinse

Rinse all the soap off the block with cold, pressurized water. Start with rinsing the oil galleries, coolant passages, and crankcase. Rotate the engine a couple of times while rinsing. Use compressed air to blow off the water, but don't dry the engine. Before it dries, spray the block with rust inhibitor. Start by protecting the cylinder bores and other machined areas (don't forget the lifter bores), then move to the oil gallery passages. Now you're going to protect the cylinders by running towels soaked with ATF (automatic transmission fluid) or light oil thoroughly up and down the cylinder bores.

12 Re-Inspection

Make another inspection to confirm the block is clean. If you find debris on your fingers, you have to start the cleaning process over again. It's possible you'll have to clean the block a few times to get it truly clean. Once the debris test comes up negative, it's almost time to move onto the internal parts.

13 Bore Preparation and Storage

Bore cleaning and preparation is highly critical. Your piston rings are counting on you to clean them completely. Get your ATF-soaked towels out again. Thoroughly scrub the bores one at a time. Start with a clean towel and keep checking the towel for brown and black discoloration. When your new towels stay fairly clean, it's time to move to the next bore. Then touch up with rust inhibitor and put a clean engine bag over the engine. Don't use an old bag that has debris trapped in it, or you're wasting all your effort. Don't seal the bag. The moisture in the block needs to escape somehow.

14 Thoroughly Clean the Caps

Because you have to clean the block without main caps so you can clean the main crankshaft oiling passages, clean the caps by themselves. Spray them with warm water and solvent, then scrub them and keep the caps wet.

Use your small bore brushes to clean the oil passage and oil pump bolt boss in the rear main cap and brush through the bolt holes in all five main caps. Before they dry, scrub them thoroughly with soapy detergent. Spray them with rust inhibitor, blow the water off them, and then re-coat with rust inhibitor. Put them in a plastic bag that is open for breathing.

15 Clean Your Crank

Be very careful handling and washing the crank. If you drop it or knock it over when washing it, you can easily bend the crank. Spray the crank with cool

solvent-fed pressurized water or give the crank a solvent bath beforehand. Spray in the bolt holes in both ends of the crank as well as the oil passages. Use your small-diameter brushes to clean out the bolt holes on both ends of the crank and its passages with solvent, until the brushes stay clean. Brush the exterior of the crank with a softer brush and soapy water and make sure not to scratch the machined surfaces. Use your compressed air to spray the water off the crank, out of the oil passages, and out of the bolt holes. Then spray the crank with rust inhibitor (in the bolt holes and passages, too) and store it in a clean vented bag so it can dry further.

16 Cylinder Head Cleaning

Heads as well as the intake manifolds are media/bead blasted at many machine shops, to get them clean. They don't always get them as clean as you want and they trap an amount of media inside them, which your engine does not like. Work on the heads and intake manifold one piece at a time, but start with the heads. Be careful with the heads and don't set them on end and blow them over with the pressurized water spray; this damages the gasket surface or valve guides. Spray out the guides with pressurized water and solvent, then use the smaller-diameter brush to clean the valve guides with solvent, being sure not to scratch the guides. Get a large piece of wood and knock the head (only on the end of the head) as shown, to break loose any debris that may be stuck to the head (including sand from the original casting process). Don't drop the head, you may damage it—just knock it against the wood. Now follow the same steps used to clean the engine block, making sure you keep the machined surfaces wet and soaked with rust inhibitor. When done with each part, store them in a vented plastic bag.

17 Cleaning Rods

Your connecting rods are small enough to soak in a solvent bath separately, so they don't knock into each other and get damaged. Set up a solvent bath and a separate soap bath made for a faster process. Clean out all the bolt holes in the rod caps with a round brush. After the solvent bath, give them a soapy water bath and scrub thoroughly with a brush; spend some extra energy scrubbing the bearing saddles. Blow them off with compressed air, cover them with rust inhibitor, and place them in a vented plastic bag.

Professional Mechanic Tip

18 Cleaning Small Parts

The small parts are extremely easy to clean in a solvent dip, such as Berryman Chem-Dip. It's non-corrosive to metals, but extremely good at cleaning off carbon, grease, and oil. It practically cleans by itself without agitation. Place the parts in the supplied basket, dip them for the suggested time, and pull them out. Some scrubbing may be necessary, but this product really cuts your prep time. After the parts are clean, blow them off with air, spray with some rust inhibitor, and put them back in a clean (and marked) bag. Some of your tools, like sockets and wrenches, could also use a dip, so debris doesn't transfer to the engine parts during assembly.

PRE-ASSEMBLY

Today's society thrives on instant gratification but building an engine is an exacting process that must not be rushed. Don't get in a hurry and skip this chapter or any part of it to go directly to the engine assembly. The fact that your engine parts are back from the machine shop, does not mean that the machine shop perfectly performed all the work or everything was done correctly. They are human, after all, and you have to ensure that everything is done correctly at each stage of the project.

You've probably purchased all the parts you need to complete your engine. If you are building a performance engine that will most likely require special-length pushrods and specific valvesprings, you will buy those later, when you get the proper measurements. If you are building a basically stock engine you should have all your parts by now.

Since you are assembling the engine yourself, you are taking responsibility for how it turns out. If you skip a step or forget something, your machine shop is not going to warranty anything for you. This fact makes the pre-assembly inspection one of the very important steps along the way. It's the last of the checks and balances before actual assembly. You can't assume everyone else along the way has done his or her job correctly. If your engine runs for five minutes and throws a rod out the side of the block, you are solely responsible for not double checking the parts. Accepting your role, you can then call the machine shop and have them assemble your engine for you; or, you can proceed with caution and have a long-lasting sense of accomplishment from successfully building your own engine. There's a high probability that if you follow along with all these steps, confirm that all the parts and clearances are correct, and assemble your engine as instructed, it will run well and will do so for a long time.

Inventory

Take a few minutes to make sure you have everything you need for pre-assembly. The following are lists of parts, tools, and chemicals that you should gather and use.

If you have a workbench, make some space on it for building an engine. If you don't have a bench, find a way to make a strong and level horizontal surface near your engine, so you can keep your supplies and parts clean and close by.

Cleanliness during the pre-assembly is just as important as it is during final assembly.

Parts

Check that you have all your parts close by and in boxes, plastic bags, or protected in some way from the elements and the environment. Most of the parts needed for final assembly will be needed for the pre-assembly steps.

You will need your block (on a stand), cylinder heads (and their components), crankshaft, connecting rods, pistons, camshaft, lifters, timing chain set, fasteners, intake manifold, head gaskets, intake manifold gasket, oil pan, pan gasket, oil pump, oil pump pickup, oil pump drive-shaft, and bearings.

Tools

Equip yourself with these common assembly tools:

- Torque Wrench; lots of fasteners and components will be torqued in this chapter. This is where we check to make sure the machine shop did all the work correctly.

- Plastigage; this handy tool is easy to use, and it's going to possibly save your engine from disaster.

- Rod Bolt Protectors; not everyone plans on building more than one engine in their life, so purchasing some rod bolt protectors or making some out of some 3/8-inch fuel hose is a cost-effective solution to protecting the crankshaft during this engine build.

- Rod Guide; after building engines with and without a rod guide, I prefer using a rod guide rather than rod bolt protectors. It allows you a little more insurance that you won't damage the crankshaft journals during assembly.

- Dial Indicator; you will be using this to check critical clearances.

- Cam Degree Wheel; if you don't have access to a cam degree kit, you can get by with a cam degree wheel, a dial indicator, and a set of valve-checking springs, which mimic the valve springs but won't apply too much pressure on the lifters during pre-assembly checking. You'll use this to degree the cam for optimum performance.

Bench vises come with hardened steel jaws. The knurl on the vice jaws is very damaging to most car parts, especially engine parts, so it's important to protect your parts when you clamp them in a vise.

Machined parts are fully protected with these rubber-padded Lisle soft jaws. Now you can clamp your parts in a vise without worrying about damaging them. These jaws can be used to protect plenty of other parts and projects. They even work well protecting threads on bolts. You can make a set with a few small pieces of .120-inch-thick aluminum bent over the jaws.

- Soft Bench Vise Jaws; I guess this assumes that you have a bench vise. Hopefully you do. You can purchase soft jaws that are made for a vise or you can get a few pieces of 1/8-inch sheet aluminum and bend it over the jaws of your vise to make a set of soft jaws yourself.

Precision Tools

In order to check all the work done by your machine shop and the factory that produced your parts, you're going to need some precision measuring tools. You also need the tools to confirm that your combination of parts will work with each other. The tools will be used to check journal sizes, bearing clearances, bore sizes, piston clearances, cam timing, valvetrain clearances as well as function, and more.

The measurements to be taken during pre-assembly are measured in the thousandths. I'm talking about measuring parts and being precise to 1/1,000 (.001) inch, where 1/8 inch is .0125 inch. If you've never measured anything that a tape measure wasn't precise enough for, then you are in for a change of pace. The tools you use in this chapter need to be precision instruments and the more precise they are, the more they cost. Some of the ones you need for this chapter include tools that you may never use again. If you believe this is the case, you have a few options on how to approach the requirements of this chapter.

Read through all the steps and decide which tools you can justify purchasing and which ones you can't. Borrow them from friends or rent the tools you aren't going to buy. Pay your machine shop to perform specific measurements you won't have the ones for and check the clearances you will be able to make. One tool used in the following chapter in particular is a dial bore gauge. If you have your machine shop check the main- and connecting-rod bearing bores and the sizing of your bearings, you can double check their work with the Plastigage steps. The shop can also confirm the size of your cylinder bores as an extra service, and then you can double check piston wall clearance with feeler gauges.

Don't forget that relying on a shop to perform every clearance test does not mean they take any responsibility if something is wrong after you assemble the engine. After you take the engine parts from a shop, you are responsible for anything that goes wrong. You should always double check a technician's work on bearing clearance surfaces with Plastigage. If a bearing fails they have no reason to warranty an engine because they don't know if you torqued the bolt correctly.

When going through this chapter, there are many important steps, but not every step may pertain to your application. Take into consideration what the steps are asking you to perform because you could be mixing aftermarket and factory parts that may not work well together. If you're building a completely stock engine with stock pistons and a stock camshaft, you may skip the step of checking the piston-to-valve clearance. Good engine builders trying to get the best performance out of an engine will dial-in every performance cam. If you are building an engine with a stock cam, you can take the chance and skip the degree process, but you're better off checking it anyway. If you're new to engines, the degree process will give you more insight into camshaft dynamics. There's nothing wrong with learning more about an engine.

Instead of skipping steps requiring a dial bore gauge because you don't have access to one, you can get a less-expensive snap gauge used for the task. These are less accurate because you have to check the bore with a less-accurate snap gauge and then transfer the reading to an outside micrometer or a caliper. Every precision tool has accuracy rated to plus or minus a small margin of error. Each time you transfer a reading from one tool to another you may be "stacking" those margins and end up being off by more than you think. The snap gauge is a viable alternative to checking bore sizes with a bore gauge because you have the backup checks as insurance.

I can't stress enough that as soon as you turn a wrench on building your engine, the responsibility is yours. So if you want to be sure everything turns out great, you should follow the steps even if they don't apply to you. You can ask your machine shop if you can skip a specific step but if there's any reservation it's better to not skip it; it's better to be safe than sorry.

Lubricants

You're not sealing anything yet, at this inventory stage, but you need lubricants for coating components so you can check clearances without damaging parts. You need a hand-held squirt can filled with 30W non-synthetic oil and a bottle of Royal Purple Max-Tuff Assembly Lube.

Paper Towels

You're going to need a good supply of paper shop towels to clean and wipe parts as you work through this chapter. As stressed in Chapter 2 (Tools), don't use regular towels for cleaning. A regular towel can leave threads from the fabric behind that don't break down in the oil and can cause bearing damage. The paper fibers will break down in the oil. In order to clean up small amounts of oil and chemicals, cut the towels into smaller pieces instead of ripping them apart. This keeps paper fiber dust to a minimum.

Inspection

Pull all the machined parts out of their boxes and wrappers and inspect them. If you've followed along with this whole book, you've already done some of these inspections. Do them again because these parts may have been out of your possession for a few days. Always inspect your parts before assembly.

Start with the block. Look at all the machined surfaces and make sure they are smooth. The deck should be free of nicks and dings. Pull out your straight edge and move it across the head mating surface with a .002-inch feeler gauge and make sure the surface is machined flat. Inspect the lifter bores by carefully using your finger to check for burrs that may interfere with the life of the lifters. The machined surface on the front of the block behind the camshaft sprocket should be smooth and flat. Peer into the camshaft journals and make sure all bearings appear to be installed and in good shape. Turn the block over and inspect the cam bearings with a light touch of a finger to be sure there are no gouges or burrs on them. Run your fingers in the main bearing saddles and make sure there aren't any burrs. Visually inspect the bearing caps for nicks or evidence that they had been dropped or damaged. The mating surfaces between the block and the main caps should be flat and in good shape so they do not distort the bearings when torqued into place.

Cylinder Heads

The head gasket surface should be smooth and free of burrs. Check the heads as you did the block deck with a straight edge and feeler gauge to be sure they are flat. If the heads are already assembled, visually check all the parts of the head for defects. If the heads are not assembled, inspect the valve seats and guides for nicks. I've had heads given to me and been told they were ready to bolt on, but had a large gouge in the tip of a valve. It appeared as if the head had fallen against something solid. Missing a problem like this can lead to engine failure, or at least valvetrain failure.

Crankshaft

Check the bearing surfaces on the crankshaft for nicks and dings.

Inspect the threads in the front of the crank and on the rear flange for damage. The snout of the crank should be in good shape to ensure ease of installing the harmonic dampener.

Rods and pistons

The pistons should be checked to make sure the ring lands are in good shape, and that there aren't any dents or dings on the faces or skirts that may cause premature engine failure or wear. The rods should be visually inspected for damage or imperfections. The sides of the bearing journals and bearing surfaces should be smooth and in good shape. Manufacturers and/or machine shops grind material off the rod bearing cap while attempting to balance them. I've seen loose metal barely hanging on the bottom of a connecting rod, after this process, which could have fallen off inside the engine after startup. Make sure there aren't any issues like this on your connecting rods. If your rods had been numbered, make sure your rods and rod caps are correctly mated and that you have numbers one through eight. If you have two number sevens and no number five, there's a problem.

Make sure the pistons are correctly installed on the rods.

The Remaining Parts

Inspect all your other parts such as camshaft, lifters, bearings, and pushrods, for defects, too.

If there were any problems with the parts the shop machined for you, contact them for resolution before using the parts. In some cases they can walk you through a quick repair. Everything needs to be correct to work right. Basically all the planets have to align between the intake

manifold and the oil pan for your engine to work correctly.

Don't forget to inspect each part for dirt and debris before assembly. A little dirt or a small piece of metal left in the engine during assembly can be catastrophic.

Precision Inspection

Every engine builder uses micrometers, feeler gauges, and Plastigage. Good engine builders do not rely on only one method of measuring bearing tolerances while building an engine. Use two methods to ensure your engine will be assembled correctly. The first method of checking the bearings, with a dial bore gauge and micrometer, ensures that you have the correct bearings to start with so you don't go directly to the second step of using Plastigage and damage a perfectly good set of bearings.

Hydraulic Problems

When assembling an engine and installing a hydraulic camshaft, you will be faced with an extra task when performing checks on valve-to-piston clearance and valve lift. Hydraulic lifters have a piston inside the body, which is pushed up by a spring (when the engine lacks oil pressure) and kept in the lifter with a retaining clip. That piston has a cup where the pushrod seats into it. While the engine is running, pressurized oil in the lifter keeps the piston pressed up against the retaining clip while the pushrod presses down against it. When performing checks using hydraulic lifters, they will be a little spongy since the engine won't have oil pressure to firm up the lifter.

Professionals have two ways to solve this problem and get accurate valvetrain readings. One way is to

find a solid lifter with the same pushrod cup height as the hydraulic lifter. The other way is to disassemble the lifter and replace the internal spring with washers or shims to restore proper cup height. Do this to two lifters specifically used for checking. Be extremely careful with the lifter face that rides on the camshaft and the outside cylinder of the lifter. Place the lifter on a non-marring surface and gently push the piston down a little while carefully removing the retaining clip inside the lifter. Slowly release the pressure on the piston. Turn the lifter over and remove the piston and spring. In some cases, suction in the lifter keeps the internal piston in the lifter. With just a little force, push a paper clip down into the center of the lifter bleed hole to release suction on the small valve in the bottom of the lifter; too much force will damage the lifter. If you're not able to get the lifter apart, contact your machine shop.

You need to keep note of how the lifter is installed so you can put it back in the same position from which you removed it. Stack washers or shims under the piston to mimic the original piston height in the lifter. A good gauge of the height is making sure the retaining clip is a tight fit when reinstalled. When you put the lifter back together, make sure you are careful with the face of it and that there isn't any debris inside the lifter from the washers or the valve checking process. Debris means quick death to a lifter.

Clean Up Your Act

Every engine part you'll be working with is a precision-machined or manufactured part.

Take care while handling each part when pre-assembling it, checking it's measurements, and storing it back in its container or box until it's installed during final assembly. The parts should be kept clean as well as damage-free. If parts get dusty and dirty while being stored, that debris is going to end up in your engine. The area you designate for engine work should be a clean environment, so there shouldn't be drafts that can blow debris into your work, or rafters above that can drop dirt into the engine. I realize not everyone hasa perfect area to build their engine but you need to be aware of your environment and cover your parts with clean plastic when you're not working on them. If your garage or shop is damp, keep parts like the crankshaft and engine block lightly oiled with penetrating oil, such as WD40, to keep rust from forming. Keep boxed parts off of cold, damp floors with a moisture-proof barrier under them. If you find debris on a part during pre-assembly, clean the part right away to keep the matter from contaminating the engine.

Head Games

Your machine shop should have spent the time it takes to get the guides, seats, seals, and valves in good working order. Any of this work should be preserved if you need to disassemble the head for any reason. This is a good reason to have a Goodson Cylinder Head Organizer. If you take a valve out of the head, make sure you put it back in the exact spot you pulled it from. You could have had the machine shop set the installed height on your valve springs too. If you did, it's important to put them back in the position you pulled them from, as well as the retainers, keepers, and any shims that were installed under each spring. Keep them organized!

Hopefully, if you have press-on-type valve seals, your shop did not install valve seals while they were doing your head work. A few steps in this chapter require you to remove the valves. It's important to know that the edge of the valve lock groove on the valve is sharp and usually damages the press-on valve seal during removal of the valve. These type valve seals should never be used once they have had a valve pulled through them. These seals are so delicate that they typically come with a special protector sleeve just to install them. Only install the valve seals when you are finished with this chapter. Talk to your machine shop if you have any questions about replacing the valve seals or if you don't know if they have performed the valve seat checking and clearances covered in the following steps 2 through 6.

Step-by-Step Pre-Assembly

Use Special Tool

1 Inspect Cylinder Head

By this stage, your machine shop should have assembled the cylinder heads, with the exception of the press-on valve seals. If you remember my warning in the previous chapter, you recall that you need to inspect the heads, so the valve seals need to be removed. If you don't have them removed, you cannot check valve-to-guide clearance and valve-stem seal concentricity. The heads should be disassembled for final inspection. The valves, retainers, locks, springs, and spring shims that come off the head should be kept in order so they can go back on in the same place. Make sure the valves and guides are free of any lubricant and slide them back in the guides so the valve sits about a 1/2 inch off the seat. Set up your dial indicator on the edge of the valve, try to move the valve up and down, and write the amount of movement on your worksheet. If you don't have a dial indicator, you shouldn't feel any wobble. The valve should not have more than .002 inch of play. Any more than that and a lot of oil will pass into the cylinder—causing excessive oil consumption; smoking out of the tail pipe; pressure on the valve seat, causing premature valve seat failure; and, in severe cases, overheating the valve until it breaks.

Use Special Tool

2 Test Valveseat Seal

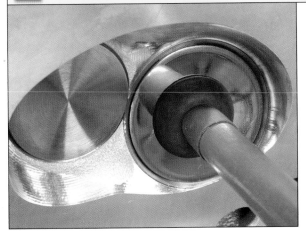

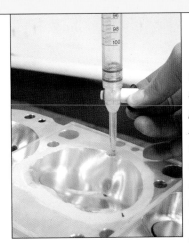

 Most likely your machine shop used lapping compound to confirm the quality of the valve seats. Clean the seat and valve of possible leftover lapping compound. Apply a thin coat of layout dye to the valve faces and seats and let it dry. Use a lapping stick to press and turn the valve against the seat for about three seconds. Check the marks in the compound on the seat and valve to confirm there is a

uniform pattern on both. Completely clean the dye and install the valves with light valve-checking springs and spark plugs, and set the head with valves facing up. Fill the combustion chamber with enough solvent to cover the valve faces. Using an inspection flashlight, peer into the ports and confirm there isn't any solvent leaking past the valve seats. If there is, confirm the seats are clean and try again. A good-quality valve job won't leak.

Use Special Tool, Precision Measurement

3 Check Valve Guide Quality

  The valve guides must be concentric in order for the press-on valve-stem seals to work correctly. The seal should be centered over the top of the guide. Use your caliper to measure the thickness of each guide at twelve, three, six, and nine o'clock positions to confirm the seal concentricity to the guide. If the seal is not centered on the guide, the valve could be forced to the side of the guide (shown exaggerated in the

left picture) and cause premature wear of the guide and the seal. Once you've confirmed the guides are correctly machined, clean the seat and valve for cylinder number-1 and slide them into their guides. If your valve-stem seals come with a protective cover that slides over the stem to protect the seal from getting damaged upon installation, put the cover on and carefully slide the seal over the stem without allowing the valve to slide out of the guide. Seat the seal all the way down on the guide.

Set up your dial indicator over the top of the tip of the stem and zero it with the valve pressed all the way up. Install the retainer and locks on the stem (without the spring) and move the valve down the exact amount of valve lift listed on your cam card (listed as "at valve"). Be sure you get the specs correct because "single-pattern" cams have matching lift at the intake and exhaust valve and "dual-pattern" cams have a different lift for intake and exhaust. Check the distance between the bottom of the retainer and the top of the valve-stem seal once the valve is down the correct "lift" amount. The clearance should be at least .070 inch. If it's close, you're going to need to check all the valves this way.

4 Valvespring Checks

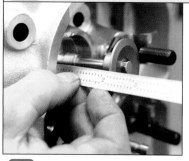

Check every valvespring for its "installed height," to confirm they all match and meet the requirements of the camshaft (specs listed on your cam card). Start by using a valvespring-height gauge installed on the valve with the locks and retainer. You can also get away with a snap gauge or caliper with less accuracy.

Use any shims necessary to meet the installed height specified by the spring manufacturer. This gauge (second photo from left) is reading 1.9 inches and needs to be shimmed. There should be one thin, hardened, flat washer (or in some cases it's a rotating washer) between the spring and the spring pocket in the head, to keep the spring from digging through the softer material. Additional shims may be necessary to get the correct installed height; they go under the hardened washer. Now move to your spring tester. They come in two styles: low-cost style for your bench vise, or expensive freestanding ram-type. To get an accurate reading, compress and relax the spring at least 10 times to allow it to stabilize. If you have more than single springs, compress all springs and use the retainer in the vise to keep the springs in place. Then compress the spring in the tester to match the spring height gauge. Write down the seat pressure on your worksheet, then check the springs to confirm their seat pressures match within + / -10% of requirements listed on your cam card. Repeat the installed height shimming and checking as well as seat pressure testing on each spring because these are different with each one. Lightly grind the spring with a cone (in the far right photo) if it's a snug fit to the retainer or if the spring has sharp edges on the end of the windings.

5 Check Compressed Spring Clearance

After seat pressure has been confirmed you can check for "compressed spring clearance." Calculate the compressed spring height by subtracting the maximum valve lift (on your cam card) from your installed height (taken from the spring installed height from the previous steps). If you are using anything other than standard rocker ratios, be sure to adjust your maximum valve lift accordingly. Then compress the spring in your bench vise just until the coils completely bind and measure this "stack" height and record it. If you have more than single springs, compress all springs and use the retainer in the vise to keep the springs in place. Last, subtract the stack height from the compressed height to get the compressed spring clearance, which for optimum reliability should be at least + .100 inch. Repeat this check on the rest of the springs.

6 Check the Main Bore

The block should be on a flat surface with the bottom facing upward to properly check the main bearing bore alignment. Use a precision straight edge and feeler gauges. If you are able to slide more than a .001-inch blade under the straight edge, the main bore needs to be machined.

7 Seat Main Caps in Registers

Important!

While installing the main caps in the following steps, make sure they are seated in the registers of the block before torquing the cap into its place. Failure to do so damages the cap and the register in the block.

8 Main Bearing Orientation

Big-blocks have two different main bearing shells: grooved, and non-grooved. The grooved bearings go in the block saddles and the non-grooved bearings go in the main caps.

9 Main Cap Orientation

The four front main caps have arrows and the letter "F" cast in them from the factory. The F designates front, so all the arrows should be pointing forward. If the machine shop installed the main caps backward, they may have performed the line bore or hone incorrectly. If that's the case, the work must be redone. By now you or the machine shop should have numbered the four front caps "1" through "4." The rear main cap is obvious and doesn't need an arrow or to be numbered.

10 Check Rod Bore

Before installing the rod and main bearings, check the bores to confirm they are machined correctly, to ensure the bearings are correct and have the right bearing crush. In order to check bore sizes, you need a dial bore gauge or a snap gauge (which isn't as accurate) and a 2- to 3-inch outside micrometer to transfer snap gauge readings. These readings need to be done, so if you don't have these tools you should have a professional check them for you. Clean the mating surfaces of the rods and mains. Lubricate the rod and main bolts to achieve the correct torque and clamping force. One at a time, put the connecting rods in the vise jaws with your soft jaws in place. Install the rod caps and take a reading with your dial bore gauge. Check bore taper from front to rear. Do this a few times on each rod to confirm accuracy. Record your findings.

Precision Measurement

11 Check Main Journal Bore

Install the main bearings in the proper location and in the correct direction. Make sure they are completely seated in their registers before applying torque. Torque them into place. Take the readings with your tools in the same manner as the rods. There should be no more than .0002-inch taper (from front to rear) and no more the .0007-inch out-of-round. If they are out of spec, you should call your machine shop to remedy the problem. When you have your measurements remove the main and rod caps. Standard production rod housing bore is 2.3247 to 2.3252 inches, standard production GM main bore is 2.9370 to 2.9380 inches.

Proper Bearing Installation

There's a right way to install a bearing shell and quite a few wrong ways. Carefully check the bearing saddle for burrs and defects with your finger. Bearings should be installed dry. Wipe the saddle and back side of the bearing shell with a clean and dry paper towel. Make sure the surfaces are oil and lubricant free. Any debris stuck between the bearing saddle and bearing shell will cause the bearing to not seat all the way into the saddle, will cause uneven wear, and can cause premature bearing failure. A human hair or a dirt particle is all it takes. Lay the bearing shell into the saddle with the bearing tab lined up with the notch in the saddle. Evenly press the shell down into the saddle but don't force it.

When it comes to connecting rod bearings, it's important to pay attention to how they are installed. Standard Clevite 77 rod bearings are not designated as "upper" and "lower" halves, but H-series rod bearings do have the designation. The upper goes in the connecting rod and the lower goes in the rod cap.

Make a quick inspection for burrs and defects. If there are any burrs you can remove them with a burr knife or a quick swipe with the blade of an old knife. Anything more stubborn should be looked at by your machine shop.

Wipe the saddle with a clean paper towel. The smallest left over debris or remnant of paper can cause damage to the bearings or premature bearing failure.

Never lubricate the back side of the bearing. The back side of the bearing and the saddle it fits in should be free of any problem-causing debris or lubricant. The only oil on a bearing should be on the side where the moving part rotates.

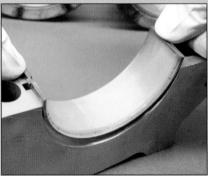

Line up the tangs and press the bearing into the saddle. If the tang does not line up correctly, don't force the bearing or tweak it into place.

12 Rifle Brush Crankshaft

Before installing the crank with new bearings, you need to make a pass through the oil passages in the crankshaft with a rifle brush. If debris falls out of the crank during pre-assembly, you'll damage the bearings.

Precision Measurement

13 Check Crankshaft for Straightness

 The crank needs to be checked for straightness. Clean the front and rear main bearings and their saddles along with the main journals of the crankshaft with a clean and dry paper towel. Install the front and rear main bearings. Lubricate the crank side of the two bearings with some assembly lube. Carefully and gently place the crankshaft on the bearings. Using your adjustable stand, place the dial indicator on the top of the crankshaft's number-3 main journal. Make sure the tip won't fall into the oil hole on the crank while it's being rotated. Slowly rotate the crank and take note of the runout on the dial indicator. A crankshaft should not have more than .0005-inch runout. The crank should be as close to zero as possible. Anything more and you're taking a chance of damaging your bearings. If your crank is not straight enough for your application, it's time to straighten it or get a replacement unit. Before removing the crankshaft, check to make sure the runout on the damper and timing sprocket surfaces, as well as the rear main seal surfaces, is not more than .001 inch.

14 Clean Bearings

Clean the main bearings, main caps, and main cap areas on the block with a clean and dry paper towel. Any lubricant or debris on the bearings throws off the readings. While doing that, go ahead and check these areas for nicks and burrs with your finger. For proper bearing installation see page 88.

Torque Fasteners

15 Install Main Caps

 Place the main caps on the block in their designated registers and with all their arrows facing the front of the engine, and then make sure they fit down into their registers. If you tighten the caps before they are seated in their registers, you will damage the block, the cap, or both. Install the bolts with some ARP moly assembly lubricant on the threads. Tighten the mains to a torque of 90 ft-lbs by alternating in 10 ft-lb increments for the nuts, and 45 ft-lbs for the outer Allen bolts. The nuts require a 3/4-inch socket and the Allen bolts require a 5/16-inch bit socket. If you're using stock hardware with 30W oil, continue to torque the 2-bolt mains to 95 ft-lbs and the 4-bolt mains to 110 ft-lbs. If you are using studs or lubricants that change the bolt torque, refer to the information that accompanies the hardware.

Precision Measurement

16 Measure Crankshaft

 Check the diameter of the main and rod journals with a micrometer. The crankshaft main journals should match each other and the rod journals should match each other. If they are different, contact your machine shop and have them fix the problem. You are going to need to subtract the crank journals from the specs you gathered in steps 10 and 11. That gives you the amount of clearance between the crank and bearings in the mains and rods.

Precision Measurement

17 Dial Bore Main Bearings

Use your micrometer to transfer measurement of the crankshaft main journals to the dial bore gauge so you know what your clearance is when you read the mains. Use your dial bore gauge to read the inside diameter of each of the main bearings. Write down all your measurements. The four front main bearing clearances should all be within .0004 inch of each other. The rear main usually has about .0005-inch-larger clearance than the other mains. If the main bearing are not in this range, you must remove the main caps and bearings, clean them and start back at step 14. If that didn't fix the problem, you then need to contact your machine shop and have them fix the crankshaft bore.

Precision Measurement

18 Plastigage Main Bearings

For this step, you don't want to put any lubricant on the bearings because the lubricant can take up space in the bearing surface and give an improper clearance reading. With the main bearings installed in the block, carefully set the crank into place. Cut a strip of Plastigage the width of the bearing and lay it across each journal as seen here. You can put a tiny smear of assembly lube in the journal to keep the Plastigage from moving during this process. Place the main caps in their designated places on the block with the bearings installed. Do not turn the crankshaft while checking the clearances with Plastigage because it destroys the plastic and you'll have to start over again.

Put ARP moly assembly lubricant or a light coat of oil on the hardware (including the surface between any washers and the hardware) so you can achieve proper torque. If you're installing nuts and they are stamped, make sure the stamping faces away from the surface of the washer. Start tightening all the main cap hardware before fully seating the main caps or torquing anything. If the main cap registers in the block are tight, you may need to tap them with a soft-faced hammer to get them to seat. Make sure they are fully seated before starting to torque them into place. If you are installing 4-bolt main caps, torque all the hardware closest to the crankshaft and then go back and torque the outer main bolts last. Torque the main caps to their proper spec in the proper sequence on page 152. Remove the main caps and check the Plastigage width against the gauge markings on the Plastigage wrapper. Their readings should all be really close to each other. If there is a large gap in the readings from main caps number-1 through 4, clean the Plastigage out completely and repeat the steps; start by removing the bearings, cleaning them, and re-installing them. According to Clevite Oil, clearance on mains number-1 through 4 should be from .0007 to .0032 inch, and the rear mains should be from .0012 to .0038 inch. This can vary by bearing type and application, so consult your machinist and paperwork with the bearing set.

Bearing clearances are different for different applications. Stock engines have tighter tolerances than performance engines.

Professional Mechanic Tip

19 Bearings for Every Application

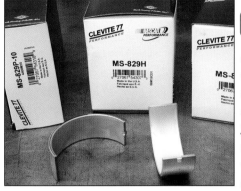

Clevite makes bearings for every application. The main set on the left are bearings you would put in general engine building applications.

They have a "P" after the part number (MS-829P). These bearings look really pretty when you pull them out of the box, unlike the "washed" look you get on the "H" bearings. The center set is bearings for performance applications and are denoted with the "H" after the part number (MS-829H). If the clearance is too small and you could use an extra .001-inch clearance, you can get that clearance back by installing a set of "HX" bearings (MS-829HX). The 496 project needed HX rod and main bearings because the clearances were too tight, due to the line-bore done on the block with the 4-bolt main caps installed. These bearings saved the project from having to go back to the machine shop for an additional line-hone or having to grind the crank to remove a small amount of material. This is proof that you really do need to check every part before you install it.

Torque Fasteners

20 Lubricate and Spin Crankshaft

Once all the readings are within spec, remove the crank and carefully clean all remnants of Plastigage off the journals and bearings.

Be sure not to damage the coating layers on the bearing shells or the machined surfaces on the rotating parts when removing the Plastigage. Make sure the crank and all main bearings are clean of debris. Lubricate the bearing surfaces in the block as well as the ones in the bearing caps. Do not install the rear main seal. Carefully place the crank into the block on the bearings. Install and tighten the main caps by using only your fingers. Take a soft hammer and lightly tap the rear of the crank forward to seat the thrust flange up against the thrust bearing surfaces on the rear main bearing. Torque the main caps to 20 ft-lbs using the sequence in step 22, then torque in 20 ft-lbs increments until full torque is reached. Tighten the rest of the main caps and torque them to spec. Now the crank should spin with an easy twist with your thumb and index finger on the snout of the crank. If you've done the previous checks and it doesn't turn freely, your mains need an align bore.

Precision Measurement

21 Check Crankshaft End Play

Use your dial indicator or feeler gauges to check backward and forward movement of the crankshaft in the block. Dial Indicator: Place the dial indicator inline with the crank with the tip on the front of the snout. Use a screwdriver to carefully pry the crank forward and backward while reading the movement on the gauge. Feeler gauge: Gently pry the crank backward and hold it there. Carefully use your feeler gauges between the thrust flange and the bearing. Start with a .003-inch feeler gauge and move up from there in .001-inch increments until the gauge won't slide in without force. Don't force the gauge; you'll damage the bearing. Clearance should be between .005 inch and .007 inch. If it's not, contact your machine shop for guidance.

22 Rod Installation Information

Connecting rods have a specific order in which they go onto the crankshaft. On the crankshaft end of the rods, there is a chamfered side and a flat side. The chamfered side is clearanced for the fillet on the crankshaft's rod journal. The flat side of the connecting rod faces the flat side of the other connecting rod when they are installed on the crankshaft. The piston-wrist-pin end of the rod is considered the reciprocating end and the rotating end is the bearing end, which clamps onto the crankshaft. The chamfer on the stock rod (right) is not as large as the one on the aftermarket rod.

23 Piston and Rod Orientation Rules

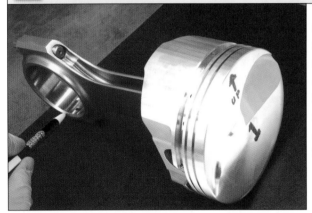

Pistons and rods are assembled in a specific way. Unless you're running low-compression flat tops, your pistons have a valve relief in the two o'clock position on the face for the intake valve. Looking at the piston face, the rods are installed on all eight pistons with the chamfer on the left side. This put the chamfer for the odd-numbered cylinders (1, 3, 5, and 7) facing the front of the engine and the chamfers for the even-numbered cylinders (2, 4, 6, and 8) facing toward the flywheel.

24 Match Rods and Pistons

The connecting rods and pistons use pressed-in wrist pins, which should have been assembled at the machine shop. The numbers on the connecting rods should determine which cylinder the piston goes in. If the pistons are numbered, make sure they match the number on the rods. Mark the top of the piston with a felt-tip marker so that at a glance you know if they are in the correct bore.

25 Install Pistons on Rods

If you are using aftermarket connecting rods with floating wrist pins, check the wrist pin and the wrist pin bore in the rod. These Eagle rod pin bores had .0005-inch clearance, which is unacceptable. These connecting rods need to be taken to the machine shop to have the bores honed out to .0012 inch. Eagle leaves them tight so the builder can machine to desired clearance.

If your rotating assembly uses pressed-in wrist pins, apply assembly lube to the wrist pin bores in the pistons and move on to the next step. If you have floating pins, install the clip or ring in one side of each piston, the snap ring with snap ring pliers, or the spiral lock ring worked into the bore, one loop at a time with a small screwdriver or a blunt-tipped probe. Most Spiral lock ring applications use two locks per side of the piston, such as these SRP pistons; so if you're installing them, put two in one side of the piston. Oil the wrist pins with 30W oil, then lubricate the wrist pin bores and the connecting rod wrist pin bores with Royal Purple Max Tuff assembly lube. Use the previous steps of piston and rod orientation guidelines to position the rod with your pistons. Slide the pin through the piston and connecting rod end. Install the pin-locking clip on the other side of the pin. Use a feeler gauge to ensure the pin end play between the clip and wrist pin is between .001 inch and .008 inch. Locks can work their way out of the piston while the engine is running if the gap is larger or smaller.

Perfect Circle Performance Ring Gap Recommendations		
Top Compression Ring		
Ductile, Gray Iron and Steel	4.25-inch (454 CID) Bore Example	Recommended Minimum Gap Factor
Moderate Performance	.017–.019	.004 per inch of bore diameter
Drag Racing——Oval Track	.019–.021	.0045 per inch of bore diameter
Nitrous Oxide——Street	.021–.023	.005 per inch of bore diameter
Nitrous Oxide—Drag Racing	.029–.031	.007 per inch of bore diameter
Supercharged	.025–.027	.006 per inch of bore diameter
Intermediate Compression Ring		
Gray Iron	4.25-inch (454 CID) Bore Example	Recommended Minimum Gap Factor
Moderate Performance	.021–.023	.005 per inch of bore diameter
Drag Racing——Oval Track	.023–.025	.0055 per inch of bore diameter
Nitrous Oxide——Street	.025–.027	.006 per inch of bore diameter
Nitrous Oxide—Drag Racing	.029–.031	.007 per inch of bore diameter
Supercharged	.025–.027	.006 per inch of bore diameter

These ring gap recommendations are for the 4.25-inch bore of a 454-ci engine. You can use the recommended ring gap factor to determine what ring gap you should be using for the bore of your engine, but the best solution to determining proper ring gap is to consult your machine shop or the paperwork accompanied with your ring set.

You may notice that the intermediate (second) ring gap recommendations are larger than the top compression ring. After much testing, Perfect Circle has determined this method increases the stability of the top ring for a better seal. It increases horsepower gains in upper RPM ranges and reduces blow-by. The larger gap on the intermediate ring allows inter-ring pressure to escape past it, rather than lifting the top compression ring off the cylinder wall allowing even more pressure to squeeze by.

26 Measure Pistons

Grab the piston assembly for cylinder number-1. Use your outside micrometer to check the piston skirt according to the position specified by the piston manufacturer. Use your bore gauge to measure the minimum bore diameter in the corresponding cylinder. Subtract the piston measurement from the cylinder bore, and you have your piston-to-cylinder-wall clearance, also known as skirt clearance. Write down your clearance. Perform this process on all eight pistons and their designated cylinder. Piston manufacturing irregularities can and do occur, so check each piston twice. To check skirt clearance with a feeler gauge, slide the piston into its designated cylinder upside down with a feeler gauge between the skirt and the cylinder wall. Start with a .001-inch gauge and move up in size until the piston gets snug in the bore, then subtract .001 inch from that gauge thickness and you have your skirt clearance.

Precision Measurement
27 Hypereutectic Ring Gap Requirement

Even if you find ring gap information with your piston rings, you also need to check with your piston manufacturer.

According to Keith Black Pistons, hypereutectic pistons require a larger gap on the top compression ring because of their design. They make more power by reflecting heat energy into the combustion process, which puts extra heat in the top of the piston and top piston ring. An extra gap in the top ring is required to keep it from expanding too far and breaking the ring and/or the piston. Consult your piston manufacturer to confirm specific gap changes for your application. According to the formula on www.kb-silvolite.com: bore x .0065 = top ring gap. These KB hypereutectic pistons for this .030-inch over 402 are .027-inch top ring gap. If your application is not a .030-inch over 402, your gap will be different.

28 Insert Ring in Cylinder

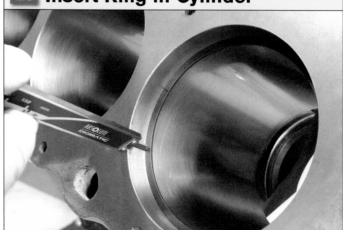

If your machine shop gapped your rings, they should be labeled by cylinder. If you have pre-gapped rings you should perform this step to ensure your rings are correct. Make sure each ring has been deburred, and the ends are free of chips. Slide one compression ring at a time into its designated cylinder and make sure the ring is at equal depth all the way around the cylinder. In order to get a correct ring gap, the ring must be square in the bore, which means it must be pressed evenly down into the bore. If you don't have a ring squaring tool, try using your caliper to set depth. Use a feeler gauge to confirm the gaps are correct and that the ends of the ring are parallel. Don't forget that the "top" and "second" compression rings have different gaps. If your pre-gapped rings are not correct, confirm your bore size and have the parts store get you the proper set.

Precision Measurement

29 Measure Ring Gaps

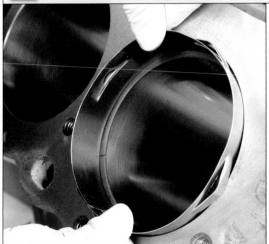

 If you are gapping your own rings, designate a "top" and "second" compression ring for each cylinder. Keep them in the order you fit them to each bore. Keep them separated with a paper towel while not working with them. Because you probably don't have an expensive power ring filer, you need a manual ring filer, a ring squaring tool (it speeds up the process compared to using your caliper), a fine metal file, and a set of feeler gauges. In order to get a correct ring gap, the ring must be square in the bore, which means it must be pressed evenly down into the bore. Because .001 inch can make the difference in how an engine runs, use a ring squaring tool, such as this Goodson unit. Put a compression ring in the cylinder. Once the ring is square in the cylinder, you can get your feeler gauge and check the gap. If your machine shop has not suggested a ring gap, use the chart on page 95.

Professional Mechanic Tip, Important!

30 File Rings

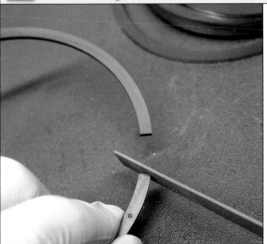

Pull the ring out of the cylinder and file it down until it has the correct gap. Be careful not to file off too much material. Continually re-insert the ring in the cylinder but make sure there aren't any burrs on the ring that can scratch the cylinder wall. If there is a burr, lightly touch the corner with a file to remove it. Use the squaring tool and check the gap every time. If you file too much, you can usually purchase single rings. When you're done with one ring, confirm the gap is parallel, that there are no chips or burrs in the gap, and move on to the next ring. When the compression rings are done, put the oil rings in the bores one at a time and check to make sure they have gaps between .015 and .060 inch. The oil rings are controlling oil, not compression, so they are more forgiving. Pack up the rings in labeled sets and put them aside for later assembly.

Precision Measurement

31 Measure Rods

While you have the rods torqued, use your caliper to measure the width of rods number-1 and 2 together and write the measurement for a later step of measuring side clearances. Do the same for rod pairs numbered-3 and 4, 5 and 6, 7 and 8. Put the rods back in the soft jaws and remove the rod caps.

32 Plastigage Rod Bearings

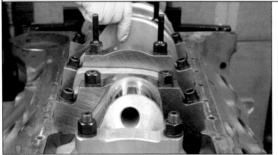

 Rod bearings are somewhat trickier to check clearances on with Plastigage than is the crank. The rod and crank want to move while trying to torque the rod cap. Any movement of the rod or crank distorts the Plastigage and gives an incorrect reading. Start at the front of the block and work your way to the rear, installing only two rods at a time. Move the crank so the front rod journal is sticking up as far as it can out of the block. Install and check clearances for only two rods at a time. Install piston and rod assemblies for cylinders number-1 and 2 with the chamfer of the rods facing the fillets on the crank and the two flat sides of the rods are facing each other. Put a strip of Plastigage on the connecting rod bearing surface. Carefully slide both rods and pistons into place on the journal, making sure that you don't hit the crank or block with the rod bolts. Slide the connecting rod caps into place on their designated rod and install the nuts by hand, but don't tighten them yet.

33 Improper Rod Torque

If you torque the rod from side to side, it will twist the connecting rod on the journal and also force the crankshaft to turn in the block. Any movement destroys your Plastigage and you will have to start over. This method produces a false Plastigage reading for your connecting rods and possibly damages your new bearings.

34 Proper Rod Torque

 Stand directly in front of the engine, and put pressure on the torque wrench toward the front of the engine to torque the cylinder number 1 connecting rod. This puts all the pressure of the rod against the crankshaft, while it limits the rod from twisting and keeps the Plastigage from giving a false reading.

Tighten each nut evenly back and forth a couple of times before you reach full torque. With aftermarket rods using alignment sleeves around the bolts to locate the rod cap, pay special attention to the parting line of the rod caps, to ensure they are even as you tighten them, because if they're slightly crooked, you can damage the rod. The Eagle rods have special caps crew-style rod bolts that required a 7/16-inch 13-point socket on the 1/2-inch-drive torque wrench.

Torque Fasteners, Use Special Tool

35 Proper Rod Torque CONTINUED

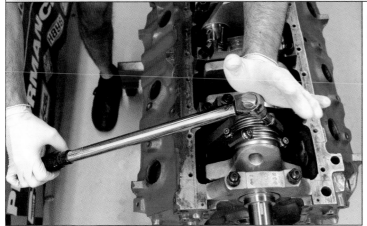

 *Stand behind the engine and torque the rod for cylinder number-2 by putting all the force on the torque wrench toward the back of the block. This pulls the rod up against the crankshaft, keeps the rod from twisting, and keeps the crankshaft from wanting to turn.*

Precision Measurement

36 Check Rod Side Clearance

This is a feeler gauge method for measuring the rod bearing side clearance. A more precise way to check, with precision measuring tools, should be done in following steps to confirm what you find here. Use your feeler gauge between the two connecting rods without rotating the crank. Take note of the gauge size needed to take up the gap between the rods without having to force it. The gap should be .015 to .025 inch per pair of rods (unless otherwise specified by the manufacturer), making the total gap .020 to .028 inch for the two rods. These Eagle rods came in at .024 inch. When you get all the rods installed, check the side clearance on every journal.

Steel Rod Applications (per rod)	Rod Side Clearance
Stock and Hi Perf	.010–.014 inch
Hi Perf——6,000+RPM	.010–.017 inch

Some performance rod manufacturers have specific recommended side clearances, so consult any instructions that accompany aftermarket rods.

37 Remove Rod Bolts

To remove the rod bolts, you must use the opposite procedure from the way these were installed, while still pushing the rods against the crank. To remove the nuts for cylinder number-2, stand in front of the engine and put all the pressure toward the back of the engine. To remove the nuts for cylinder number-1 stand behind the engine and put all the pressure on the wrench toward the front of the engine. Use a 12-point 7/16-inch socket and a flex-handle ratchet.

38 Remove Rod Cap

Because Plastigage is a pliable piece of plastic, you have to be extremely careful not to rotate the crankshaft during this process. If you have rod cap bolts (on performance rods), loosen the rod bolts a few threads and use a soft-faced hammer to gently tap the rod bolts. Tap each side evenly until the rod and rod cap separate. If you have stock-type rod bolts and nuts, loosen the nuts a few turns and use a pair of channel-lock pliers to gently pry the cap off the rod bolts without disturbing the parting line (faces of the cap and rod that touch each other when installed). Remove the nuts (or bolts in the case of aftermarket rods) while being careful not to allow the piston and rod to fall on the floor. If you have bolts sticking out of the connecting rod (as with stock), you should install your rod bolt protection now. Carefully slide the rod out of the bore without damaging the crank or cylinder wall. Follow the same method and remove the other rod on the journal without turning the crankshaft.

Precision Measurement

39 Check Plastigage for Rods

The Plastigage gets wider as it is crushed. The tighter the tolerance on your bearings, the wider the Plastigage ends up when you remove the bearing cap. Compare the width with the chart on the Plastigage package. Clevite suggests oil clearance to be .009 to .0034 inch. This will change with some bearing sets and applications, so consult your machinist and paperwork with your bearings. If your clearance is not within spec, consult your machine shop to see if you can remedy the problem by installing some undersized or oversized bearings. The 496 Eagle rods and mains required "X" Clevite bearings to give extra clearance.

40 Measure Crankshaft Rod Journal Clearance

Using your caliper, measure the width of each of the crank journals. Measure with the caliper tangs positioned flat against the journal thrust faces. Refer back to the measurements you took in step 36. Subtract the rod pair widths from the journal widths and you have your rod bearing side clearance. Refer to the clearance chart on page 99. If the specs are not in the proper range, check everything again and contact your machine shop.

41 Install First Pair of Pistons

Now we're going to be checking for TDC. We're going to be working with cylinders number-1 and 2. To get to this step, the crank has been installed and lubed. The pistons have been installed on the rods and the bearings are installed in them. First check the crank to make sure you can slowly rotate it a couple of revolutions. Grab number-1 piston and pivot the connecting rod back and forth (without knocking the skirt on the rod beam) to make sure there isn't any bind, then check number-2. Lightly oil the piston skirts and the cylinder walls. Lubricate the rod bearings and the front rod journal on the crank. Install rods and pistons (without rings) number-1 and 2 in their correct bores and torque them to spec. Slowly rotate the crankshaft by hand. If it doesn't spin easily or binds, don't force it. Something has gone wrong with the installation of the rods or the rods may be hanging up on the engine block. Check for possible interference problems with the rods or, if necessary, check the rods and bearings for damage.

42 Install Camshaft

 Put a thin coat of engine oil on the cam bearings and on the cam journals. You can use a long bolt, the cam sprocket, or a camshaft handle like this Goodson tool. Carefully insert the cam straight into the the block. Turn the cam gently as you install it to ease it into the block. Be sure to support it, so the cam lobes don't fall and knock the bearings, especially when the journals slide past the bearings. If the cam doesn't slide into the bearings easily or turn freely, there could be a problem with the installation of the bearings or the bearings could have been damaged upon installation. If this happens, carefully remove the cam and check it for straightness. Inspect the bearings for shiny high spots. If there are a few small high spots, sometimes you can remove them by carefully scraping them with a bearing knife. If the cam isn't bent and removing high spots doesn't work, the machine shop must check and repair the cam bore.

43 Install Keys and Sprocket

Once the cam fits correctly, remove it, put more oil on the journals and put more assembly lubricant on the lobes, and then carefully put it back in the block. If you're installing a Milodon gear drive, follow the steps for doing so in the "Milodon Gear Drive Install" sidebar on page 100; if not, continue this step. The keys should already be installed in the crank but if not, go ahead and install them by tapping them gently with a non-marring hammer. Once installed, put a small amount of anti-seize on the snout of the crank and slide the small timing sprocket onto the snout, positioned so the flat side with the timing marks is facing away from the block. Some sprockets have more than one keyway and different marks, such as triangles, round dots, and other shapes. With the crank key installed, align the keyway with the zero ("0") mark and drive the sprocket onto the snout with a crank socket or a brass drift by tapping it lightly with a hammer around the flat surface of the sprocket.

44 Install Timing Set

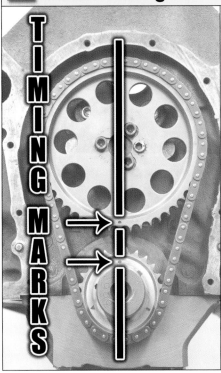

Rotate the camshaft so the dowel pin is in the three o'clock position and the crankshaft key is also in the three o'clock position. Put the timing chain on the cam sprocket and let the chain hang down. Hold the cam sprocket with the timing mark in the six o'clock position. Loop the chain under the crank sprocket, and slide the cam sprocket onto the cam dowel pin. The timing mark positioning is critical. The timing marks on the cam and crank sprockets should be lined up as shown. If they don't, reposition the chain and/or sprockets until they do, then install the three bolts snugly.

Milodon Gear Drive Install

Gear drives come in different types. There are ones with two idlers that "float" between the cam and crank gears. The Milodon gear drive was chosen for this project because it's the best one on the market for a big-block. It has a single idler solidly mounted to the timing cover to eliminate wear associated with "walking" found in floating gear drives. This gear drive is also equipped with an access panel, which can be removed without having to remove the harmonic balancer, timing cover, or without disturbing the oil pan seal in order to adjust timing or swap camshafts. Follow along to find out how to install the Milodon gear drive on the 496 project engine.

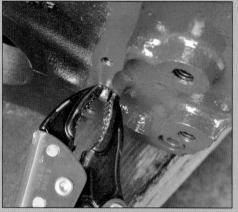

Remove the two stock dowel pins from the front of the block with a special slide-hammer. Locking pliers were used as an alternative. They were locked onto the dowel pin and rotated back and forth while slowly pulling the pliers away from the block.

Make sure the crankshaft keys are installed. Put a little anti-seize on the crankshaft snout. Install the concave side of the gear against the raised snout on the crank.

Drive the crank gear onto the crank using a brass drift, so you don't damage the gear and its teeth. Think of the gear as a clock face and drive at three, nine, six, and twelve o'clock and repeat until the gear is fully seated.

Layer the thrust washer, bearing, and washer on the camshaft on the front of the block, and then install the cam gear hub over the bearings. Install the three bolts supplied hand tight. Torque the bolts later. Remove the access cover from the timing cover.

Install the timing cover on the front of the engine block and install all 10 small Allen bolts. If they don't all thread into the block, you may need to get a rat-tail file to file out the mounting holes in the cover in order to get enough play to properly adjust the lash between the gears. Timing cover bolt location has slight variances from the factory and some custom fitting may be required. With all 10 bolts installed, you should be able to move the cover from the right and left slightly, enough to feel the difference in play between the crank gear and the idler gear when doing so. Once all the bolts freely screw into the block and slight gear lash change can be felt, you can remove them and the cover.

Place a (single thickness) narrow strip of newspaper on the crank gear. This helps to bend the paper to conform to the gear. Carefully lay the timing cover over the strip of newspaper making sure it does not slip off. Install all the bolts to hold the timing cover to the block. Place another (single thickness) narrow strip of newspaper on the top of the idler gear and place the upper timing gear into the cover, making sure the newspaper stays between the idler and cam gear. Bolt the cam gear to the cam hub with two of the seven bolts. Now there is paper between all three gears. Thread all the cover bolts into the block hand tight but loose enough to move the cover.

Push the cover toward the number-1 cylinder to apply pressure on the cover to take the lash out between the gears. If you leave too much lash in the gears, you will have a much louder gear drive than you may have planned. While holding pressure on the cover, torque all the bolts holding the cover to the block to 7 ft-lbs, in order to lock it in place with the tension on the gears. With your crank socket, turn the crank clockwise enough to get one end of the newspaper strip to feed out from between the idler and crank gear. If the paper shreds, the clearance is too tight. If the paper only has a small hole from each gear tooth, the clearance is correct. If the clearance is too tight, the idler bearing will fail prematurely.

The dowel pins are slightly undersized on one end. Place the dowel pins in the dowel pin guides through the back side of the timing cover. One end of the pins go into the holes. Measure how far they stick out the back to find out how deep to drill the holes into the face of the block. Ours had to be drilled .350-inch deep. Cover any other holes with paper towels to keep metal shavings out of the engine. Drill the front of the block with a 5/16-inch drill bit by using the hardened bushings in the front cover as drill guides. Do not damage the drill guides; they remain in the cover to locate the timing cover. Remove the timing cover and carefully clean up all the metal shavings.

Tap the 5/16-inch dowel pins into the block. Ours were slightly loose so we put some hard-setting No. 1 Form-A-Gasket on the pins before installing them. We used a sharp-tipped punch to lightly punch the surface around the pins to help lock them into place. Now you can remove the entire timing cover and pull out the strips of paper. Now the lash is always the same, any time you remove or re-install the cover.

Milodon Gear Drive Install *CONTINUED*

Get your timing cover gasket and cut new dowel pin holes in it. If you are installing the gear drive for pre-assembly, install the timing cover hand tight so you can take it off for the rest of the chapter. If you are leaving it installed, you can put a thin coat of black Permatex on both sides of the gasket and torque all the timing cover bolts to 7 ft-lbs. Install the cam gear hub without the cam gear.

Milodon does not put timing marks on their gears, so we start by installing the gear drive at zero, without any timing advance or retard (those adjustments are simple after zero is found). Use a dial indicator and degree wheel for timing because these tools are more accurate than aligning generic marks. Set the degree wheel on TDC for number-1 cylinder. Grab a lifter and lightly oil its body and put some assembly grease on the face of the lifter to protect the camshaft and lifter. Install the dial indicator (at zero) on the cylinder number-1 intake lifter. Make sure the lifter is all the way down on the camshaft. Use the spec card that came with your camshaft and locate the cam timing spec at .050-inch lift. If the spec were 12-degrees BTDC at .050-inch lift, you would move the crank until the pointer was positioned on 12 degrees. Position the camshaft so that the lifter would be lifted .050 inch. Now the crank and cam are in straight-up position exactly, with zero advanced and zero retarded timing.

There are seven Allen bolts that mount the cam timing gear to the hub attached to the camshaft. Only one position of the timing gear will be the correct zero position on the hub. You know that you have the correct position when all seven bolt-holes line up with the hub, you have not moved the camshaft from its .050-inch lift, and you have not moved the crankshaft. It may take several tries to find the exact position.

Scribe a mark on the cam hub next to any one of the seven Allen bolts and put a corresponding number "1" on the cam gear next to the bolt you picked to mark on the hub. Now, in a clockwise direction, mark the gear for the next Allen bolt with a "2." Continue going clockwise and mark numbers "3" through "7." We chose to remove the hub and gear to stamp the numbers rather than scratch them with a scribe. When you're ready for final assembly, put a drop of Red Loctite on each bolt as you torque the cam hub bolts and the seven cam gear bolts to 22 ft-lbs.

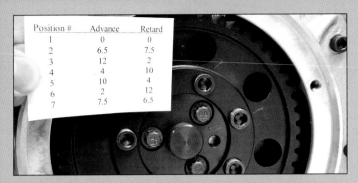

Position #	Advance	Retard
1	0	0
2	6.5	7.5
3	12	2
4	4	10
5	10	4
6	2	12
7	7.5	6.5

If you choose to advance or retard the timing, you must read the chart supplied with the cam to find the amount of advance or retard that corresponds with the numbers "1" through "7" on the cam gear. Keep the crank in the original zero position. There is slight clockwise or counterclockwise cam movement in order to line up the numbers "2" through "7" with your mark on the hub. A slight clockwise movement of the cam to line up the teeth advances the timing, and a slight counterclockwise movement of the cam to line up the teeth retards the timing.

Carefully pull the O-ring off the cover plate and test fit the cover on the timing cover. If it does not fit all the way against the timing cover, you need to have the thrust button on the cam hub adjusted. It can be ground down on a lathe, or you can lay some emery cloth down on a flat surface and sand it down until you have .005-inch clearance between the cover and the button. It's plastic, so it isn't too tough to work with. When you are within spec, put the O-ring back on with a little engine oil and re-install the cover. Install the timing pointer and the Allen bolt with a little Ultra Black sealer to save from having a leak.

45 Install Cam Degree Kit and Final TDC

Important!

If the crank turns freely, go ahead and rotate the crank until the number-1 piston is as close to TDC as possible. Install your cam degree wheel, such as this one that came in a complete kit from Crane Cams. Install your pointer (or bent coat hanger with a pointed end) on the zero mark of the wheel. There are many methods to find exact TDC; I prefer not binding the piston with a stop by using a dial bore gauge on a magnetic base on the deck surface. Set the dial at zero. Rotate the crank counterclockwise to where the gauge reads .070 inch down, then rotate the crank clockwise until the gauge reads .050 inch down, and then record the reading on the degree wheel. Then continue clockwise past TDC to .050 inch down on the dial gauge and record the reading. Adjust the pointer or degree wheel until the degree on the wheel matches at .050 inch down before and after TDC and you have found TDC.

Precision Measurement
46 Piston-to-Deck Clearance

R To start with, the piston dome needs to match the combustion chamber configuration for your heads. Next, there should be a minimum of .060 inch between the piston and chamber. If the piston is .030 inch below the deck, you need to run a head gasket that compresses to .030 inch below the deck. If the piston is .040 inch below the deck, your head gasket needs to compress to a minimum of .020 inch. If your piston is less than .050 inch below the deck surface, you need to be concerned with the piston hitting the head.

Piston-to-head clearance is calculated by adding the piston-to-deck clearance and the thickness of your compressed head gasket. To determine the piston-to-deck clearance, bring number-1 piston to TDC. Mount your dial indicator to a deck stand like this one from Goodson and stick it to the deck as shown. Without moving the crankshaft, gently rock the piston by pushing down on the bottom of the piston and take your reading, then push down on the top of the piston near the gauge to rock the piston the other direction and take your reading. Take the average of the two readings and add the result (or subtract if your piston is higher than the deck surface) to the compressed head gasket thickness and you have your piston-to-head clearance. This measurement can be found by using a straight edge and some feeler gauges.

Precision Measurement
47 Piston-to-Head Clearance

R Many big-block pistons have a domed face and need to be checked for clearance to the head. Hopefully you read my warnings in Chapter 5 and didn't purchase open-chamber pop-up pistons for closed-chamber heads, or you will have interference problems in this step. Using a few head bolts, lightly bolt the left cylinder head on the block without the head gasket. Bring the number-1 piston to TDC. If the piston binds, don't force it (install shims the thickness of your compressed head gasket in place of the head gasket).

Remove the rod cap from number-1 rod. Make sure the rod bearing is still contacting the crank, place the dial indicator on the top of the rod bolt, and zero the gauge. Slowly push the rod into the cylinder toward the head. When the piston contacts the head, you have the piston dome-to-head clearance on the gauge. Add the reading to the head gasket thickness and you have your dome-to-head clearance If it's less than .050 inch, contact the machine shop and find out if a thicker head gasket will fix the problem. When you're done, re-install the rod cap and remove the cylinder head and dial indicator.

48 Hydraulic Lifter How-To

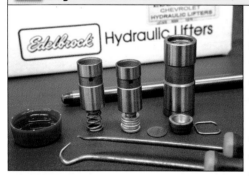

If you are installing a hydraulic cam, modify a few of the lifters so you can use them in the following steps. Hydraulic lifters have a spring inside that compresses when you need the plunger inside the lifter to stay stationary, while you check clearances to the thousandth of an inch. Professional engine builders swap in a couple of solid lifters for these tasks, but if you don't have access to some that are the same "cup" height as the hydraulic lifters, you can take apart a pair of old lifters that are still in great shape (no scuff or scars on the face of the lifter-to-cam surface) and modify them. Place the lifter on a non-marring but solid surface, push the piston cup down with a pushrod, and remove the snap ring. Sometimes suction in the lifter won't release the piston, so you can carefully push the end of a paper clip into the small hole in the bottom of the internal piston, so the internal valve opens. This releases the suction in the lifter and causes the pistons to slide out of the lift bore. Remove the spring under the piston and add spacers or washers so the clip just fits back in the lifter.

49 Find Camshaft Base Circle

Important!

! *Apply engine oil to the outside and face of two lifters and slide them into the exhaust and intake lifter bores for number-1 cylinder. If the lifter hangs up in the bore, don't force it; pull it out and resolve the problem. Using your magnetic stand, place the dial indicator on the top edge of the intake lifter. Make sure it is parallel to the lifter. Rotate the crankshaft until the intake lifter is at its lowest position in its bore (the base circle of the camshaft). Gently push the lifter down to confirm it is touching the camshaft lobe.*

Precision Measurement

50 Confirm Cam Specs

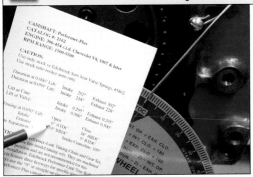

R *Pull out your cam card (the spec sheet that comes with your camshaft) and check the valve timing specs. Most cam timing specs are measured at .050 inch. Slowly rotate the crank clockwise, which is the way the crank turns while it's running, until the intake lifter raises the correct amount (.050 inch, in this case). Write down the degree indicated on the wheel and continue clockwise until the lifter reaches the same lift (.050 inch, in this case) as it goes back down on the other side of the cam lobe. You must always go through this cycle in a clockwise motion; so if you miss the reading on the back side of the cam, you can go back but you have to*
go past the reading, perhaps to .060 inch. Then go clockwise again to get the reading again. The opening and closing readings should match the ones on the cam card. Perform the same procedure on the exhaust lifter. Our cam card showed opening at 0 degrees, which matched our reading.

Professional Mechanic Tip

51 Find Optimal Timing

🔧 *Many companies offer timing chain sets for setting them with advanced timing, at zero, or with retarded timing. Some timing sets allow you to interchange a bushing on the camshaft dowel pin for fine tuning and some sets, such as this Hex-A-Just chain offered by Edelbrock, allow you to adjust the cam timing with a turn of the adjustment screw before tightening the cam gear bolts. These adjustable*
sets allow the builder to correct timing if your cam doesn't match the specs of your cam card. The adjustments also allow you to alter your timing for increased power at different RPM ranges. Without a good grasp on the effects of deviating from a zero setting, and without space to devote a few chapters to camshafts, you should set the cam at zero and leave it. Engine builder Paul Caselas says, "Hopefully you purchased the cam you wanted and you can install it without altering the timing." When you've set your timing, record the settings and keyways by marking the gears and writing your changes on your worksheet for reassembly in the next chapter. Take the lifters out of the block and put them away for now.

52 Check Stroker Clearance

Install the other six pistons and rods using the instructions in step 41. Stock engine rebuilds won't have rotating assembly clearance issues but when you are changing the stroke and installing performance pistons, you need to check for internal interference. Carefully turn the crank and make sure to stop at any sign of bind. If there is any bind or drag on the crank, find the offending culprit and fix it. It could be rod bolts hitting the block near the oil pan rail, the rods hitting the bottom of the cylinder walls, or the crank counterweight hitting the bottom of the piston or the inside of the block. If you have to remove any material from the block or modify any parts for clearance, refer to Engine Blueprinting by Rick Voegelin. If the rotating assembly is not contacting the areas mentioned, make sure you installed the rods correctly.

53 Install Windage Tray and Fit Oil Pan

Now that you know the block and rotating assembly are free of interference, it's time to confirm that your windage tray (if you have one) and pan fit. Install the windage tray and adjust its height with the double nuts on the ends of the main studs and rotate the crank to make sure there is at least .10-inch clearance between the rotating assembly and the tray and/or screen. Once that's adjusted, thread a couple of bolts in the oil pan without the oil pan gasket. If the pan doesn't fit over the tray, you may need to adjust the tray height or trim the excess threads off the mounting studs and possibly trim the edges of the tray. Be careful when cutting the studs; don't damage the threads. Carefully chamfer the ends with a fine file to ensure the threads are in good shape. You can lay a shop towel over the tray, place the oil pan over it, and lift it off. The towel has marks showing where the interference may exist. Once the pan clears the tray, put it back on and rotate the crank; if it binds, the pan moves, or the crank doesn't easily turn, identify where it's hitting and address the issue. If you are building a stroker, you may need an oil pan with stroker clearance at the rail, such as this Milodon oil pan. If the clearance is very tight, you can place a washer between the block and the pan to simulate an installed oil pan gasket. Some dimpling of the pan may be necessary on some pans; but if your pan needs a lot of work, you may consider buying another that may fit better. When you are done checking clearances, pull the pan off and write notes on your worksheet as to where you had set your windage tray, but leave the tray in place for now.

Important! ❗

54 Check Crankshaft Index

❗ This step verifies that the rod journals are correctly indexed on the crankshaft. Start by using the instructions in step 45 to re-check the accuracy of the pointer on the degree wheel and TDC of number-1 piston. Perform the same steps on pistons number-3, 5 and 7. TDC for the following pistons should index on their perspective degree marks on the degree wheel: number-3 at 90 degrees ABDC, number-5 at 90 degrees ATDC, and number-7 at 180 degrees BDC. Because pistons number-2, 4, 6, and 8 share journals with pistons number-1, 3, 5 and 7, you don't need to check their TDC. However, you should check the piston height on all eight cylinders with the dial caliper to make sure they all match. It's acceptable to have up to .005-inch difference between all eight pistons in stock and light-duty applications. High-performance applications have closer tolerances and require zero difference.

55 CC Chamber

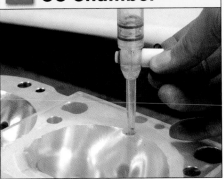

You can always use the pistons you ordered as a guideline for your engine's compression ratio, but the head's combustion chamber cc can significantly change your compression ratio.

56 Keep Valves in Place

Ready the heads for the next steps to check clearances. Because low-tension "checking springs" are typically sold in pairs (except the Crane degree kit that comes with eight springs), you must install them on cylinder number-1 and put O-rings on the other valves to keep them in the seated position. If they drop into the cylinder during this process, you'll have to remove the head to fish the valve out of the cylinder. Using checking springs keeps you from needing to remove and re-install the head each time you want to run the following checks for each cylinder. When moving the checking spring to the next set of valves, position the piston at TDC for that cylinder to ensure the valve doesn't drop while in the process. The only other way to get around this is to get enough checking springs for each valve.

Precision Measurement

57 Check Rocker Geometry

Not all head castings are perfect, so the rocker arm stud and valve location geometry can be off enough to cause improper rocker-to-valve contact, which can cause rocker failure and/or the rocker to wear on the valve retainer. It's suggested to check all 16 rockers, but at least check intake and exhaust rockers' cylinders number-1 and 2 (one on each head). Install both heads with a few bolts hand tightened (without head gaskets) with low-pressure valve checking springs installed. If you have

mechanical lifters, you're set, but if you have hydraulic lifters, you have to perform step 48 on page 106 to remove the hydraulic function, or temporarily use mechanical lifters with the same cup height as your hydraulic lifters for the following steps: Check all four lifter bores on cylinders number-1 and 2 for burrs and debris; apply Royal Purple Max Tuff assembly lubricant to the face and sides of the lifters and gently re-install them for cylinders-1 and 2—if they hang up, don't force them; install the pushrods and rocker arms for cylinders number-1 and 2, using non-locking nuts; and, rotate the crankshaft and if there is any bind, stop moving the crank!

Because your engine passed bind checkups to this step, there are two new possible interferences: rocker arm bind on the stud, or valve-to-piston interference. If you are using stock-style stamped rocker arms, make sure there is at least .040-inch clearance between the rocker slot and the rocker stud at maximum lift (refer to arrow). If the rocker is too close or bound on the stud, you need long-slot rockers as discussed in Chapter 5. If the rocker clearance is okay, remove the rocker arms and see if that fixes the problem. If the valves are hitting the pistons you should contact your machine shop or refer to Engine Blueprinting *by Rick Voegelin before modifying anything.*

With hydraulic lifters for cylinder number-1 on the heel (the section of the cam without lift), the rockers should barely touch the valve tips but not compress the valve. The rocker should be on the inside tip of the valve. Turn the crankshaft and the rocker should move from the inside of the valve tip to the middle and then to the outside of the valve tip. The rocker should be in the center of the tip when the cam is half way through its valve lift (according to the cam card). At no time should the rocker tip be off the edge of the valve tip.

58 Check Pushrod Length

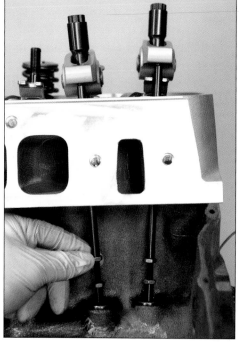

The last part to purchase for your engine should be the pushrods, after you get through this step. Obtain a set of adjustable pushrods like these from Crane Cams to find the optimum length. Put the cam on the base circle, and adjust the pushrod out (including your lash setting at the valve), or pre-load on the lifter (generally .030 inch to .060 inch). Rotate the camshaft and watch the rocker tip; it should never roll off the tip of the valve. It should always favor the center of the valve tip through its travel. For guide and seal life, you are looking for the shortest travel on the valve tip.

59 Rocker Position

Make a quick visual inspection to be sure the rockers are square on the tips of the valves. They should not be hanging way off the side of the tip because this could cause extra side loading on the valve, cause extreme premature wear, or, at higher RPM, the rocker tip could move off the tip of the valve and hit the retainer.

60 Seal Clearance and Rocker Ratio

At maximum lift, the retainer should have at least .070 inch of clearance to the top of the valve seal or valve guide. The rockers should not contact the outside edge (closest to the rocker stud) of the retainers during full articulation. Mount the dial indicator so the point is pushing on the valve retainer, and measure the actual lift at the valve to confirm you have the right rocker arm ratio for your application. Aftermarket rockers come in ratios ranging from 1.6:1 to 1.9:1, so checking ratios is important so you can change the performance of an engine as well as piston-to-valve clearance.

Precision Measurement

61 | Check Piston-to-Valve Clearance

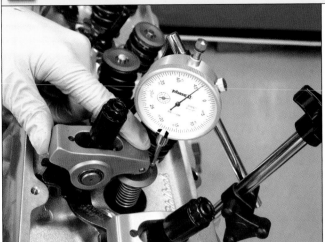

At this point, the valves should clear the pistons and it's time to confirm how much piston-to-valve clearance (PTVC) you actually have. Rotate the crank clockwise until the number-1 piston is at TDC while both valves are open (valve overlap). Mount the dial indicator on the head, so it's riding on the intake valve retainer and parallel to the valve. Push the tip of the rocker arm down until the retainer hits the valve seal or valve guide, or the valve hits the piston. Take notes on the PTVC on your worksheet. Release the pressure and confirm the pushrod tip falls back into the cup of the lifter plunger. Rotate the crank 2 degrees and check the PTVC, and take notes. Continue this procedure until you get to 12 degrees ATDC. In that range, you should have read your minimum PTVC. If you move the crank past the degree mark at any point, you need to back up 10 degrees and approach the mark in a clockwise direction. Repeat this procedure for the exhaust valve and, then, if you don't perform this check on all the other cylinders, do at least cylinder number-2, so you know both sides of the engine have enough clearance. Minimum safe PTVC on the intake is .100 inch and .080 inch on the exhaust. Check clearances on all cylinders if any clearances are close to minimum specs because some may be closer than others. Remove the rockers, pushrods, and lifters and put them away for now.

Critical Inspection, Precision Measurement

62 | Check Distributor and Oil Pump Fitment

Without intake gaskets on the heads, install the intake manifold with the four corner bolts hand tightened. You are going to install your distributor without an ignition cap or gasket. Lightly oil the distributor gear and carefully slide it down into the hole in the back of the intake manifold. With a slight turn of the distributor shaft or rotor, it should mesh with the gear on the camshaft and drop against the intake manifold. Tighten the distribu-tor hold-down bracket. Carefully rotate the engine upside down. Hopefully you took my advice from the oil pumps section on page 57 and replaced your stock oil pump drive shaft. Slide the shaft down into its hole in the rear main cap and turn it to make sure its two forks completely drop into the tab in the center of the distributor gear. Hand tighten the oil pump on the rear main cap. The oil pump should sit all the way down on the main cap and the shaft should move up and down a little bit. Mark the oil pump shaft with a fine-tipped marker, with the driveshaft down, and then use your finger to lift the driveshaft and mark the oil pump shaft again. When you remove the pump, you can measure the distance between the two marks for your clearance. There should be .010 inch to .040 inch of play in the shaft. If the shaft is too long, the oil pump won't even tighten down all the way. If this happens, refer to "Setting Distributor Height" on page 139.

Torque Fasteners

63 Install Oil Pump Pickup

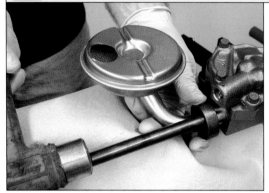

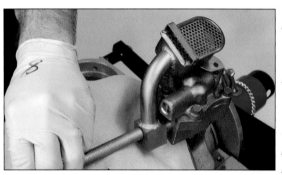

Pull the oil pump off and remove the oil pump drive shaft, then re-install the oil pump to full torque. If you are building a big stroker, slowly rotate the crankshaft one revolution to confirm the crank clears the pump. Lay a couple of paper towels over the rotating assembly to catch shavings of metal that usually come off the pickup tube during installation. Get your oil pump pickup, and a pickup installation tool (like this one from Goodson). Stick the pickup in a plastic bag and into the freezer for a couple of hours next to the taquitos, to help shrink the pickup tube. Lubricate the end of the pickup and the pickup opening on the pump. Drive the pickup onto the pump as level as possible to start.

If you are installing an aftermarket oil pan, install the pickup designated by the manufacturer to go with the pan. Some aftermarket pickups have a tab that locates it to the pump by using one of the pump cover bolts, like this Milodon pickup. If this is the case, go ahead and remove the correct bolt. This pickup had a sturdy square tube joint so we were able to use a brass drift to drive it onto the pump. Some pickups use the same manner of installation as a stock pickup; torque the cover bolt to 10 ft-lbs.

64 Tack Weld Oil Pump Pickup

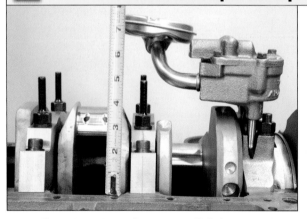

Lay the oil pan on the engine without the pan gasket to confirm the pan clears the pickup. If you have a pickup without a mounting strap, turn the pump slightly upward and lay the pan over it until the pickup barely holds the pan off the block. Push the pan down, which pivots the pickup down on the pump. Unlike factory pickups, Milodon takes the time to weld a clearance strap on its pickups. This ensures adequate clearance between the pickup and oil pan during installation and just in case the oil pan were to get dented upward while driving on the street. Pull the pan off and lay a 1/4-inch-thick piece of wood on the screen part of the pickup, lay the pan over the engine again, and push the pan down to where the pan rails touch the block. This makes sure you have 1/4-inch clearance between the pickup and the pan before installing the pan gasket. According to Ken Sink at Milodon, the optimal clearance between the pan and the pickup (with oil pan gasket installed) is between 1/4 inch and 3/8 inch. Anything more and your pump could become a suction vortex at the pickup and air could enter the system in extreme cases, resulting in bearing failure.

64 Tack Weld Oil Pump Pickup *CONTINUED*

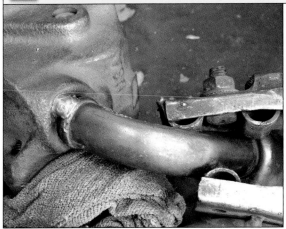

If you have an oil pickup with a mounting tab, confirm that there is a proper gap between the pan and the pickup and that the pickup doesn't interfere with bolting the pan to the block. To fit correctly, some aftermarket pans require the same company's oil pump as well as their pickup. Mark the position of the pickup and for welding it into position. The best practice for welding the pickup to the pump is to take the cover off, pull the gears out, and remove the spring from the body. This ensures that heat does not distort any components and won't damage the spring by overheating it. I took this pump to Vic DeLeon at Goodies Speed Shop of San Jose, California, and he had a tried-and-true technique of welding the pickup without heat soaking the pump. First, he used a die grinder to give a good welding surface. Then he connected the grounding strap for the welder to the pickup to pull the heat away from the pump, and he wrapped a cold and wet shop towel around the pressure spring area of the housing to reduce heat soaking the spring. A quick tack weld kept the heat from causing problems. The pump was cool enough to handle within seconds. Strapped pickups don't require welding because the strap keeps the pickup in place, but if movement was necessary you can usually do some tweaking with a soft-faced hammer.

Precision Measurement

65 Check Intake Manifold Fitment

 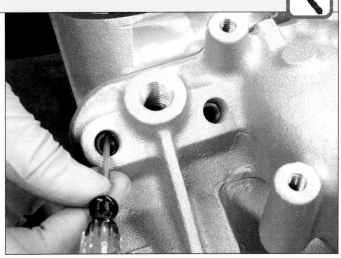

Remove the heads from the block. Clean any oil off the head gasket mating surfaces on the block and heads, lay your new head gaskets on the block and install eight head bolts (distributed evenly around the head) hand tight (less than 5 ft-lbs of torque). Lay the intake manifold in place without the intake gaskets. Check the angles of the intake manifold against the angles of the heads. If the angles are even 1/2 degree off in one direction or the other, the intake manifold gasket will not seal properly, causing vacuum and coolant leaks under the intake into the engine block or on top of the intake. These problems can be tough to diagnose. Inaccurate or improper machining causes these incompatible angles. Pull the intake manifold off and make sure the intake gasket surfaces are clean. Temporarily lay the two side gaskets (intake-to-head gaskets) on the heads and carefully lower the intake on the block. Use a small Philips screwdriver in the bolt holes to reposition the gasket while barely lifting the intake. Hand thread all the intake bolts two or three threads to confirm the bolt holes all line up. Lightly hand-tighten the bolts at all four corners. Use your feeler gauges to confirm the gap between the ends of the intake manifold and the front and rear block rails is at least .060 inch. Consult your machine shop if this clearance doesn't meet the requirements.

Valvetrain Insurance

There are a few parts you can install in an engine that do nothing more than act as an insurance policy against damage. Installing magnets and a lifter valley screen kit ensures that any large debris stays out of the crankcase. That debris is not limited to pushrods, lifters and/or valvetrain bits. These parts should be installed before assembling anything in the block since epoxy can possibly drip on the cam.

Screen kits are available from Milodon and a few other companies. The kit consists of two-part epoxy and stainless screens for the four drain holes in the lifter valley and one round screen to stick in the port behind the camshaft timing gear. Magnet kits can be purchased from Moroso or you can purchase some from an electronics store and use some of the epoxy from the lifter valley screen kit to stick them to the heads.

The epoxy won't adhere to the block unless you clean all the oil off the block in the lifter valley area, the upper timing gear port, and where you are going to epoxy the magnets. Use your brake cleaner and paper towels to clean the surfaces and then test fit the screens. Spend a couple of minutes tweaking the screens to fit around the lifter bosses and sit down against the block as much as possible.

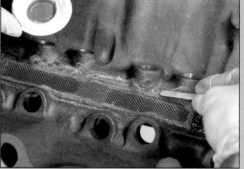

Place the screens in the block. Mix the two-part epoxy as the instructions indicate. Apply the epoxy around the edges of the screens. Milodon supplies just enough epoxy to do the job, but, if you are using another manufacturer's screen kit, be careful and don't put so much on that it dribbles down into the cam bearings; if it does start to drip, keep it off the bearings.

The Milodon kit also comes with a round screen to cover the hole leading to the timing gear. It's a tight fit, so you need a minute or two to tap it into place. When it's about 1/16 inch from being flush with the lifter valley wall, it's far enough. Use some of the left over epoxy to smear around the edges of the ring to lock it into place. Clean up any metal shavings that came off the ring during installation.

Here's an old trick that works: Go to an electronics store and purchase four small (about 1/2-inch-diameter) magnets and use some of that two-part epoxy to glue them in each corner of both heads where the oil drains back into the block. Don't block the hole; glue the magnet about an inch upstream from the oil return hole. This ensures most of the oil has to go around the magnet as it travels back to the pan. The magnets can also be wiped off by simply popping off the valve covers.

Important!

66 Check Accessory Fitment & Re-Check Changes

Any custom bracketry or stock bracketry that may have changed during the rebuild process can be temporarily bolted to the block and heads to ensure a hassle-free assembly in the next chapter. Double-check the threads in the heads to make sure you can easily thread your bolts into them because it would be easier to take a head to the machine shop than the entire engine. Any parts that may get mixed up or clearances you forgot to check should be noted and marked during this step, before heading off to the next chapter when everything is installed for good. At this point, also re-check any clearances that may be changed by any additional machine work that has to be performed. It would be a pain to start over in this chapter, but it's an even bigger pain to have your engine only last 10 seconds because you took a chance on something. Take everything apart carefully and clean up everything before going to the next step. It makes the engine building process much easier.

67 Install Valve Seals

Now you are completely done with all clearances and checks so you can fully assemble your cylinder heads. Make sure you put all the parts exactly where they were pulled from, especially any shims that were under the valvesprings. Because you won't be removing the valves again, you can install the valve-stem seals. There are a few different types of valve seals. Umbrella- and press-on-type seals are the most common. Umbrella seals simply slip over the valve stem and valve guide, but don't actually attach to the top of the guide. Press-on-type seals actually have to be pressed over the valve guide. If you are using press-on-type seals, the machine shop should have made sure that any required machining has already been done. You can carefully drive it onto the guide with a socket that sits on the outer edge of the metal body of the seal and then install the valve. Most valve seals come with a protective sleeve that you slide over the tip of the valve stem before sliding the seal over the tip, where sharp edges can damage the seal.

Oil Pump Checking and Modifying

It's really easy to take a brand-new oil pump out of its box, bolt it on the rear main cap, and continue building your big-block, but you really should take a few minutes to take the pump apart for your own insurance. It's better to be safe than sorry. At a minimum you should remove the oil pump cover, check for defects, lube up the parts, and re-install the cover.

This checking was done after the oil pump pickup was installed, but it's much better to perform these checks before installing the pickup.

Take the cover off the pump and inspect all the parts for burrs and debris. This new Melling pump looked really good on the inside; the pump bolts were metric 10-mm instead of the 3/8-inch in old pumps.

Oil Pump Checking and Modifying *CONTINUED*

Use a straight edge and a feeler gauge or a depth micrometer to find the clearance between the cover and the gears. Set the straight edge on the housing surfaces and check the gap between the gears and the height of the pump cover. This is the pump gear clearance. Normal clearance is between .002 inch and .006 inch. Racing engine builder Robert Cancilla prefers .0015- to .002-inch clearance for all his wet sump oil pumps. With your straight edge, check the cover and body to confirm both surfaces are flat, especially after the pickup has been welded to the pump.

If the clearance is out of spec, you can correct it by taking some material off the height of the body or the gears. You can do this by having a shop machine the surfaces necessary or you can carefully take matters into your own hands: Lay a sheet of 400 grit wet/dry sandpaper on an extremely flat surface and carefully sand the housing or gears by keeping them flat. Material comes off the parts in a hurry, so sand a little, clean the parts, reassemble, and check the clearances often.

When the parts are within spec, re-check for burrs and clean all the parts (housing, passages, spring, pressure relief valve, and gears) with solvent. Apply only assembly lube to the gears and the internal surfaces of the housing. Don't use assembly grease or anything thicker than assembly lube here! Assembly grease simply moves around in the gears and keeps the pump from priming the oil galleries.

When installing the cover bolts, go ahead and apply a drop of Permatex Red Loctite to the thread of each bolt and then torque them to 10 ft-lbs. Now check to make sure the pump gears turn freely. If they do, you've successfully blueprinted your oil pump and you can feel good about installing it.

STEP-BY-STEP FINAL ASSEMBLY

Are you ready? You've carefully followed all the instructions up to this page? Every word was written because it's important. You're familiar with what tools, supplies, manuals, and parts you need to start? All your parts are easily accessible and ready to assemble? If you were going to paint or detail your parts, they've all been addressed? All your bolts and hardware have been cleaned and are in specifically marked bags to ease assembly? Your work area is clean and well lit, and you have time to start assembly without being distracted or rushed? If you answered, "No," to any of these questions, you're not ready and you have some work to do. If you answered, "Yes," to all the questions, you're ready to start final assembly. This can be a long process, so don't rush. When you need to take a break, finish the step you are working on and protect your engine from dirt and debris with an engine bag. Have fun!

Torque Fasteners

1 Install Rear Oil Gallery Plugs and Freeze Plugs

Before your block can be mounted on the engine stand, install the rear oil gallery plugs and freeze plugs. First, get your freeze plug kit out. Don't be fooled by thinking the freeze plug kit has all the plugs needed for the oil galleries. The freeze plug kit is for the cooling system, not the oiling system (even though they usually include enough 3/8-inch plugs to block the front and rear camshaft oil galleries). Depending on the block, you may need four 1/8-inch plugs and one 3/8-inch plug for the rear main oil gallery. Make sure the plugs you install in the oil gallery don't have holes in them. If they do, you have mixed up the plugs that go behind the camshaft sprocket and you need to install them in the front of the engine. If you install them in the rear, you'll be surprised with a large oil leak upon fire up.

I'm a firm believer that pipe threads need Teflon tape, not liquid Teflon sealer or silicone. Wrap the plugs a couple of times with tape and tighten them into the block to 20 ft-lbs. Make sure no stray strands of tape get into the oil gallery when you're installing the plugs. Carefully apply a thin coat of Permatex Form-A-Gasket Number-1 Sealant around the outside edge of the freeze plugs before installing them. Find a socket in your toolbox that has an outside diameter about 1/8 inch smaller than the inside diameter of the cup side of the plug. Using a hammer, squarely drive the plug into the block until the outside edge of the plug lines up with the chamfer of the hole in the block. Wipe excess sealant from the plug.

2 Install Rear Camshaft Plug

To prevent sealant from getting into the rear camshaft journal and on the bearing, you can put a thin layer of Permatex Number-1-Sealant on the lip of the rear cam plug and using a hammer, drive the plug in with a socket that has a 1/8-inch-smaller diameter than the inside diameter of the cup side of the plug. It's important not to drive the plug in too far because the camshaft may come into contact with it. Only drive the plug into the block until the lip is about 1/32 inch below the machined surface of the block. Some engine builders don't put sealant on the plug, but carefully smear a thin layer of Permatex Ultra Black around the edge of the plug after it has been installed.

3 The Big-Block Takes a Stand

Now that you're done installing the parts in the back of the block, you can install the big-block on your heavy-duty engine stand. Make sure the four bolts that thread into the transmission-mounting flange actually thread into the block at least seven full turns. Anything less than that and the threads can pull out of the block and you could get maimed when your engine falls on the ground, or at minimum your engine crashes to the ground damaging everything on it.

4 Install Front Oil Gallery Plugs

If you removed the two 1/4-inch front gallery plugs and they had a small hole in each one, you want to put them back in the front. If you accidentally put them in the back of the engine block, you'll have to swap them out. The holes in the plugs are for extra lubrication of the timing chain and gear. If you don't have holes in the plugs, you can drill a 1/32-inch hole in the middle of these two or buy a pair from your machine shop. If you don't have the holes, it's not required, but you're better off having them to lubricate the timing chain. Wrap the plugs a couple of times with Teflon tape and torque them into the block to 20 ft-lbs. Make sure no stray strands of Teflon tape get into the oil gallery when you're installing the plugs because you don't want it getting loose in the oiling system.

5 Install Other Block Plugs

Install the oil gallery plugs from the front of the block on the lower right-hand side (when looking at the front of the block). Install the brass freeze plugs on the left and right sides of the block, the same way you installed them in the back of the block. If you had plugs and/or an oil-pressure sender to install in the block above the oil filter boss, you can install them now with Teflon tape, along with brass or steel plugs in the cooling system drains above the oil pan rails on both sides of the block. If you don't have the proper plumbing for the oil gallery ports over the oil filter, go ahead and thread a couple of plugs in the holes temporarily to keep debris out during the build; it prevents an oil leak later if you forget to plug them before priming the oil system.

6 Install Main Studs (if applicable)

If you are installing main studs in your engine you need to install them now. If you are installing main bolts, you can move on to the next step. In the previous chapter you made sure the studs were trimmed if necessary. If they are cut to different lengths, make sure you re-install them correctly the first time. You can use red Loctite to permanently install the studs in the block, but you have to torque the caps in place before the Loctite sets or else you could have main cap alignment problems and experience bearing failure. You're better off threading the studs into the block hand tight without Loctite. Only use tools to tighten the studs if they fail to thread in all the way into the block, but don't lock them down into the block with tools, they should only be hand tightened for correct cap alignment. Each of these ARP studs are broached and therefore have an Allen wrench hole in the end of the stud. We opted to use ARP assembly lube (instead of Loctite) on the threads and hand tighten them into the block. A couple of studs needed extra help with a 3/16-inch Allen wrench.

7 Install Main Bearings & Prepare Main Bolts

Thoroughly clean the main bearing saddles in the block and the back side of the bearings to make sure they are free of oil and debris. Then install the grooved bearings in the block. Make sure the tang on the bearing lines up with the relief in the saddle. Carefully with your fingers, try to move the bearings back and forth to make sure they are completely seated and that the oil holes match the holes in the block. Now do the same with the bearings for the main caps. Remember, it's imperative that there isn't any oil or debris under the bearings. The wide bearings are for the rear main and the other four are interchangeable with the four front main saddles. Set out all of your main bolts (or nuts if you are installing studs) and lubricate the threads. If you're using studs, lubricate the stud thread and the washer between the nut and washer for correct torque.

8 Lubricate Cam Bearings

Because you won't have access to the cam bearings once you install the crankshaft, you need to apply a nice coat of thick assembly lube to the cam bearings now. Generously coat all five cam bearings with Royal Purple assembly lube or engine oil.

9 Install Rear Main Seal

Make sure the rear main seal groove in the block and the rear main cap are free of oil and debris. Make sure the backside of the two halves of the rear main seal are clean and oil free. Before going further, confirm that there is only one way to install the rear main seal. The seal "flap" needs to face toward the front of the engine as shown in the picture. If you do it wrong, you'll have a major leak and have to remove the pan and rear main cap to fix it later. Install the seal sticking up about 3/8 inch above the parting line on the block, which makes the other side sit below the parting line. Don't apply any sealant to the seal or its surfaces. When the rear main cap is installed, its seal will match up with the one in the block as shown. The seal just slips into the saddle, and this offset helps deter any oil that may make its way through the parting line in the rear main.

10 Install Crankshaft

Apply a film of oil to the main bearings and to the main bearing surfaces on the crank. Only lubricate the bearings and try not to get oil in the main bearing mating surfaces. Lightly oil the rear main seal surface that rides on the crankshaft, but not enough to get it on the area of the mating surfaces of the seal. Apply a light film of lubricant to the rear main seal surface on the crankshaft. Get some help lifting the crank if it's too heavy. Installation can be especially tricky if you are running main studs. Carefully and slowly lower the crankshaft into the block. Be careful not to bind the thrust surface of the crank on the rear main bearing. If you don't feel confident lifting the crankshaft over the studs, you can remove the five studs on one side, install the crank, and re-install the five studs.

Torque Fasteners

11 Install Rear Main Cap

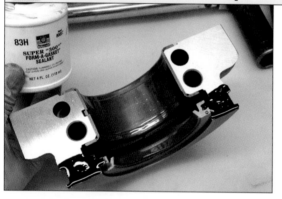

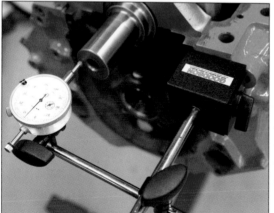

Apply a thin film of oil on the bearing in the rear main cap and the rear main seal lip where it rides on the crankshaft. Clean the cap mating surface with some carb cleaner to make sure it is oil-free, then apply a thin film of Permatex Super 300 Form-A-Gasket on the rear main cap only to the darkened areas shown.

Check the mating surfaces of the rear main cap and block to ensure they are free from debris and oil and then place the rear main cap on the block. Lightly tap the cap into position in the registers in the block. Make sure the cap is fully engaged in the block; if it's not, and you tighten it down, you'll damage your parts. When the cap is seated properly, thread the ARP moly-lubed fasteners finger tight to about 5 ft-lbs. Hit the rear of the crankshaft forward a few times with a soft-faced hammer in order to align the thrust bearings in the rear main. Torque the rear main to 20 ft-lbs.

It's a good idea to set up your dial indicator on the crank to confirm your end play is correct, then torque the caps into place to 20 ft-lbs, using the torque sequence diagram on page 152. Because this engine has splayed 4-bolt main studs, the torque specs are different from other configurations. If you have a different setup, consult the instructions that accompanied your hardware or get your specs from the bolt torque recommendation chart on page 151. Torque your main fasteners in 20 ft-lb increments until they reach full torque. These main stud nuts were torqued to 90 ft-lbs with a 3/4-inch socket. The outer main Allen bolts were torqued to 45 ft-lbs with a 5/16-inch Allen bit-socket. After the caps are fully torqued, the crankshaft should spin freely. Check the crankshaft end play one last time after full torque is reached.

12 Assemble Pistons with Floating Pins Onto Connecting Rods

If you have press-fit wrist pins, they were already assembled by your machine shop and you can move to the next step. Apply Royal Purple Max Tuff assembly lubricant into the wrist pin bores in the pistons, then assemble the pistons and connecting rods in the correct orientation using the instructions in the Chapter 8 (steps 22 and 23 on page 94). Use your internal snap ring pliers to install Tru-Arc snap ring retainers. The open ends should either face up or down in the piston and make sure the flat side with the sharp corners face outward. Never use old lock rings because they may fail during operation. If your pistons require Spirolox retaining rings, work them into place one loop at a time with a small screwdriver or blunt-tipped probe. They require some stretching and twisting to get them into place, but don't stretch them too far. Make sure all rings are fully seated in the piston grooves so they won't come out while the engine is running. Two Spirolox retainers were required for each side.

13 Ring Gap Locations for Cylinders

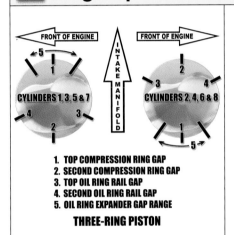

FRONT OF ENGINE   INTAKE MANIFOLD   FRONT OF ENGINE

5

1

CYLINDERS 1, 3, 5 & 7

4   3

2

2

3   4

CYLINDERS 2, 4, 6 & 8

1

5

1. TOP COMPRESSION RING GAP
2. SECOND COMPRESSION RING GAP
3. TOP OIL RING RAIL GAP
4. SECOND OIL RING RAIL GAP
5. OIL RING EXPANDER GAP RANGE

THREE-RING PISTON

FRONT OF ENGINE   INTAKE MANIFOLD   FRONT OF ENGINE

1

2   3

CYLINDERS 1, 3, 5 & 7

4   1

4

1

CYLINDERS 2, 4, 6 & 8

2   3

1. TOP COMPRESSION RING GAP
2. SECOND COMPRESSION RING GAP
3. THIRD COMPRESSION RING GAP
4. OIL RING GAP

FOUR-RING 366 & 427 TRUCK

Ring manufacturers include recommended ring-gap orientation instructions with piston ring sets. Follow the sheet for ring gap locations because they are very important to how your engine performs. Incorrect gap locations can result in loss of compression and/or lack of oil control. The instructions included with your ring set may be specific to the ring set you are installing. The gap information in this step was supplied by Perfect Circle.

14 Install Oil Rings

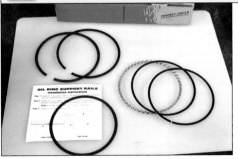

Gently clamp the number-1 piston and rod assembly in the soft jaws of your vise with the intake valve relief pointing to the right. Some aftermarket pistons, such as these SRP pistons for the 496 project, require an oil ring support rail because the wrist pin is above the oil ring land and the oil ring needs additional support. Follow the instructions on their installation. They are very difficult and require powerful fingers to get them into place. Start them in the oil ring groove and slowly feed them into the groove around the piston while you pull the rail down into place. Check the diagram in the previous step and install the rings, using the rules as you install them. Install the wavy oil expander ring in its groove. The ends should not overlap but they can touch. Slide one end of the lower oil ring below the bottom oil ring "land" and the oil expander ring. Wrap the ring around the piston until it's installed. Install the upper oil ring. Double-check to make sure the expander ring ends have not overlapped. Properly installed oil ring and expander assemblies should slide smoothly in the piston groove with a slight drag.

15 Install Compression Rings

Refer to the instruction card included with your ring set to determine which rings are top compression rings and which ones are second compression rings, and which side of the rings should face upward in the piston. The majority of rings have the word "TOP" or a dimple stamped in the top of the ring, but some are not marked and require the sheet to determine if a bevel or step faces up or down in the groove. Don't take chances by guessing; if necessary, call the ring manufacturer or check their website. Using your ring expander, carefully spread your second ring just enough to get it over the face of your piston and install it in the second ring groove. Now install the top compression ring in the top ring groove. If you don't have a ring expander, you can spread the rings apart with your fingertips. Or, you can wrap the rings around the piston like you did to install the oil rings, but only wrap the rings down the piston one groove at a time because they are too brittle to traverse two or three grooves at a time. Using a ring expander is suggested. Call your machine shop if you break a ring. Don't forget to perform and follow previous gapping procedures for any replacement rings. If you are working on a 366 big-block with three compression rings, install the compression rings in this order: third, second, and then top.

16 Install Rod Bearings

Remove the rod and piston assembly from the vise. Make sure the rod bearing mating surfaces on the rod, rod cap, and the two bearing shells are clean of oil and debris. Carefully install the bearing shells into the rod and its cap. Make sure the tang in the bearings line up with their designated notches.

17 Ready to Install Piston/Rod Assembly

The easiest way to install the rods and pistons is to have the block positioned with the deck surface of odd-numbered cylinders completely horizontal, so you can easily install pistons number-1, 3, 5, and 7. Rotate the block to the opposite direction to install the even-numbered pistons. Peer down into the cylinder you're working on and rotate the crankshaft until the journal you're working on is centered in the bottom of the bore (toward the floor). Slide rod bolt protectors over the bolts. If you don't have specific covers you can use 3/8-inch hose that's cut 3/4 inch longer than the bolts. If you have performance rods with cap-screw-style rod bolts that thread into the rod (rather than conventional rod bolt and nut combination), you only need to be careful of catching the counterweight of the crank with the rod. Rod guides are available that also protect the crankshaft rod journal.

18 Ring Compressor Choices and Procedures

The two most common types of ring compressors are the adjustable overlapping-steel-band-type and the tapered-bore ring compressor. The tapered-bore compressor is the best choice because its bore is smooth. Place the compressor on the deck surface and lower the piston into the compressor. Tap the piston lightly to compress the rings as the piston slides into the bore. The adjustable steel band has a harsh edge where the band overlaps and has been known to damage rings in some cases. If you use this type, you tighten the band around the piston enough to compress the rings slightly smaller than the cylinder bore diameter, then place the compressor against the deck surface and gently tap the piston into the bore.

19 Lubricate Piston and Rod Assembly

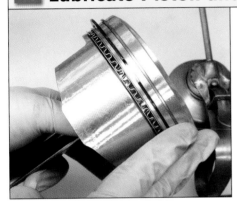

The piston wrist pins should have enough lubricant from assembling them. You can add more oil if needed. Pat some oil on the piston skirts and the entire face of the rings so they have some lubrication against the cylinder walls. Put oil on the bearing shells and the rod journals. Use a lint-free shop towel saturated with engine oil to thoroughly lubricate the cylinder bore.

20 End Gap Check and Compressor Install

Make sure all your ring gaps are in the location by using the instructions that came with your rings (as a backup you can refer to the diagram in step 13. Now carefully install the ring compressor. Keep the compressor against the deck surface. If it's the adjustable tapered-bore type, lay it on the deck surface and adjust it slightly smaller than the bore. Test fit it to the piston. If it's an overlapping band type, carefully compress the rings while being sure they all stay in their ring lands. If they pop out, you can break a ring or damage the piston by continuing to tighten the band.

Professional Mechanic Tip

21 Installing the Piston

Install the cylinder number-1 piston in the bore. Then move on to cylinders number-3, 5 and 7. After the odd-numbered piston/rod assemblies are installed, move on to cylinders number-2, 4, 6, and 8. Triple check piston orientation in the cylinder before inserting the piston into the block. The rod slides side to side under the piston on the wrist pin. Slide odd-numbered rods toward the back of the block and even-numbered rods toward the front to help the rod clear the crank counterweights. Here, the Wildman Rod Guide was placed over the crankshaft journal and placed over the rod bolts on our 402 project because

21 Installing the Piston CONTINUED

it's using standard-style rod hardware. The rod is safely guided all the way over the journal to help prevent damage to parts while installing the piston and rod. If you have other forms of rod bolt protection, be careful to guide the rod from the bottom of the block while lowering it into the bore. If you have performance connecting rods with only rod cap bolts, you need to pay close attention to the rod end while installing it. Place the ring compressor on the face of the block and firmly hold it against the block. Lower the rod and piston assembly into the compressor and slide the piston down until the compressor and all the rings are at least partially compressed, making sure the rings all stay in their ring lands. Using your hammer handle or piston hammer, firmly but softly tap the piston into the cylinder. If the piston halts, stop and check the next step to identify the problem.

Important!

22 Identifying Piston/Rod Interference Issues

If the piston hangs up during installation, look for these possible problems: 1) A ring has come out of the compressor and has hung up on the top of the cylinder bore or in the valve relief notch at the top of the cylinder; 2) The rod or rod bolt got caught on the crankshaft counterweight or rod journal (check to make sure the crank journal is still in the six o'clock position); 3) Your ring compressor is the wrong size (too tight or too loose); or, 4) Ring gaps are set incorrectly.

23 Continue Installing Piston

Once all the rings have entered the bore, you can remove the ring compressor. Reach into the bottom of the bore to guide the rod and continue tapping the piston down into the bore. When the rod gets close to the journal, you may see that the rod needs to be slightly turned to fully engage on the crank. Confirm the rod bearing shell is still in the rod because it can pop out while tapping the piston with the hammer. Carefully continue to tap the piston until the rod is fully seated on the journal.

Torque Fasteners

24 Install the Rod Cap

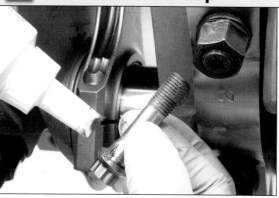

Confirm that the bearing shells in the connecting rod have stayed in place during the installation process. Make sure the rod is numbered correctly for its location. Make sure the chamfer of the rods are facing the counterweights and the non-chamfered sides are facing the center of the journal. Remove the protective covers from the rod bolts if they are still in place. Confirm there's oil on the bearing shell in the rod cap. Apply ARP assembly lube to the rod bolt threads and under the bolt head or nut. Use any specific instructions accompanying your rod bolts for lubrication suggestion. Put the rod caps on their number-matched rod in the correct direction (bearings tangs should mate to each other). A torque wrench with a 7/16-inch 12-point socket was used to torque the rod-cap-screw-style bolts to 63 ft-lbs.

Torque Fasteners

25 Check Rotation Torque

 *The crank was easy to rotate before you installed the first piston. Every piston creates more drag from friction from the rings in the cylinder. Use a beam-type torque wrench to rotate the crankshaft after installing each pair of pistons and rod assemblies to confirm resistance does not increase more than 3 to 5 ft-lbs per piston/rod assembly installed. If rotating resistance is outside this range, it's likely something has gone wrong. You need to check for the following: rings are in good shape, pistons are in the correct bores and they are clocked right, rods are in the right position, and bearings have proper clearance and are properly lubed. With all pistons and rods installed there shouldn't be more than 35 to 40 ft-lbs of rotating resistance.*

Critical Inspection

26 Check Cylinder Wall

 After installing each piston, rotate the crank a couple of times then position the crankshaft at BDC for that piston. Inspect the cylinder wall for scratches. If there are any grooves deep enough to catch your fingernail on, you need to remove the piston and confirm there aren't any broken piston rings. Superficial surface scratches are normal, but anything deeper is a concern and needs to be addressed by a machine shop. If everything has gone smoothly, install your remaining pistons.

Torque Fasteners

27 Install Remaining Pistons and Check Torque

 When you're done installing the odd-numbered pistons, rotate the block so the even side (cylinders number-2, 4, 6, and 8) deck is horizontal, and install the remaining pistons by going back to step 17. As an extra precaution when installing the pistons, you need to be aware that the rods can now catch on the other rod on the same journal as well as the crankshaft and its counterweights. When the rods have been installed, re-check the torque on rod bolts and mains; start on number-1 connecting rod and check each one as you move toward the back of the block, then re-check the torque on the mains in the same fashion. Use a 7/16-inch 12-point socket for the rod bolts and torque the main nuts to 90 ft-lbs with a 3/4-inch socket. Torque the outer main Allen bolts to 45 ft-lbs with a 5/16-inch Allen-bit socket.

Use Special Tool

28 Camshaft Lubrication

 Start by attaching a camshaft handle and a bolt at least 4 inches long, or temporarily install the upper cam sprocket to ease installation. The next part can be a mess or it can be clean. The messy way is to grab the cam and the assembly grease or cam break-in lube, slather the entire cam in one shot with as much lubricant as you can and carefully slide it into the block. The clean method (covered here) is to lubricate the number-4 and 5 cam bearing journals with assembly lube and apply a generous amount of assembly lube or cam break-in lube to the four rearmost camshaft lobes and distributor gear with your finger.

29 Camshaft Installation

Don't forget that the cam bearings can be easily damaged so be careful not to knock, scrape, or scratch them. The cam should be placed on its bearing journals if it's resting in the block for any reason. Carefully thread the needle by installing the camshaft into the front of the engine and rest the number-4 and 5 lubed journals in the two front cam bearings. Apply a liberal amount of JGR assembly grease to the next four cam lobes and assembly lube to the number-3 cam journal. Be careful when the cam journal initially slides out of the bearing, because the cam could fall onto the bearing and damage it. Carefully slide the cam into the block until the number-3 cam lobe is in the front cam bearing and rest the cam. Continue this process of lubricating the lobes and journals one-by-one until the camshaft is fully installed in the block. Don't forget to coat the fuel pump lobe (the last lobe before the number-1 cam journal) with JGR assembly grease, as if it is another cam lifter lobe.

30 Install Timing Chain Cam Drive

If you want information on installing a gear driven setup see the "Milodon Gear Drive Install" sidebar on page 102. Both crank keys and the lower cam gear have been installed during pre-assembly on page 101, so you've already started this install. Rotate the crank until the timing mark is in the 12 o'clock position and then rotate the cam until the dowel pin is lined up in about the three o'clock position. Apply assembly lube to the thrust surfaces on the face of the block around the camshaft and the back of the timing upper gear. Hold the cam gear up as if you're going to install it on the cam and hang the chain over it. Remember the important marks you made on the timing gears after you dialed in your camshaft. Rotate the gear until the timing marks you made are lined up. Loop the hanging chain under the crankshaft timing gear and feed the upper timing gear over the dowel pin. Install the crank gear set at zero ("0") on the crank keyway, position the zero mark or dot straight up at the camshaft, and (with the chain installed) position the cam gear with its zero mark or dot pointing down directly at the crank gear. Either dots or marks need to be lined up in a straight, vertical line.

Torque Fasteners

31 Bolt-on Cam Gear and Lube

If you are installing a cam bolt locking plate, it's time to install it. Without any lubricant, install the three cam bolts hand tight (with cam bolt locking plate if applicable) and confirm that your timing marks are still in the correct position. Once the timing marks are perfect, unscrew the three bolts one at a time and put a drop or two of red Loctite on each bolt and thread it back in the cam. Now torque the bolts to 20 ft-lbs with a 1/2-inch socket on your torque wrench. If you installed a locking plate, go ahead and bend the locking tabs on the sides of the bolts. Lubricate the timing chain with a light coat of assembly lube. Apply just enough to coat it but not to make a mess on the floor.

32 Install Timing Cover Seal

Smear a thin coat of silicone sealer inside the recessed seal boss in the timing cover. Set your timing cover on a flat, wooden or protective surface. Evenly position the seal into the cover and lay a flat piece of wood over the seal (or you can use an actual seal installation tool). Use a mallet to carefully drive the seal straight into the cover. Be sure the wood completely covers the edges of the seal, otherwise, you'll bend or tear the seal and have to replace it before going further.

Torque Fasteners

33 Install Timing Chain Cover

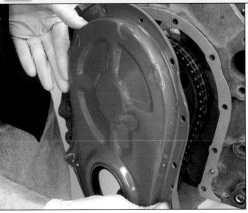

 Oil the timing chain so it has some lubricant upon fire up. Inspect the timing cover mounting surface for flatness and straighten any high spots with a small hammer and a block of wood. Clean the timing cover gasket surface of the block and the timing cover with a paper towel wet with brake cleaner until it's oil-free. Apply a thin film of Permatex Ultra Black to the block side of the timing cover gasket and push the sealant side against the block to hold it in place. Apply a thin film of the same sealant to the gasket surface on the timing cover and push it in place on the block. Place the timing tab in the correct location and install all ten bolts. Torque all ten bolts to 6 to 8 ft-lbs. Use a 3-/16-inch Allen-bit socket on your beam-style torque wrench.

Use Special Tool

34 Harmonic Damper Install

A special tool is required to properly and safely install the harmonic damper. Don't try to draw the damper onto the snout of the crank by tightening a bolt in the snout of the crank. This pulls the threads out of the crank. Rent, borrow, or buy the correct damper installation tool. Thoroughly lubricate all threads of the tool with anti-seize as well as the threads in the crank, the snout of the crank, and the bore of the damper. Using your finger, lubricate the sealing surface of the damper on the timing cover with oil. If you have a performance damper, it may have an interference fit and require some muscle to get installed, but you can help with the install by setting the damper in the sun for a while, or, heat the hub to expand it slightly so it slides over the snout easier. Don't overheat the damper with a torch or you'll damage the elastomer band. Squarely position the damper on the crank snout. Thread the shaft of the tool into the front of the crank without applying pressure on the damper. Adjust the large nut until the tools thrust bearing evenly applies pressure to the damper. Tighten the adjusting nut until the damper is fully seated against the lower timing chain gear. If you feel resistance before installation is complete, stop! Confirm that the damper is not cocked on the crank snout. If you have concerns, remove the damper and inspect it for damage and address any problems. This BHJ Performance damper was a tight fit. Stock replacement dampers have more tolerance than performance versions.

35 Oil Pump and Shaft Install

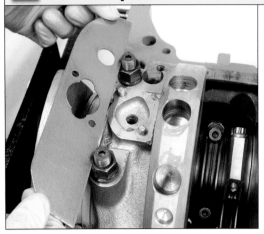

If you are installing a pan baffle, you need to install if between the pump and main cap. This Milodon pan baffle keeps oil from climbing up the back of the rear of the pan during acceleration and robbing you of horsepower. You can see that it has holes for the pump and the driveshaft but not for main studs, so if you have studs, you can drill two large holes in the baffle to clear the nuts. Be sure the mounting surfaces of the oil pump and main cap are in good shape and clean. Install the oil pump driveshaft. If it's a stock one, make sure it has a new plastic sleeve because after years of service they get brittle, and you wouldn't want it to fail. Snap the bushing onto the pump drive and snap the driveshaft into the bushing, meshing their tangs. Brand-new, high-performance driveshafts (highly recommended) have a collar permanently attached to the shaft, and these don't snap on the oil pump. Slide the pump and shaft into the main cap and place pump on main cap. Oil the threads of the 7/16-inch mounting bolt and torque it to 65 ft-lbs. If you're installing a stud, put some ARP assembly lube on the stud and hand thread it into the main cap and torque the nut to 56 ft-lbs.

36 Install Oil Filter Adapter

There are at least two different factory-style oil filter adapters available. The standard one is short and fits down into the oil filter boss. This one requires no gasket and can be installed with the relief valve close to or away from the crankshaft. Apply some oil to the threads of the two 5/16-inch bolts and torque them to 13 ft-lbs. If you have the heavy-duty oil filter adapter you install the gasket and install the two long, 5/16-inch bolts.

37 Prepare Oil Pan Gasket Surface

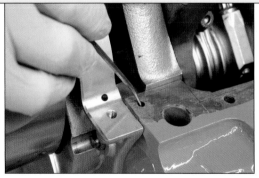

There are two types of oil pan gaskets: one-piece and four-piece. Fel-pro Gaskets sells this great one-piece oil pan gasket. All other manufacturers offer the standard four-piece gasket that has two rail gaskets and two rubber end seals. Before installing the oil pan gasket, the surfaces need to be completely oil free. Get some paper towels and your carb cleaner and start cleaning all the gasket surfaces on the block, timing cover, rear main cap, and oil pan. Be sure the little holes in the timing cover and the gasket surface in the block are clean, because the gasket uses those holes.

38 Install the Front and Rear Pan Gaskets

Apply a thin layer of Ultra Black sealant to the seal surface of the timing cover and block where the front rubber seal goes. Place the gasket over the timing cover, making sure the alignment nubs go into the block on both sides, and that they also feed through the timing cover arch. Carefully pull the nubs through with some needle-nose pliers if it helps get the gasket seated. This Victor Reinz gasket has side rail gaskets made of heavy-duty layered cork and metal gasket. Add some extra Ultra Black at the interlocking joint with the rubber gasket. Do the same for the rear oil pan seal.

39 Install Side Rail Pan Gaskets

Apply a dab of sealant on the rubber where the side rail gaskets meet the rubber seals. Spray both sides of the pan rail gaskets with Permatex High-Tack Spray-A-Gasket to help keep it from sliding, or you can add a thin layer of Ultra Black, and place them on the block in their correct locations interlocked with the rubber gaskets and lined up with the bolt holes. Apply a thin film of Ultra Black on the top of the rubber gaskets.

Torque Fasteners

40 Install Oil Pan

 Lay the oil pan over the gaskets, being sure not to shift them. Install the oil pan hardware. If the pan sits too high to start the hardware, you can push down on the pan or get four longer bolts and install them at all four corners of the block to draw the pan close enough to the block to start your oil pan bolts (don't forget to swap out the longer bolts). Torque the larger 1/2-inch socket-size bolts to 12 ft-lbs and the two smaller 7/16-inch socket-size front bolts to 7 ft-lbs.

41 Fel-Pro One-Piece Oil Pan Gasket

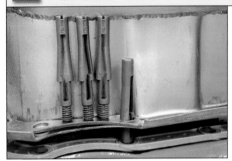  

Installation of this one-piece gasket is simple because the gasket requires almost no sealant. When installing Fel-Pro PN OS30061T, you get the gasket and four installation guide studs. Thread the studs into four opposite corners of the block. Here you can see the ARP oil pan studs are threaded into the block to help hold the gasket in place to ease pan installation. Apply small dabs of Permatex Ultra Black in the corners where the rear main cap meets the block, where the timing cover meets the block and both tight corners of the timing cover, and then slide the gasket over the guide studs. Make sure the gasket is seated in the rear main cap groove and the little nubs fit in the holes in the timing cover. Apply one small dab of sealant to each of the four corners of the gasket where the flat rails meet the arches. Slide the oil pan over the guide studs and install the pan bolts.

In order to check your engine oil for pre-oiling the engine, install the oil dipstick temporarily. It must be removed later when you are installing the headers because the factory-mounting location utilizes one of the exhaust manifold bolts. Simply slide the dipstick tube into the pan and hand thread a 2-inch bolt into the head where the mounting tab can rest comfortably. Leave the bolt loose; this is just a temporary mount.

Professional Mechanic Tip 🔧 PRO TIP

42 Install Valve and Seal

🔧 PRO TIP *Slide the designated shims over the valve guide. Be sure the shim-to-spring contact is thicker than .030 inch or is hardened. If your heads have already been assembled at the machine shop, you can move onto step 44. Lubricate valve guides with assembly lube and slide the valves into their designated places in the heads. Slide them in and out a few times to lubricate the entire valve guide. If you are using valve seals that press onto the guides, install the seals one at a time. These seals must be driven onto the guide. I've used a socket that's the same diameter as the seal to drive it into place. Then install the valves by placing the protective sleeve in the seal to protect it from being damaged by sharp edges on the valve. There are also umbrella seals, which simply slide over the valve stem and float over the guide but don't do a great job of keeping the oil sealed in the engine in performance applications.*

43 Install Valvesprings

If you are running heavy dual valvesprings (the damper spring is not considered a second spring) accompanied by a flat tappet camshaft, leave the second spring off for break-in. Install them after break-in, otherwise there is too much spring pressure and the cam flattens during break-in. Compress the spring and retainer designated for each valve and shim set enough to install the valve locks in the groove correctly. Slowly release pressure on each valvespring, making sure the locks don't pop out of their groove.

44 Prepare Heads, Gaskets, and Bolts

Turn the block so the deck surface you're working with is completely horizontal, or else some of your sealers in the next step will run across the surface and make a mess. Thoroughly clean the head gasket surface on the block and the cylinder heads with a paper towel and carb cleaner. Inspect your gaskets to make sure there aren't any flaws in the rings around the cylinders, and check for other bad spots. Gather all your head hardware.

45 Install Head Hardware

Tap the dowel pins to install them into place. Use the brush applicator in your Permatex Super 300 Form-A-Gasket to get the sealant into the head threads in the block. Be clean about using the Super 300; it's messy. If you are installing head bolts, apply a light coat to the threads before installing them. If you are installing head studs, you're going to need some more Super 300 on the coarse threads. When the stud is installed, there should be a small pool of Super 300 at the base, but not so much that is affects the head gasket seal. All the threads in big-block Chevy heads go into water jackets and coolant could get through the threads and get into the engine oil. Thread the studs into the block. Make sure you put the short studs across the bottom and, depending on the head manufacturer, there could be two or more intermediate-length studs for the holes where the dowel pins are located. If thread sealant oozes onto the head gasket surface, clean off the head surface with a paper towel and carb cleaner but leave some sealant around the base of the stud. Thread them all the way in but only thread them in hand tight. Test the straightness of the studs and threads in the block by attempting to place the head gasket over the studs. If the studs need some tweaking to freely install the gasket, you can thread a nut on the end of the stud to protect the threads and lightly tap the nut with a hammer to nudge it into position.

46 Check Your Heads

Before installing your heads in the next step, you should inspect every intake and exhaust port for parts, debris, and rags. It sounds strange, but the simplest little part that might have fallen into a port can destroy an engine on startup. If you can't see into every port, you can turn the heads over to see if anything falls out.

47 Cylinder Head Safety

Important!

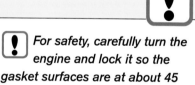

For safety, carefully turn the engine and lock it so the gasket surfaces are at about 45 degrees before installing the head on each side of the engine. This decreases the possibility that the head will slide off the block and land on you or the floor. If you are installing head studs, the studs help to guide the head into place without worrying about it sliding off the block. To lift the head, place your right index and middle fingers in the last intake port and your left index and middle finger in the exhaust port on the other end of the head. Don't pick up the head with your fingers under the head, because you may smash your fingers and damage the head gasket during assembly. Get a second person if you need help.

48 Install Cylinder Heads

Place the head gaskets over the head dowel pin sleeves in the correct orientation according to the words "up" and "front" stamped in the gasket. If your gaskets aren't stamped, that's okay because they only install one way. If you're using head bolts (not studs), get two head bolts ready for safety. Carefully and slowly place the head on the block, making sure not to knock the gasket. Fully engage the head on the two dowel rings and start the two bolts to keep the head in place before completely releasing hold of the head. Install the remaining head bolts. Verify that the head sits down on the block.

49 Head Bolt Torque Sequence

Torque Fasteners

Torque head bolts in proper sequence and correct specifications according to your application or your head gaskets won't seal correctly. Head bolts should be torqued with a 5/8-inch socket to 25 ft-lbs and then in 20 ft-lb increments until full torque of 65 ft-lbs is reached. For ARP hardware and lubed applications, read the instructions accompanying your bolts or check the chart on page 151. Go back to step 45 and start installing the second cylinder head. When you've installed both heads, re-torque them to 65 ft-lbs one last time.

50 Install Lifters

Give the lifters an oil bath for a couple of minutes before installing them in their bores. It's best to use a plastic container and soak two at a time. You can soak more than two at a time but be careful not to knock them into each other to avoid damaging their critical surfaces. If you are using the old cam, you need to re-install all the old lifters—they have to be installed on the exact same lifter bore. Generously apply assembly grease to the face of the flat tappet lifters and then assembly lube or oil to the outside diameter of the lifters and install them in their bores. Squirt JGR assembly grease into the lifter pushrod cups. Roller lifters get a dose of oil on the roller, the tie-bar pivot points, and lifter body.

51 Install Pushrods

If you are installing the old pushrods, they have to be installed with the same lifters and in the passages they came out of. In addition, the right end needs to be in the lifter (wear on the pushrod from the guide plate helps determine the ends). Apply a dab of JGR assembly grease to the tips of the pushrods and in the pushrod guide plate; then slide the long ones into the lifters for the exhaust valves and the shorter ones for the intake lifters. Make sure the pushrods seat in the center of the lifter cups.

52 Rocker Arm Installation

If you are installing the old rocker arms, they must be installed accompanying their original pushrods. These parts all wear into each other. If the rockers are new, install them in any order. Apply JGR assembly grease to the tip of the valve stem. Dab some JGR assembly grease on the contact surfaces of the rocker arms and slide them over the rocker studs. Apply assembly grease to the rocker pivot balls and slide them over the stud's ball, face down. If the fulcrum balls are used, they should be re-installed with the rocker they were previously mated with.

53 Rocker Locking Nuts

Apply some ARP assembly lube to the rocker stud threads. If you are using original locking nuts, which require using a 5/8-inch socket to tighten, be sure they aren't worn so much that they won't keep your valves adjusted. If they are too loose, you can purchase new replacement nuts or you can install new aftermarket nuts with the center set-screw. For best results, the set-screw is designed to work best on studs with flat-tipped studs. The tips of the stock rocker studs are typically pitted and uneven. The nuts require a 9/16-inch wrench and the center set-screw requires a 3/16-inch Allen wrench.

54 Adjust Valves

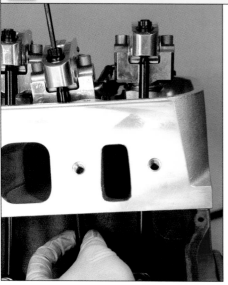

There are methods available to adjust valves while only rotating the engine a couple of revolutions, but with the availability of custom-ground camshafts and increasing advances in camshaft technology, some of those methods can fall short and create headaches for engine builders. This is the reason for using the following tried-and-true method of adjusting lifters. This suggested method won't have you jumping back and forth adjusting valves out of order, which can lead to confusion and oversights.

The additional revolutions of the engine from using this method aren't going to flatten your flat-tappet cam as long as you have followed my instructions on leaving secondary inner valvesprings off the heads until after camshaft break-in, all of your parts are in good working order, and you used a heavy-duty camshaft lube like Joe Gibbs Racing Assembly Grease.

For adjusting hydraulic lifters, use your thumb and index finger to turn the pushrod while tightening the rocker nut. When the pushrod starts to drag because of rocker arm pressure, only tighten the nut another 1/8 turn. Tighten the rocker set-screws if your rocker nuts are equipped with them. Check your cam card for proper lash settings for solid lifter cams and adjust them while using a set of feeler gauges and, when the lash is set, don't tighten the nut any farther. Rotate the crankshaft clockwise until the mark on the damper is on TDC and both valves on the number-1 cylinder are closed (lifters are both down inside their bores). For reference while adjusting the valves, the intake valves are closer to the intake manifold. Rotate the crank until the number-1 cylinder exhaust valve starts to open and adjust the intake valve. Rotate the crank until the position when the number-1 cylinder intake valve completely closes and adjust the exhaust valve. Continue down the line to the cylinders in this order: number-3, 5, 7, 2, 4, 6, and 8 until all the valves are adjusted.

55 Install Fuel Pump

Apply a thin coat of JGR assembly grease to the fuel pump pushrod shaft and liberal amounts on both tips, and slide it into the access hole and push it up as far as it goes. The grease should be thick enough to keep it up inside its bore. Put some Teflon tape on the 3/8-inch access plug and install it with a 5/16-inch Allen wrench. Apply a thin layer of Ultra Black on both sides of the fuel pump gasket surface and stick it to the fuel pump. Put assembly grease on the fuel pump arm. If necessary, use a screwdriver to prop the pushrod up in its bore and slide the pump arm under the rod. Pull the screwdriver out and push the pump up against the block and install the bolts. If the bolts don't line up, the rod and pump arm have become misaligned; so try again. Torque the two bolts to 30 ft-lbs with a 3/8-inch 12-point socket.

56 Pre-Oiling Checks

Warning! Once you add oil to the engine in this step, don't turn the engine upside down again! Check to make sure there aren't any open oil galleries. If you have an oil filter adapter, make sure you have the lines and cooler plumbed into the adapter installed. Confirm that you have tightened the oil pan drain plug. If the plug has a plastic gasket, tighten the plug but don't bear down on it too much, or you'll crack the gasket and cause a leak. Hold the oil filter upright and fill it with your break-in oil up to the passage holes. Rub some oil on the gasket. Spin the filter onto the block and, as soon as the gasket contacts the block, spin the filter another half turn.

If you have a stock oil pan, pour five quarts of break-in oil into the distributor hole; that way the oil doesn't wash the assembly grease off the camshaft. By the way, this huge Microdon pan requires 8 quarts of oil. Pour the bottle as shown for better control of the flow.

57 Prepare Intake Manifold and Gaskets

If your stock intake manifold was equipped with an underside heat shield, it should've been re-installed (see page 36, step 4). Use a paper towel and carb cleaner to clean the intake manifold gasket surfaces on the block, heads, and intake. If you're installing a cast-iron intake manifold, you should install steel-core gaskets; if you're installing an aluminum intake, you should have paper gaskets. Intake manifold gasket kits come with rubber or cork end-seals. Almost all Chevy engine builders throw these in the garbage because they slip and pop out of place, causing vacuum and oil leaks. Professionals apply a 1/4-inch-diameter bead of Ultra Black Silicone in their place. If you feel compelled to use the supplied end-seals, apply a thin layer of Ultra Black to both sides, place the gaskets on them, and add a dab on each end where they interlock with the side gaskets.

58 Apply Intake Manifold Silicone

Apply a thin film of Permatex Water Pump RTV sealer to the coolant ports (not around the intake ports) on the head surface. The gaskets already have a bead seal around the ports on the intake manifold side so you can leave the intake manifold side of the gasket without sealant, but if you feel compelled you can add a small bead there too. If your side gaskets have optional heat riser block-off or restrictor plates, you need to install the right one for your application. For performance applications, use the heat riser blocks. For cold climates and smog purposes, use the open ones or no restrictors. Set the side gaskets in place. Edelbrock and Victor Reinz sell gaskets specifically designed for aluminum intake manifolds. The dark-colored layered-steel composite gasket is best suited for cast-iron intake manifolds and the center-graphite-layered gasket is good for both. Add an extra dab of Ultra Black at each of the four corners where the intake gaskets meet the block.

59 Install Intake Manifold

Before the silicone dries, carefully place the intake manifold on the gaskets without moving them around. To help position the gaskets, stick a small screwdriver through the intake bolt holes while slightly lifting the intake, then reposition the gaskets. Install the intake manifold bolts and their washers. If there are four that are different (as on this ARP bolt kit) they are for the four locations centered above the intake runners. Apply ARP thread sealer to the eight bolts that go around coolant ports.

Torque Fasteners

60 Intake Manifold Torque Sequence

Follow this torque sequence to torque the intake manifold bolts to 30 ft-lbs in 10 ft-lbs increments. Some intake manifolds don't give you access to get a torque wrench on bolts number-1, 2, 3, and 4. You may need to use a wrench to tighten them to your best estimate of torque. As you tighten the bolts, others become loose. After you torque the bolts to 30 ft-lbs, go back a few times until all the bolts are tight. Use 3/8-inch 12-point socket to install these ARP bolts.

61 Seal Open Ports

Open ports on the engine, like the intake manifold, exhaust ports, distributor hole, thermostat port, and spark plug holes, should be covered as soon as possible. Loose hardware loves to go in these openings. Nobody wins in a fight between a stray screw and a piston. If you don't have a really nice kit of port covers, at least use some duct tape to cover the holes to keep dirt and junk out of the engine.

Torque Fasteners

62 Install Water Pump

Test fit the pump to the block to ensure all the bolts thread all the way into the block without bottoming out. Apply thread sealant to the threads. Apply a thin film of water-pump silicone to the gasket

surfaces of the water pump, press the gaskets onto the pump and apply a thin layer of RTV to the exposed side of the gasket. Apply ARP thread sealant to the threads of all four 9/16-inch bolts and torque them to 30 ft-lbs.

Torque Fasteners

63 Install Valve Covers

If you're using cork gaskets, run a thin bead of Ultra Black around the gasket surface on the valve covers and press the gasket onto the covers. Don't put sealant between the gasket and the cylinder head. Tighten the valve covers to the heads to about 5 ft-lbs. If you're using rubber gaskets like these Victor Reinz Gaskets, you don't need to use any sealant. Just tighten them down and go!

Torque Fasteners

64 Install Thermostat and Housing

Place the thermostat into the recessed area in the intake. Most thermostats are stamped showing which side is up. If your thermostat housing has a rubber O-ring like this stainless steel unit from Performance Stainless Steel, it shouldn't require sealant as long as the sealing surface on the intake manifold is in good shape. Housings that require gaskets require a thin film of water-pump silicone on both sides of the gasket. Put Teflon thread sealer on the threads of both bolts and torque them to 30 ft-lbs with a ratchet and a 9/16-inch socket.

65 Distributor Preparation

Install all the ignition parts on the distributor (except ignition cap) because it's harder to install these parts later. Stick a long standard screwdriver or the oil pump primer down the distributor hole and turn the oil pump intermediate shaft until the slot points toward the number-5 cylinder. Liberally coat the distributor gear with JGR assembly grease.

66 Install Distributor

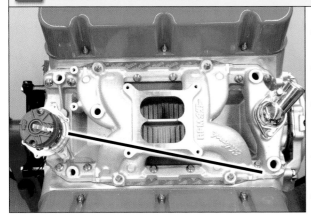

As you install a distributor, take into consideration that, because the helical gears mesh, they rotate the distributor shaft (approximately 45-degrees clockwise). Point the rotor's electrode toward the number-3 cylinder and slowly lower the distributor into place. Before the distributor seats against the intake manifold, it needs to completely engage with the cam gear and oil pump shaft. It could take some movement of the rotor and/or the oil pump shaft to fully seat the distributor. The rotor should point toward cylinder number-2 when it is fully seated against the intake manifold as shown in the picture. Once the distributor is in the correct position, install the clamp in the intake manifold and tighten the 9/16-inch nut to hold the distributor from moving. Number "1" on the distributor cap should be pointing toward cylinder number-2.

Torque Fasteners

67 Install Exhaust Manifolds

If you are installing headers, you should test fit them on the engine now, even though you'll probably need to remove them to install the engine in your vehicle. This helps confirm the header flanges fit over the tops of your head bolts. The heads on most aftermarket head bolts are taller than stock bolts and most of these taller fasteners interfere with header flanges. The only way to cure this problem is to grind the header flanges for clearance. It's much faster to perform this task before installing the engine in your vehicle. Test fitting the headers or exhaust manifolds at this point also gives you a chance to check the route of your spark plug wires. Use good gaskets when you install your headers, or you'll be under the hood again before you know it. Remflex gaskets are made from flexible graphite material that seals even the worst warped flanges and need no re-torquing. They offer gaskets for every big-block head configuration. Coat the threads with anti-seize compound before installing them. Snug the bolt by hand if you are only test fitting the headers or exhaust manifolds. If you are installing the manifold bolts for final assembly, torque them to 20 ft-lbs. We eventually used ARP stainless steel bolts with 3/8-inch 12-point heads.

68 Firing Order

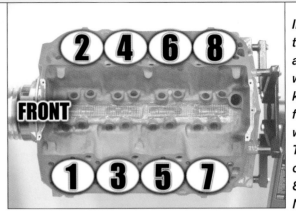

In order to install the distributor and spark plug wires you need to know what the firing order is and where to start. The firing order is cylinder number-1, 8, 4, 3, 6, 5, 7, 2. Number-1 spark plug wire is located toward the front of the cap, as shown. The ignition rotor rotates clockwise as the engine is running. The cylinders are numbered with the odd numbers on the driver's side of the engine and the even numbers on the passenger's side of the engine, as shown.

69 Install Spark Plugs and Ignition Wires

Gap your plugs for your application, apply anti-seize on the plug threads and hand thread the plugs all the way into the head to ensure you don't cross-thread them. Don't forget to add anti-seize to the threads of the plugs. That rule goes for cast-iron heads as well as aluminum heads. You can purchase spark plug wires that are pre-made or you can custom tailor wires to fit your own requirements. We are custom building our own wires from an MSD Ignition universal wire set. We're using MSD crimpers to make crimping the ends a breeze. It's much easier to perform this task with the engine on a stand. This should be done after all the accessories and wire looms are installed, for correct routing around the valve covers. If you need to install the engine without the exhaust manifolds, don't install the spark plugs until the engine is installed because spark plugs break easily and often during engine installs.

Torque Fasteners

70 Install Carburetor

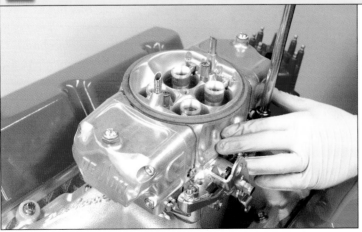

Only permanently install the carburetor at this point if you don't need the carburetor removed to install the engine in your vehicle. If it needs to be removed, temporarily set the carb in place for correct hose routing. Always use a new base gasket. If you're going to use a thick gasket, make sure it has a non-crushing insert to keep from overtightening the carb and warping or cracking the base plate. The carb bolts are torqued to 7 ft-lbs with a 1/2-inch socket.

Setting Distributor Height

Critical first step: Check installed distributor height. Many books on the market omit this step. If I save one engine with this step, I'll sleep well at night.

This preliminary check will keep you from wiping out your oil pump and bearings on start-up. Put a little cam lube on the drive gear. Lower the distributor into the distributor hole without the distributor cap or the distributor gasket in place. When the distributor shaft base gets close to the intake manifold's mounting boss the distributor may need a little turn so the gear meshes with the gear on the camshaft. You're not setting the timing, so don't worry about pointing the rotor in a specific direction. The second obstacle to ensure the distributor seats correctly is the oil pump driveshaft. It has a slot in the center of the shaft that has to mesh with the blade in the end of the distributor shaft. It takes some finesse to get them to line up correctly. If the distributor is still raised 1/4 inch, you need to lift the distributor and turn the shaft 1/16 of a turn clockwise by rotating the top plate (the flange on top of the distributor shaft where the weights and springs attach) or rotor while holding the distributor body. You may have to repeat the movement a few times until the distributor shaft meshes with the oil pump shaft. When it's seated, the distributor will either rest on the intake manifold or have less than 1/8-inch gap. Grab the distributor body with one hand and the top plate with your other hand. While holding the body down, pull up on the top plate. If the plate doesn't pull up, it is already bottomed out on the oil pump shaft. You will need a distributor shim kit, like the Mr. Gasket kit shown here, with three nylon shims (.030 inch, .060 inch, and .090 inch). Pull the distributor and re-install with a shim until you find which size you need. Do not stack distributor gaskets (in place of shims) to correct distributor height. The gaskets will compress over time and damage you engine components. Remove the distributor and pull the proper shim off the shaft. Apply a thin coat of gasket sealer between the distributor flange and distributor gasket to hold it in place, and then add the nylon shim (without sealer).

Install the distributor as far as it will go down against the intake manifold, without the gasket in place. If the gap is more than 1/8 inch, you don't have the distributor all the way down, somehow you have acquired a distributor for a truck block and are trying to install it in your passenger car block, or your block and heads have been shaved a lot.

If you have a gap between the distributor and the intake manifold, you need to install some shims to take up that space. Mr. Gasket and other companies sell specific nylon shims with thicknesses of .030 inch, .060 inch, and .090 inch. Use your feeler gauges to measure the gap and write the spec in your notes for future use. Add .030 inch to that measurement, and install the correct thickness shims to correct the distributor-to-manifold gap created by not using the gasket.

Ignition Components

Two designers from a missile range founded Autotronic Controls Corporation in 1970. They were working with partners to design lean-burning fuel systems to help fuel the economy of new and older cars. As they were working on the fuel system, they had to develop an ignition system to ignite the lean mixture because archaic breaker points ignition systems just couldn't handle the job. They developed Capacitive Technology (CD), which allowed for Multiple Spark Discharge (MSD) and hence the name of the company. The MSD ignition not only ignited the lean fuel system, it also improved the engine's performance by improving starting, idle, dropped emissions, and made more power. Trucks, automobiles, and racing cars were able to take advantage of this new system.

When it comes to ignition products, MSD Ignition is the first company that comes to mind because its products have made a name for themselves with top shelf parts made with only the best materials and the latest technology. MSD is always on the forefront of technology with an extensive R&D division. MSD's testing facility is constantly testing products on-site with a "shake-table"

to confirm its products can take 5 g of force; the punishment its parts may endure on an off-road racing truck or tire-shaking dragster. MSD also thermal loads its products to make sure they don't miss a beat in extreme temps from -60 degrees F to +275 degrees F. Testing is also done on vehicles that are flogged on its five on-site dynos. All this engineering, design, and testing ensures that its customers are only getting the best parts.

MSD Ignition produces just about any product associated with the automotive electrical system. This includes ignition control boxes for just about every automotive application, high-performance distributors, ignition coils, crank trigger systems, timing boxes, racing matgnetos, ignition tune-up accessories, ignition wires, fuel system components, alternators, starters, and more. With its huge R&D staff working in top-gear, MSD Ignition is constantly adding new parts to its catalog; so, I'm sure there are more new parts available since this book was written. To learn more about these products and ignition accessories in general and how they work, get a copy of *How to Build High Performance Ignition Systems* by Todd Ryden.

MSD offers many different distributors for the big-block Chevy. It is the distinguished holder of the No. 1 Selling Distributor in the World with the Pro-Billet Chevy distributor PN 85551. This distributor must be used with an MSD 6, 7, 8, or 10 Series Ignition box. MSD also offers a Pro-Billet Ready-To-Run distributor, which has its own internal ignition amplifier and does not require the additional MSD "box."

MSD has the coolest wire-crimping tool on the market; it's called Pro-Crimp Tool II. It's a ratcheting crimp tool that comes with the correct dies for stripping ignition wire and two crimping slots, one for a standard crimp and the additional slot for crimping the smaller section of MSD's Dual Crimp terminal. MSD also sells additional Pro-Crimp dies for crimping AMP, AMP Lugs, Deutsch, and Weathertight (Weather Pack) connectors.

Torque Fasteners

71 Install External Accessories

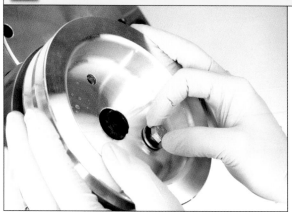

 Put some blue Loctite on the damper bolt threads and torque the bolt to 85 ft-lbs with a 13/16-inch socket and torque wrench. Wedge a clean 2 x 4 between the block and crank on the back end of the engine to hold the crank from spinning. Add blue Loctite to the three 9/16-inch lower crank pulley bolts and start them by hand, then torque them to 35 ft-lbs.

Unless you need the parts off the engine before installing it in the vehicle, install all remaining front accessories, including power steering pump, smog pump, alternator, pulleys, and fan. The original alternators were crusty and questionable, so they were replaced with some quality Powermaster units. When installing accessories, if you have doubts about how the accessories mount, check your detailed photos taken earlier. After pulleys are in place, install new fan belts. Be sure all your pulleys are aligned so you won't have fan belts flying off when driving. Mr. Gasket and Moroso sell shims to align water pump and crankshaft pulleys. Some other accessories can be shimmed out with washers for proper alignment.

72 Install Remaining Top Accessories

Refer back to your original pictures to correctly install the ignition system, route hoses, vacuum lines, and all the accessories on the carburetor, or else you'll have serious running issues. For break-in, you want the engine to fire right away and stay running without fussing with the tune or with vacuum leaks. Turning the engine on and off multiple times during break-in is extremely bad for flat tappet cams. Double check that all bolts and accessories are correctly installed and tight.

Torque Fasteners

73 Install Flywheel or Flexplate

 Once you've pulled your project off the engine stand, you can install the flywheel or flexplate. Put some ARP assembly lube on the bolt threads and under the head of the bolts and torque them to 70 ft-lbs. If you're installing anything other than ARP large-shouldered bolts here, make sure you're installing star-type lock washers. Brace the ring gear with a large screwdriver if you don't have the proper flywheel turning tool.

74 Install Starter

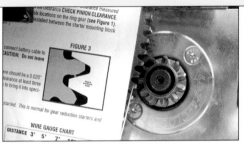

R *Your block may only be drilled for staggered mounting, but most have staggered and non-staggered bolt patterns. Confirm the starter fits the block and is correct for the ring gear (153- or 168-tooth). Our* original starter had seen better days, and we expect more cranking power is needed with this new higher-HP engine, so we are installing a Powermaster MasterTorque starter. This starter is designed to work with both ring gear sizes and has their Infi-Clock option, which allows the starter to be infinitely adjusted for the ultimate in clearance for tight headers. After the starter is installed, follow the instructions and engage the solenoid to mesh the teeth with the ring gear without spinning the starter. We were able to pull the gear out by hand (using some serious muscle). Check the gap between the flank of the ring gear and the starter pinion with a wire gauge. The gap should be between .020 inch and .025 inch. Check the gap in three positions on the ring gear. If necessary, you can change the gap by using the shim and instructions included with the starter.*

Stud Girdles

High-performance engines, with their additional valve spring pressures, high RPM, and aggressive camshaft profiles, produce extreme loads and stress on rocker studs and make the stud girdle necessary. The girdle gives rocker studs rigidity because it solidly mounts to the rocker, adjusting across all eight studs. The girdle greatly reduces valvetrain deflection, which translates into reduction in power loss and more horsepower for you.

Girdles also lock the adjusting nuts in place so they don't come loose. You can get the adjusting nuts as tight as possible (without going past their torque yield) and still have them vibrate loose. It's very annoying to be driving down the street or racing at the track and have a rocker arm come loose because an adjusting nut spontaneously backed off.

Big-block stud girdles require special, tall adjusting nuts for the girdle to lock onto. The drawback to the girdles are that they are a lot taller and don't fit under standard-height valve covers. Tall valve covers are required when using stud girdles.

Power output in high-performance engines suffers from rocker stud deflection induced by aggressive cam profiles, high valvespring pressures, and high RPM. These Jomar Performance girdles are the best way to reduce stud deflection, by rigidly locking all the studs together so your valvetrain can operate deflection-free.

These Ansen valve covers demonstrate valve cover heights. The standard height valve cover (left) does not fit over the stud girdle, but the tall valve cover (right) clears the stud girdle and adjusting nuts by a mile...well, by at least an inch. In some cases, the intake rocker arms for cylinders number-1 and 8 require some extra clearance on the valve covers around the bolt bosses.

START-UP

I covered some of the following items in the last chapter. As an extra precaution, though, they are being mentioned again. In the heat of the moment of wanting to fire your engine, it's easy to skip over a step or two by accident. The importance of slowing down, reviewing your plan, and making sure everything is done *before* firing the engine, can't be stressed enough. Even seasoned veterans occasionally forget some of these steps.

Lubrication

Check to make sure the oil filter is in place, the oil drain plug is tight, and the engine has enough oil. If you've skipped the pre-oiling step, it's easy to forget these and damage your engine or, at minimum, have the huge mess of a few quarts to clean up off the driveway.

Coolant

You should have connected the bypass hose between the water pump and the intake manifold, the heater

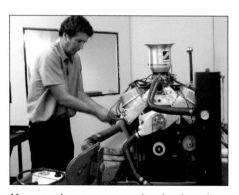

You can have your engine broken-in on the dyno like this. Robert Cancilla tests this big-block to be sure everything is in order. This way you know how the engine will perform without the hassle of installing it in your vehicle and finding out something is wrong. Dyno testing is done in a controlled environment by seasoned professionals.

Don't forget to put an oil filter on the engine. Many engine builders prefer the Wix 51069 or the racing version, Wix 51069R. Wix also offers taller versions if you have more space, the Wix 51794 and 51794R, which are 8.2 inches tall, and the 51069, which is 4.33 inches tall. The "R" series filters have thicker cases, spiral-wound center case for strength and better flow, and are individually sealed to keep contaminants out. Don't use the "R" series for break-in; stick one on after the engine is broken-in.

Don't forget to add oil! If you followed every step in this book, you have already added engine oil. If you've skipped some steps, don't forget to add oil...after you've installed the drain plug.

FilterMag

The FilterMag is one of the products that hit the market and make you think, "Why didn't I think of that first?" One of the worst things for your bearings is metal debris, and you'd be surprised how much of it is loose in your engine. Most of those particles are small enough that the oil filter mesh won't stop them. The FilterMag locks the harmful metal particles (smaller than 40 microns and down to 1 micron), which your filter cannot stop, to the case of the filter so they won't get re-circulated through your engine and bearings.

You should install one of these on every engine just to have peace of mind. It makes even more sense to put this product on a newly rebuilt engine; you can monitor how well you performed the rebuild right after the first couple of hundred miles of break in. If you find excessive shavings or large particles, you'll know that something has seriously gone wrong and you need to address it, but, if you only find what appears to be a small amount of fine metal sludge, you'll know things have gone well.

FilterMag is made up of a Zytel housing with steel shielding behind strong neodymium rare-earth magnets. They have an SS Series, which is for autos and light trucks with big-blocks (PN: SS365) with 160 lbs of approximate pulling force (magnetized to the oil filter), and they have the RA Series, which is for heavy duty and racing big-block applications (PN: RA365) with 600 lbs of pulling force. They also offer the TM and DM Series FilterMag series for automatic transmissions and differentials. You simply snap them on, use them, muscle them off the filter when you change it, and snap them onto the new filter. The FilterMags are completely re-usable.

Here is the amount of metal debris on my daily-driven stroker 433 big-block after a week of being attached to my filter. These are the sorts of metal particles that float around in an engine because you would never typically capture and pull them out during oil changes.

Put this on your engine before break-in to get a good idea of how your engine is performing after all the hard work you accomplished putting it together. The extremely strong rare-earth magnets attract metal fragments as small as 1-micron, when even the best filters only trap as small as 25 microns.

The best water you can pour into your radiator is distilled water because it has the least amount of cooling-system-damaging minerals. Filling your radiator with tap water or from a garden hose is just asking for trouble because of the minerals and foreign debris that can clog important coolant passages inside the engine.

hoses, coolant plugs in the block, heads and intake manifold, and the upper and lower radiator hoses. Once those are all connected, it's time to add coolant and water to the system. If you care about your engine, don't fill your radiator with tap water. It's really easy to grab the garden hose and add water, but fight the urge. Tap water is full of minerals that love to damage your system, and garden hoses are rarely free of bugs and debris. Tap water mineral content is different for every city. If your city tap water is "soft" (low mineral content) you can take your chances with your garden hose. For example, the water in San Jose, California, is so "hard" that my 12-month-old faucet looks like it's made of sandstone. You can be your own judge and take your chances. The best water to put in your cooling system is distilled water that you can purchase by the gallon at the grocery store.

If you are filling a system that you know is in good shape (hoses, heater core, radiator, etc.), you can confidently fill your system with a 50/50 mix of coolant and water. You can simply fill it with water only if your engine is going in a racecar or you have a hunch you may need to drain the fluid to repair the system.

There will be multiple air pockets in the system when you fill the cooling system. They give the false impression that the system is full. Big-blocks trap air in the cylinder head coolant passages. If you have a temp sender in the intake manifold next to the thermostat, you can eas-ily loosen it to release trapped air. Fill the radiator and allow it to transfer into the block multiple times before assuming the system is full. If you are on a steep driveway, be sure the front (radiator) end of vehicle is facing uphill. Don't forget to tighten the radiator cap before moving to the next step.

Throttle

Make sure the throttle cable is connected and that there are two throttle return springs. The second is a safety spring. I've seen return springs break, causing the engine to rev uncontrollably. Think of the second spring as an insurance policy.

Wires and Hoses

Connect all the wires and hoses to your engine by referencing your photos (or diagrams) and the labels on the wires. If any labels fell off, connect the ones with labels and focus on the leftover connections. Over time, wires and hoses form "memory," and they usually lay close to where they were connected. Many

Throttle springs are nothing to get cheap on because these are important safety devices. You should always use two throttle return springs. The second one is a backup. Springs break, so don't leave yourself open to the hazard of having a spring break and over-revving your engine. I've heard of many cars getting wrecked and people being maimed because a spring broke and a backup spring had not been installed.

1 Install Fuel Lines

If you're upgrading the performance of your engine, you need to consider the amount of fuel your system can deliver to the carburetor.

A 6-cylinder 1960s muscle car had 5/16-inch-diameter fuel lines. The 3/8-inch fuel lines fed the standard big-block V-8s, and 5/16-inch lines will starve the big-block, causing piston-damaging lean conditions. Any carbureted application making more than 500 hp should upgrade to 1/2-inch fuel line and 5/8-inch line if more than 750 hp, to be safe. Contact Aeromotive Fuel Systems or Barry Grant for suggested fuel system design and upgrades.

older cars came with the factory-equipped idiot lights instead of water temp and oil-pressure gauges. Keep better tabs on your new engine and install some more precise gauges. If you're connecting a mechanical oil pressure gauge, you're much better off installing copper tubing instead of the nylon tubing they supply. If the nylon burns through on something hot, you'll start pumping oil out of your engine. Copper tubing is much more reliable.

Grounds

Don't forget to make sure you have at least two ground cables connecting the engine to the chassis or body. Without them, you are asking for starting issues.

Accessories and Belts

If you haven't done so yet, install the last of the leftover accessories. Check the belts for damage and signs of aging. Replace them if necessary. Tighten the belts, but realize new belts will stretch a little and usually require re-adjustment after the engine has been running for a few hours.

Fuel

An engine won't work without fuel to ignite. Make sure the fuel lines are in good shape, are connected properly, and are the proper size for your application. If your vehicle wasn't factory equipped with a big-block, the fuel lines may be too small for your new requirements. Even big-block-equipped vehicles have 3/8-inch fuel lines, which may be too small for your new engine. The 496 engine is going to easily pro-

duce more than 550 hp. A 5/8-inch line feeds the Barry Grant 850 cfm carb and a 3/8-inch line returns to the tank. A 5/16-inch feed line is too small for a 375-hp big-block. Check your line size. A new fuel filter is a good idea and can be had for very little investment, depending on what you want. If they have a specific flow direction, there will be an arrow on the housing; so, pay attention.

Don't overlook the fuel in your fuel tank. If your car hasn't been running for a few months, and the fuel hasn't been treated with fuel stabilizer, the fuel has probably turned to shellac and isn't going to ignite well. It would be ridiculous to try to run your new engine on garbage. Do yourself a favor and siphon the old fuel out of the tank. If that garbage doesn't ignite, you're going to spend time trying to figure it out

If your vehicle has been sitting for a while, it's possible your battery has lost its charge. Check the voltage with a tester to confirm you have 12 volts. When you're all done assembling your engine, a dead battery is an irritating obstacle. Be prepared with the correct voltage. If there's plenty of voltage and the car won't turn over, there's something wrong. If something is lodged in the combustion chamber it keeps the car from turning over; so look at all possibilities if the car won't turn over.

and after a few turns of the starter all the assembly grease will be wiped off your cam lobes. Then, you're at high risk of flattening your cam on break-in. The engine needs to run *right away* and run continuously for 15 to 20 minutes for best break-in results. Put at least five gallons of fuel in the tank. The five gallons should safely get you through your break-in period and some test driving. If you add less fuel and run out of gas during break-in, you're asking for problems.

If you have an electric pump, disconnect the fuel line just before the carburetor and stick it in a fuel can and turn the electric pump on, without starting the car. This will get as much debris out of the line as possible, so it won't get into your carburetor. If you have a mechanical pump, you'd have to siphon the fuel up to the front of the vehicle.

Battery

Does it have a charge? If you have electronic ignition, you're going to need at least 11 of your 12 volts to start. Any less and you may not get your ignition to fire, unless you're using a points-type ignition. Is your battery in good condition? In some cases a battery can have a 12-volt charge, but have a bad cell that causes starting gremlins. If you have doubts about the condition of your battery, take it to a shop you trust and have them test it. If you're building a performance engine, you may consider upgrading to a performance battery like an Optima or PowerMaster.

Battery Cable

Connecting the battery is the last task when working on any part having to do with electrical

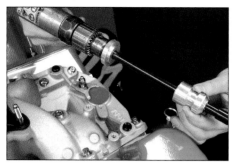

Before firing the engine, prime the oil pump one last time, especially if your engine has been sitting for a few days since the last time you primed the system. The worst thing for bearings, the cam, and the lifters is to be started dry. Don't take the chance of flattening your cam on start-up. This oil-system priming tool is only to be used when the intake manifold is installed, because of distributor gear clearances. It has an aluminum bushing that acts as a distributor housing and redirects the oil up to the camshaft oil galleries. The top bushing sets on the intake manifold.

connections. Connect the positive connection to the battery first, then the negative cable.

Pre-Oil Engine

It's time to pre-oil your engine if it's been more than seven days since you assembled your engine or if you skipped the pre-oiling step at the end of the previous chapter. Loosen the distributor and pull it out of the engine. Grab your drill and clean all the dirt and debris off its body and out of the drill chuck because metal and wood shavings love to get up into the drill chuck and fall into your engine. Insert the oil-priming tool into the drill. Insert the primer into the engine and line it up with the intermediate oil shaft. Set the drill to turn clockwise. Prime the

engine for 30 seconds. Depending on the power of your drill, you should get decent oil pressure at your oil pressure gauge while using the oil primer. Crane Cams notes that big-block Chevy engines are notorious for taking a long time to fully prime. They say it can take as much as 20 minutes, while rotating the crankshaft periodically, in order to get oil all the way up to all the lifters.

Distributor Reset

If you had to pre-oil your engine, you're going to need to re-time your engine and set the distributor back on TDC. Use the timing information in "Initial Timing" to perform this task properly. Remove the valve cover over number-1 cylinder to confirm the valves are closed while the piston is at TDC. This is not the time to take chances and accidentally re-install the distributor off by 180 degrees. During every rotation of the engine (trying to get it started) the lifters are pushing the assembly paste off the lobe. That paste is protection against intense friction. Cams and lifters get damaged while people try to get their engines started.

Transmission

If you have an automatic transmission from which fluid has been drained, you'll need to add more to keep it from burning up on break-in. Consult your local transmission shop for fluid advice on your specific transmission. The fluid level doesn't have to be perfect upon break-in but don't overfill it. Once you're done breaking in the camshaft and lifters, you can drop the idle and get the transmission fluid level correct.

Manual transmissions should

have the fluid topped off properly before firing the engine. Don't forget to do it before you drive off for your maiden voyage.

Initial Timing

With the distributor set in the instructed, correct position, go ahead and slightly rotate the damper to align the zero mark on the harmonic damper with the 12-degree before top dead center (BTDC) mark on the timing tab. Hook up all the ignition wiring, distributor cap, ignition rotor, and spark plug wires. Pull the number-1 spark plug out of the head (or you can use a spare spark plug) and connect it to the end of the number-1 spark plug wire. Ground the spark plug to a known ground. Loosen the distributor hold-down fastener enough that you can easily turn the body of the distributor. Without starting the car, turn the ignition on to energize the coil. Be careful not to shock yourself or move the distributor body clockwise and counterclockwise until you see the spark jump the spark plug electrode. As soon as the spark jumps, stop moving the distributor and snug the hold-down fastener down tight enough to hold the distributor in place (so it can't turn by itself when the engine is running), but not so tight that you can't rotate it with a little muscle. Now your ignition timing is set at approximately 12-degrees BTDC, which is accurate enough to get your car started for break-in. You can reset the timing with a timing gun later after you get the car started.

Pick Up Your Mess

Your parents tell you that a few times while you are growing up.

They were just trying to get you ready for rebuilding your big-block Chevy. Remove all the tools from your engine compartment right before you fire your engine. Tools tend to fall off of fender wells and radiator supports when the engine is running. The last thing you need is a screwdriver rolling into your fan and maiming you or your radiator. Make sure there aren't any tools or items resting on the headers or exhaust manifolds. Confirm that the cooling fan is not obstructed and is in good working order.

Put your tools on your workbench or a place nearby so you can access them if necessary. There's a good chance you'll need access to a standard screwdriver and a couple of wrenches during break-in.

Flat Tappet Cam Break-In Process

The camshaft and lifters need to go through a process of "mating-in" with each other. The lifters rotate while they glide on the face of the cam lobes to complete the "mate-in" process. The camshaft lobes are machined with a slight taper and the lifter's site slightly off-center, this and initial high RPM induce lifter rotation. If the lifters don't rotate, they simply grind into the camshaft and quickly turn into thousands of metal shavings in your oil. The damaged lifters also grind the lobes off the cam, and valve lift decreases. Without the ramps on the lobes, the cam is considered "flat." Having the RPM over 2,500 helps the lifters turn so they can mate-in to the camshaft properly. The first 20 minutes of running is the most important for flat tappet cams, hydraulic or mechanical.

Every camshaft manufacturer has a slightly different RPM and length of time required for proper cam and lifter break-in. The general rule is to start the engine and immediately adjust the idle to more than 2,500 rpm. The break-in period is typically around 25 minutes long. Over that time, the idle is very gradually lowered and raised from 1,500 rpm to 3,000 rpm. Every manufacturer has a different version of this process and you should read the information included with your camshaft. The information written here is only a general idea of what the camshaft break-in procedure will be.

Fire It Up!

Now for the moment you've been waiting for. Don't get ahead of yourself and relax yet; every engine needs two key things to run: fuel and fire. If you've followed all the steps, you should have plenty of fuel that can get to the engine, all your ignition parts installed, and the battery fully charged to power the spark or "fire." Keep in mind that the best scenario is to start the car on the first try and to keep it running for the initial break-in period.

In order to safely break in the engine, it's good to have at least one other person helping you watch the gauges for oil pressure, make sure the coolant temperature stays in the safe zone, look for oil and water leaks under the vehicle, and listen for strange noises. It's always safer to have two sets of eyes and ears focused on the break-in process.

If you hear concerning sounds or see a problem at any point during the break-in process, shut the engine off immediately. After you've addressed the problem, re-start the

engine and continue the break-in procedure.

The first thing to do after starting the engine is to get the RPM to the suggested level. Open the throttle to reach the correct RPM and adjust the idle screw on the carb until the engine sustains the break-in RPM. When you fire up the engine, it's not going to be timed correctly. You're going to need to turn the distributor to correct the timing soon after initially firing the engine. If you don't, the engine could get damaged. At sustained break-in RPM, it can start overheating within a few minutes and cause the headers to glow red unless you correct the timing. There's no way to use your timing light during this time, so you'll have to time it by ear. Slowly turn the distributor until the RPM starts to climb and the engine is running effortlessly and then turn the distributor slightly clockwise to retard the timing. Correct the idle and continue monitoring everything. Once the suggested period of break-in time has passed, lower the idle to a normal operating level and set the timing and tune.

Roller Cam Break-In

Breaking in a roller cam is much easier than a flat tappet cam because the lifters roll on the cam lobe and don't need to "mate-in" with the cam. Follow the instructions that come with your roller cam. Basically, you fire the engine and keep the idle at about 1,500 rpm for a few minutes while you check for oil pressure, leaks and noises, adjust the idle back down to normal, and then set the timing and tune.

Camshaft Break-In

Once the engine is shut off, let it cool. Check for leaks and loose hose clamps, hardware, belts, and accessories. Check the oil level and check to make sure there isn't any white foam in the crankcase. If there is, water has somehow mixed with the oil and needs to be addressed right away. It could be water getting past the head bolt threads under the valve covers, or, it could be something more serious such as a crack in a head or the block. Pull the valve covers and look for beads of water around the valve springs. When you shut off a hot engine, pressure in the cooling system increases and coolant will try to find its way out. Check the coolant for oil residue when the radiator cools enough to safely remove the radiator cap. If the oil and coolant are in good shape you're ready to move on. If you have an automatic transmission, start the car and check the fluid level. Top off the fluid level if it is low.

Crane Cams suggests changing the oil and filter after camshaft break-in and installing fresh non-synthetic oil for the first 500 miles of engine break-in. For the rest of the next 5,000 miles of break-in, they suggest running non-synthetic oil. They consider 5,000 miles enough to fully seat the rings properly and synthetic oils can then be introduced.

Break In the Rest

Before hitting the streets at full-throttle, you need to take it easy for the first 500 miles in order to make sure the piston rings seal with the cylinder walls. Without seating the rings correctly you will be plagued with low vacuum, blow-by, and loss of power potential. Take your vehicle out on the highway and drive it, without racing the engine, at highway speeds. Gradually fluctuate between the speed limit and slower speeds. Pull onto off-ramps to decelerate multiple times to promote ring seating under load and deceleration.

Tuning

After the car has run for a few hundred miles, the rings start to seat and the tune needs to be adjusted and refined. The Barry Grant carburetor installed on the high-performance 496 engine came with a very informative DVD on how to tune your carburetor. If you want to know more about tuning your carburetor, CarTech's S-A Design series offers tuning books on almost all carburetors on the market. They are a valuable resource and will be great for reference for years to come. There's a good chance you'll be making many changes on your car now that you've got a taste of the rewards of building your own engine, and just about every change can require a carb adjustment.

The best tuning tool on the market, without having your car strapped to a dynamometer, is the handheld Innovate Motorsports air/fuel ratio meter. They offer a few different models. Some are stand-alone units and some have data logging and can be hooked up to a laptop computer for additional features. It reads the air/fuel ratio by hooking up to an oxygen sensor plugged into your exhaust system. This gives the user the ability to tune the carburetor and determine how the engine is running.

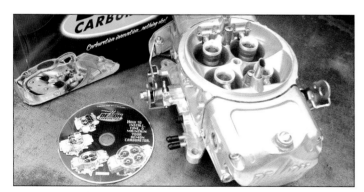

Barry Grant carburetors come with a DVD to show you how to install your new carb, tips on tuning, and some trouble shooting advice. This DVD is a huge help. This technology has come a long way since the 1980s, when you bought a carburetor and you were on your own.

This hand-held air/fuel ratio meter is almost like having your own personal dyno. The LM-1 is a wideband sensor controller and six-channel data logger for tuning carbureted and fuel-injected engines. Hook it to your laptop for graphic interface of full readout of how your engine is truly performing, so you can make effective changes to your fuel delivery. One of the many accessories is the LMA-2 RPM Converter. It converts your engines tach signal so the LM-1 can store the signal as data input and be read on your laptop.

Torque Specifications for Fasteners

Recommended Torque to Achieve Optimum Preload (Clamping Force) Using ARP Moly Assembly Lubricant or 30-wt. oil - Torque (ft./lbs.) - Preload (lbs.)								
Note: For those using Newton/meters as a torquing reference, you must multiply the appropriate ft./lbs. factor by 1.356.								
	Fastener Tensile Strength (PSI)								
	170,000/180,000 (1,171 N/mm²)			190,000/200,000 (1,309 N/mm²)			220,000 (1,515 N/mm²)		
Thread Size and Type	**Torque w/30 wt. oil** *not recommended*	**Torque w/ARP Moly**	**Preload**	**Torque w/30 wt. oil** *not recommended*	**Torque w/ARP Moly**	**Preload**	**Torque w/30 wt. oil** *not recommended*	**Torque w/ARP Moly**	**Preload**
1/4″ stud	12	10	3,804	14	11	4,280	15	12	4,755
1/4-20	13	10	3,804	14	11	4,280	16	13	4,755
1/4-28	14	11	4,344	16	13	4,887	18	14	5,430
5/16″ stud	25	20	6,264	28	22	7,047	32	25	7,830
5/16-18	26	21	6,264	29	23	7,047	32	26	7,830
5/16-24	28	22	6,948	32	25	7,817	35	28	8,685
3/8″ stud	45	35	9,276	50	39	10,436	56	44	11,595
3/8-16	46	36	9,276	51	41	10,436	57	45	11,595
3/8-24	50	39	10,512	57	44	11,826	63	49	13,140
7/16″ stud	71	56	12,720	80	63	14,310	89	70	15,900
7/16-14	73	58	12,720	82	65	14,310	91	72	15,900
7/16-20	80	62	14,220	90	70	15,998	100	78	17,775
1/2″ stud	108	84	16,992	122	95	19,116	135	105	21,240
1/2-13	111	88	16,992	125	99	19,116	138	110	21,240
1/2-20	122	95	19,164	137	107	21,560	152	119	23,955
9/16″ stud	156	122	21,792	175	137	24,516	195	152	27,240
9/16-12	159	126	21,792	179	142	24,516	199	158	27,240
9/16-18	174	136	24,312	196	153	27,351	217	170	30,390
5/8″ stud	214	167	27,072	241	187	30,456	268	208	33,840
5/8-11	220	174	27,072	247	196	30,456	275	217	33,840
5/8-18	243	189	30,660	273	212	34,493	303	236	38,325
8mm stud	25	20	6,250	28	22	7,050	32	25	7,830
8mm x 1.25	25	20	6,250	28	22	7,050	32	25	7,830
10mm stud	54	42	10,600	70	60	12,015	75	65	13,350
10mm x 1.25	54	42	10,600	70	60	12,015	75	65	13,350
10mm x 1.50	50	38	9,500	72	63	12,510	77	68	13,760
11mm stud	80	63	14,220	90	71	15,998	100	79	17,775
12mm stud	97	77	15,540	109	86	17,483	122	96	19,425

Intake Manifold Torque Sequence

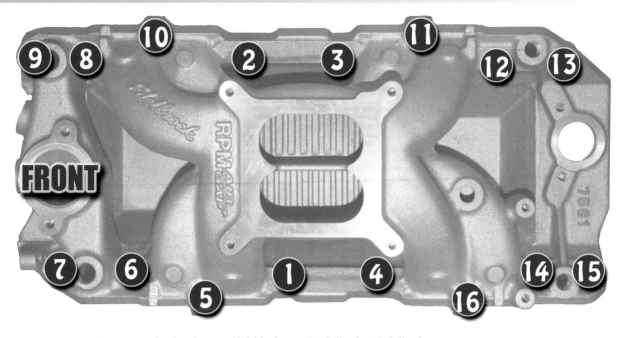

Use this torque sequence to torque the intake manifold bolts to 30 ft-lbs in 10 ft-lbs increments.

Piston Orientation for Assembly

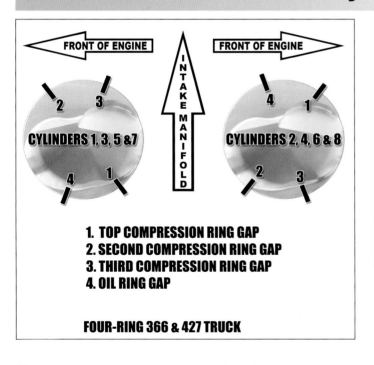

1. TOP COMPRESSION RING GAP
2. SECOND COMPRESSION RING GAP
3. THIRD COMPRESSION RING GAP
4. OIL RING GAP

FOUR-RING 366 & 427 TRUCK

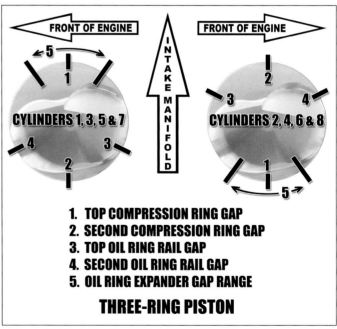

1. TOP COMPRESSION RING GAP
2. SECOND COMPRESSION RING GAP
3. TOP OIL RING RAIL GAP
4. SECOND OIL RING RAIL GAP
5. OIL RING EXPANDER GAP RANGE

THREE-RING PISTON

Pistons and rings must be correctly oriented for proper installation. Follow the appropriate illustration for your particular engine.

Bearing Cap Torque Sequence

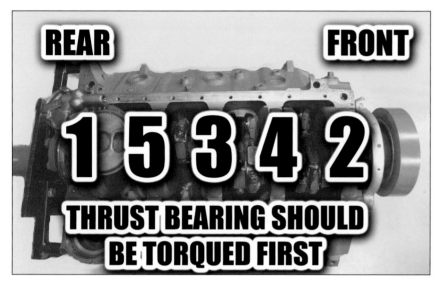

Place the main caps on the block in their designated registers and with all their arrows facing the front of the engine, and make sure they fit down into their registers. Next, torque main bearing caps according to the sequence in this photo.

Firing Order

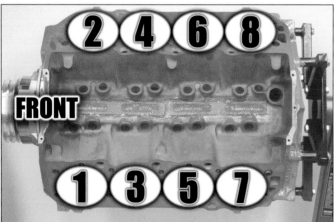

At the top is the firing order; at the botton is the location of cylinders number -1 through 8.

Timing Chain and Gear Alignment

The timing marks on the cam and crank sprockets should be lined up as shown.

Torque Specifications for Engine Fasteners

Big Block Chevy Mark IV -Fastener Torque Specifications				
Fasteners	Torque Rating	Lubricant/Sealant	Torque Rating	Lubricant/Sealant
	Factory FastenersW/30WT Oil		ARP Fasteners Used In Book	
Cam Bolts	20 ft-lbs	Permatex Red Loctite	20 ft-lbs	Permatex Red Loctite
Carb Bolts	8 ft-lbs	30 WT Oil	8 ft-lbs	ARP Assembly Lube
Distributor Hold-Down Bolt	25 ft-lbs	30 WT Oil	20 ft-lbs	Permatex Anti Seize
Exhaust Header Bolts	N/A	N/A	20 ft-lbs	Permatex Anti Seize
Exhaust Manifold Bolts (iron)	25 ft-lbs	Permatex Anti Seize	N/A	N/A
Flex Plate Bolts	60 ft-lbs	30 WT Oil	60 ft-lbs	Permatex Blue Loctite
Flywheel Bolts	60 ft-lbs	30 WT Oil	60 ft-lbs	Permatex Blue Loctite
Fuel Pump Bolts	30 ft-lbs	30 WT Oil	30 ft-lbs	ARP Thread Sealant
Harmonic Damper Bolt	85 ft-lbs	30 WT Oil	85 ft-lbs	Permatex Blue Loctite
Head Bolts	75 ft-lbs	Permatex Super 300	N/A	N/A
Head Studs (nuts)	N/A	N/A	70 ft-lbs	ARP Assembly Lube
Head Studs (threads in block)	N/A	N/A	Hand Tight Only	Permatex Super 300
Intake Manifold Bolts	25 ft-lbs	ARP Thread Sealant	30 ft-lbs	ARP Thread Sealant
Main Bolts 2-Bolt (iron block)	95 ft-lbs	30 WT Oil	N/A	N/A
Main Bolts 4-Bolt (iron block)	110 ft-lbs	30 WT Oil	N/A	N/A
Main Studs 2-Bolt (iron block)	N/A	N/A	100 ft-lbs	ARP Assembly Lube
Main Studs 4-Bolt (inner) (iron)	N/A	N/A	100 ft-lbs	ARP Assembly Lube
Main Studs 4-Bolt (outer) (iron)	N/A	N/A	45 ft-lbs	ARP Assembly Lube
Main Studs (threads in block)	N/A	N/A	Hand Tight Only	ARP Assembly Lube
Oil Filter Adapter	13 ft-lbs	30 WT Oil	13 ft-lbs	30 WT Oil
Oil Pan Bolts (except 2 front)	12 ft-lbs	30 WT Oil	12 ft-lbs	ARP Assembly Lube
Oil Pan Bolts (2 front)	6 ft-lbs	30 WT Oil	7 ft-lbs	ARP Assembly Lube
Oil Pump Mounting Bolt	65 ft-lbs	30 WT Oil	N/A	N/A
Oil Pump Mounting Stud	N/A	N/A	56 ft-lbs (nut)	ARP Assembly Lube
Oil Pump Cover Bolts	10 ft-lbs	Permatex Red Loctite	10 ft-lbs	Permatex Red Loctite
Rocker Arm Studs	50 ft-lbs	30 WT Oil	55 ft-lbs	ARP Thread Sealant
Rod Bolts 3/8"	50 ft-lbs	30 WT Oil	N/A	N/A
Rod Bolts 7/16"	70 ft-lbs	30 WT Oil	Eagle Rod Cap-screw 63 ft-lbs	ARP Assembly Lube
Spark Plug (tapered seat)	15 ft-lbs	Permatex Anti Seize	15 ft-lbs	Permatex Anti Seize
Spark Plug (gasketed seat)	15 ft-lbs	Permatex Anti Seize	15 ft-lbs	Permatex Anti Seize
Thermostat Housing Bolts	25 ft-lbs	ARP Thread Sealant	25 ft-lbs	ARP Thread Sealant
Timing Chain Cover Bolts	6 ft-lbs	30 WT Oil	6 ft-lbs	ARP Assembly Lube
Valve Cover Bolts	3 ft-lbs (stamped steel covers)	30 WT Oil	5 ft-lbs (cast valve covers)	ARP Assembly Lube
Water Pump Bolts	30 ft-lbs	ARP Thread Sealant	30 ft-lbs	ARP Thread Sealant

Torque Specifications for Engine Fasteners

Year	Displacement	RPO	Carburetor	Horsepower	Torque	Compression Ratio	Application
1965	396	L35	4V	325@4,800	410@3,200	10	Chevrolet
1965	396	L78	4V	425@6,400	415@4,000	11	Chevrolet
1965	396	L78	4V	425@6,400	415@4,000	11	Corvette
1965	396	L37	4V	375@5,600	415@3,600	11	Z16 Chevelle
1966	396	L35	4V	325@4,800	410@4,800	10.25	Chevrolet/Chevelle
1966	396	L34	4V	360@5,200	415@3,400	10.25	Chevelle
1966	396	L78	4V	375@5,600	415@3,600	11	Chevelle
1966	427	L36	4V	390@5,200	470@3,600	10.25	Chevrolet/Corvette
1966	427	L72	4V	425@5,600	460@3,600	11	Chevrolet/Corvette
1967	396	L35	4V	325@4,800	410@3,200	10.25	Chevrolet/Chevelle
1967	396	L34	4V	350@5,200	415@3,400	10.25	Chevelle/Camaro
1967	396	L78	4V	375@5,600	415@3,600	11	Chevelle/Camaro
1967	427	L36	4V	390@5,200	460@3,600	10.25	Chevrolet/Corvette
1967	427	L68	3x2V	400@5,400	460@3,600	10.25	Corvette
1967	427	L72	4V	425@5,600	460@4,000	11	Chevrolet
1967	427	L71	3x2V	435@5,800	460@4,000	11	Corvette
1967	427	L88	4V	430@4,600	485@4,000	12.5	Corvette
1967	427<1>	L89	4V	435@5,800	460@4,000	11	Corvette
1968	396	L35	4V	325@4,800	410@3,200	10.25	Camaro/
1968	396	L34	4V	350@5,200	415@3,400	10.25	Chevrolet/Chevelle
1968	396	L78	4V	375@5,600	415@3,600	11	Nova/Camaro/
1968	396<1>	L89	4V	375@5,600	415@3,600	11	Camaro/Chevelle
1968	427	L72	4V	425@6,400	460@4,000	11	Camaro/Nova
1968	427	L36	4V	390@5,400	460@3,600	11	Chevrolet
1968	427	L68	4V	400@5,400	460@3,600	10.25	Corvette
1968	427	L71	3x2V	435@5,800	460@4,000	11	Corvette
1968	427	L88	4V	430@4,600	485@4,000	12.5	Corvette
1968	427<1>	L89	3x2V	435@5,800	460@4,000	11	Corvette
1969	396	L35	4V	325@4,000	410@3,200	10.25	Camaro/Chevelle
1969	396	L34	4V	350@5,200	415@3,400	10.25	Chevelle/Camaro/Nova
1969	396	L78	4V	375@5,600	415@3,600	11	Chevelle/Camaro/Nova
1969	396<1>	L89	4V	375@5,600	415@3,600	11	Chevelle/Camaro
1969	427	L36	4V	390@5,400	460@3,600	10.25	Chevrolet/Corvette
1969	427	L72	4V	425@5,600	460@4,000	11	Chevrolet/Corvette
1969	427	LS1	4V	400@5,400	460@3,600	10.25	Chevrolet
1969	427	L72	4V	425@5,600	460@4,000	11	Chevelle<2>
1969	427	L68	4V	400@5,400	460@3,600	10.25	Corvette
1969	427	L71	3x2V	435@5,800	460@4,000	11	Corvette
1969	427	L88	4V	430@5,200	450@4,400	12	Corvette
1969	427<1>	L89	4V	435@5,800	460@4,000	11	Corvette
1969	427	ZL1	4V	425@5,600	460@4,000	12	Camaro<3>
1969	427	ZL1	4V	430@5,200	450@4,400	12	Corvette
1970	396/402	L34	4V	350@5,200	415@3,400	10.25	Camaro/Chevelle/ Nova
1970	396/402	L78	4V	375@5,600	415@3,600	11	Camaro/Chevelle/ Nova
1970	400	LS3	4V	330@4,800	410@3,200	10.25	Chevelle
1970	454	LS5	4V	390@4,800	500@3,400	10.25	Corvette
1970	454	LS6	4V	450@5,600	500@3,600	11.25	Camaro
1970	402<1>	L89	4V	375@5,600	415@3,600	11	Chevelle
1970	454	LS5	4V	360@5,400	500@3,200	10.25	Chevelle
1970	454	LS6	4V	450@5,600	500@3,200	11.25	Chevelle
1970	454	LS6	4V	460@5,600	490@3,600	11.25	Corvette
1971	402	LS3	4V	300@4,800	400@3200	8.5	Chevrolet
1971	454	LS5	4V	365@4,800	465@3,200	8.5	Chevrolet
1971	454	LS6	4V	425@5,600	475@4,000	9	Chevelle/Monte Carlo/Corvette
1972	402<4>	LS3	4V	240@4,400	345@3,200	8.5	Monte Carlo/Chevelle/ Camaro
1972	402<4>	LS5	4V	270@4,000	390@3,200	8.5	Chevelle/Chevrolet/
1973	454<4>	LS4	4V	275@4,400	395@2,800	8.5	Monte Carlo/Corvette
1974	454<4>	LS4	4V	235@4,000	360@2,800	8.5	Chevrolet/Monte Carlo/Chevelle
1974	454<4>	LS4	4V	270@4,400	380@2,800	8.5	Corvette

<1> Aluminum head engine

<2>COPO 9562, 9566, 9694 produced 430@5,200 or 450hp@4,400

<3> COPO 9561, 9560

<4>SAE net horsepower and torque

APPENDIX B: WORK-A-LONG SHEETS

DISASSEMBLY

Project Statistics

Your Name _____ Today's Date_____

Vehicle Engine Removed From _____ Engine Year _____

CI/L _____ RPO _____

Accessories Attached to Used Engine

❏ A/C Pump   ❏ AIR Pump   ❏ AIR Lines and Hoses   ❏ Water Pump   ❏ Flywheel   ❏ Clutch   ❏ Flexplate

❏ Transmission   ❏ Starter   ❏ Fuel Rails/Injectors   ❏ All Pulleys; Except _____   ❏ Alternator

❏ Coils   ❏ Intake Manifold   ❏ Exhaust Manifolds   ❏ Motor Mounts   ❏ Motor Mount Attaching Brackets

❏ Spark Plug Heat Shields   ❏ EGR Valve   ❏ Dipstick Tube ❏ All Bolts; except _____

❏ _____   ❏ _____   ❏ Items Attached to Intake Manifold (brackets, etc) _____

_____

Operational Notes

Oil consumption _____ Compression check pressure variation _____ psi

Leak-down percent _____ Other observations _____

_____

Disassembly Notations

Head gaskets   ❏ MLS   ❏ Graphite-layered

Worn/damaged lifters   ❏ No   ❏ Yes; where _____

Cam sensor location   ❏ Rear of block   ❏ Front cover

Knock sensor location   ❏ Valley   ❏ Sides of block

Coolant air bleed pipe style _____

Clutch pilot bearing present   ❏ Yes   ❏ No

Valve seal/spring seat style   ❏ 1-Piece   ❏ 2-Piece

Cylinder head plug/sensor locations _____

M11 head bolt style   ❏ All-same length   ❏ Short/long

Other signs of damage _____

INSPECTION

Initial Parts Inspection Observations

Block OK   ❏ Yes   ❏ No; describe problem _____

Heads OK   ❏ Yes   ❏ No; describe problem _____

Crank OK   ❏ Yes   ❏ No; describe problem _____

Bearings OK   ❏ Yes   ❏ No; describe problem _____

Pistons OK   ❏ Yes   ❏ No; describe problem _____

Cam/lifters OK   ❑ Yes   ❑ No; describe problem _____

Damper OK   ❑ Yes   ❑ No; describe problem _____

Intake manifold OK   ❑ Yes   ❑ No; describe problem _____

Exhaust manifold OK   ❑ Yes   ❑ No; describe problem _____

Oil pump OK   ❑ Yes   ❑ No; describe problem _____

Main cap mating surfaces damage/abnormalities   ❑ No   ❑ Yes

Identifying marks you placed on any parts (Non-intrusive method only!) _____

AT THE MACHINE SHOP

Parts Delivered to the Machine Shop

❑ Block   ❑ Main Caps   ❑ Crankshaft   ❑ Oil Pump   ❑ Oil Pump Pickup   ❑ Connecting Rods

❑ Pistons   ❑ Piston Rings   ❑ Camshaft   ❑ Lifters   ❑ Damper   ❑ Main Bearings

❑ Rod Bearings   ❑ Cam Bearings   ❑ Rod Bolts   ❑ Gasket Set   ❑ Pushrods   ❑ Rocker Arms

❑ Head Bolts   ❑ Main Bolts/Studs   ❑ Miscellaneous Nuts/Bolts/Brackets for Cleaning   ❑ Water Pump

❑ Timing Cover   ❑ Oil Pan   ❑ Flywheel/Flexplate   ❑ Clutch   ❑ Exhaust Manifolds

❑ Motor Mounts   ❑ Motor Mount Attaching Brackets   ❑ Assembled Heads

❑ Disassembled Heads with: ❑ Valves ❑ Springs ❑ Retainers ❑ Keepers

❑ Intake Manifold

❑ _____   ❑ _____   ❑ _____   ❑ _____   ❑ _____

Special Instructions for Machine Shop

❑ Bore block   ❑ Hone Block   ❑ Desired piston-to-wall clearance: 0._____-inch   ❑ Grind crank

❑ Desired rod bearing clearance: 0._____-inch   ❑ Desired main bearing clearance: 0._____-inch   ❑ Resurface block

❑ Resurface heads   ❑ Install cam bearings   ❑ Gap piston rings   ❑ Assemble cylinder heads

Is pilot bushing to be installed in crankshaft (required for manual transmission)?   ❑ Yes   ❑ No

After You Pick Up Your Parts

❑ Yes ❑ No   Threaded holes reconditioned/chased   ❑ Yes ❑ No   Cam bearings installed

❑ Yes ❑ No   Plugs installed (coolant/oil gallery)   ❑ Yes ❑ No   Crank keys installed

PRE-ASSEMBLY FITTING

Measured and Recorded During Pre-Assembly Fitting

Measured valvespring installed height:

1 _____   3 _____   5 _____   7 _____

2 _____   4 _____   6 _____   8 _____

Spring shims used to obtain correct installed height:

1 _____   3 _____   5 _____   7 _____

2 _____   4 _____   6 _____   8 _____

Measured valvespring coil bind height _____ -inches

Calculated compressed valvespring clearance:

1 _____   3 _____   5 _____   7 _____

2 _____   4 _____   6 _____   8 _____

Reluctor ring runout OK? ❑ Yes ❑ No Measured runout of 0. _____ -inch

Crank straightness OK? ❑ Yes ❑ No Runout on center main of 0. _____ -inch

Main bearing clearance OK? ❑ Yes ❑ No Measured clearance 0. _____ -inch

Crank thrust OK? ❑ Yes ❑ No Measured clearance 0. _____ -inch

Camshaft bearing fit OK? ❑ Yes ❑ No; Describe problem _____

Piston–to-wall clearance OK? ❑ Yes ❑ No Measured clearance 0. _____ -inch

    Pistons with incorrect clearance _____

Measured ring end gap:

1 Top _____ 2nd _____ 3 Top _____ 2nd _____ 5 Top _____ 2nd _____ 7 Top _____ 2nd _____

2 Top _____ 2nd _____ 4 Top _____ 2nd _____ 6 Top _____ 2nd _____ 8 Top _____ 2nd _____

Rod bearing clearance OK? ❑ Yes ❑ No Measured clearance 0. _____ -inch

Rod side clearance OK? ❑ Yes ❑ No Measured clearance 0. _____ -inch

Piston-to-head clearance OK? ❑ Yes ❑ No Measured clearance 0. _____ -inch

    Cylinders with incorrect clearance _____

Adjustable crank sprocket keyway used: ❑ + – 2 ❑ + – 4 ❑ + – 6 ❑ + – 8 ❑ + – 10 ❑ + – 12

Rotating assembly clearance OK? ❑ Yes ❑ No; Cause of interference_____

Rocker geometry OK? ❑ Yes ❑ No; Describe problem _____

Rocker-to-retainer clearance OK? ❑ Yes ❑ No Maximum 0. _____ -inch (Intake); 0. _____ -inch (Exhaust)

Piston-to-valve clearance OK? ❑ Yes ❑ No Maximum 0. _____ -inch (Intake); 0. _____ -inch (Exhaust)

Other checks/observations:

_____

_____

_____

_____

_____

_____

_____

_____

_____

_____

_____

_____

Aeromotive
7805 Barton St.
Lenexa, KS 66214
(913) 647-7300
www.aeromotiveinc.com

Ansen Enterprises
3011 W. Lomita Blvd.
Torrence, CA 90505
www.ansenusa.com

ARP
1863 Eastman Ave.
Ventura, CA 93003
(800) 826-3045
www.arp-bolts.com

Barry Grant Inc.
1450 McDonald Rd.
Dahlonega, GA 30533
(706) 864-8544
www.barrygrant.com

BHJ Products
37530 Enterprise Ct.
Newark, CA 94560
(510) 797-6780
www.bhjproducts.com

Carbon Press
920 Ridgewood Ave.
Holly Hill, FL 32117
(386) 947-1986
www.smokeyyunick.com

Clevite77
www.mahleclevite.com

Comp Cams
3406 Democrat Rd.
Memphis, TN 38118
(901) 795-2400
www.compcams.com

Crane Cams/Mikronite Technologies
530 Fentress Blvd.
Daytona Beach, FL 32114
(386) 258-6174
www.cranecams.com

Crower
6180 Business Center Ct.
San Diego, CA 92154
(619) 661-6477
www.crower.com

Detroit Speed & Engineering
185 McKenzie Rd.
Mooresville, NC 28115
(704) 662-3272
www.detroitspeed.com

Eagle Specialty Products
8530 Aaron Ln.
Southaven, MS 38671
(662) 796-7373
www.eaglerod.com

Edelbrock
2700 California St.
Torrance, CA 90503
(800) 416-8628
www.edelbrock.com

FilterMag
13260 W. Foxfire Dr. #7
Surprise, AZ 85374
(800) 345-8376
www.filtermag.com

Fitzpatrick Chevrolet
2121 Diamond Blvd.
Concord, CA 94520
(925) 674-8756
www.fitzpatrickchevrolet.com

GM Performance
www.gmperformanceparts.com

Goodies Speed Shop
345 Lincoln Ave.
San Jose, CA 95126
(408) 295-0930
www.goodies-speedshop.com

Goodson Tools
156 Galewski Dr.
PO Box 847
Winona, MN 55987
(800) 533-8010
www.goodson.com

Gromm Racing Heads,
Balancing & Engine Machine
664-J Stockton Ave.
San Jose, CA 95126
(408) 287-1301

Innovate! Technology
5 Jenner, Suite 1000
Irvine, CA 92618
(949) 502-8400
www.innovatemotorsports.com

Joe Gibbs Racing
13201 Reese Blvd. W.
Huntersville, NC 28078
(866) 611-1820
www.joegibbsdriven.com

Jomar Performance
211 N. Cass Ave.
Pontiac, MI 48342
(248) 322-3080
www.jomarperformance.com

KB Performance Pistons
4909 Goni Rd.
Carson City, NV 89706
www.kb-silvolite.com

Mahle
www.mahle-aftermarket.com

Melling Engine Parts
2620 Saradan Dr.
PO Box 1188
Jackson, MI 49204
www.melling.com

Milodon
2250 Agate Ct.
Simi Valley, CA 93065
(805) 577-5950
www.milodon.com

Motion Software
(714) 231-3801
www.motionsoftware.com

Mr. Gasket
10601 Memphis Ave. #12
Cleveland, OH 44144
(216) 688-8300
www.mrgasket.com

MSD Ignition
Autotronic Controls Corp.
1350 Pullman Dr. #14
El Paso, TX 79936
(915) 857-5200
www.msdignition.com

Optima Batteries
Johnson Controls Inc.
(888) 867-8462
www.optimabatteries.com

Performance Stainless Steel
PO Box 67266
Scotts Valley, CA 95067
(831) 335-7901
www.performancesst.com

Powermaster Motorsports
7501 Strawberry Plains Pike
Knoxville, TN 37924
(865) 688-5953
www.powermastermotorsports.com

RaceHome.com
PO Box 8232
San Jose, CA 95155-8232
www.racehome.com

Remflex
PO Box 170
Mineral, WA 98355
www.remflex.com

RPM Machine
(925) 685-8112

Robert Cancilla Machines
S&S Automotive
14127 Washington Ave.
San Leandro, CA 94578

Victor Reinz
www.victorreinz.com

XRP
5630 Imperial Hwy.
South Gate, CA 90280
(562) 861-4765
www.xrp.com

Notes